I N THIS AMBITIOUS WORK, *VICTORIOUS WOMAN!* DE-livers compelling stories full of inspiration and insight. One minute you will cry and the next you will stand in awe at the circumstances the women faced. Masterly crafted to reach each reader on their own journey, the book leads you to discover within yourself an opening for victory. This will surely be a book you passionately share with friends. Together you'll ponder the possibilities.

DEANNE BRYCE, *author of the monthly*
e-zine ReaderStength

V *ICTORIOUS WOMAN!* IS AN UPLIFTING BOOK *EVERY* woman should read. No doubt, each reader will see glimmers of her own reflection in the stories and lessons that Annmarie so beautifully shares with us. The stories are a testament to what can be achieved through the power of purpose and optimism. After reading the book, you are left with a true sense of hope that anyone in any situation can find a way to victory. Wonderful, wonderful book!

THERESA HUMMEL-KRALLINGER, *laughologist*

STORYTELLER ANNMARIE NOT ONLY PROVIDES US WITH wonderful heartwarming tales, she gives us a path to our own victory. The soul-searching questions at the end of each chapter, the excellent analysis of the characteristics that made these women victorious, and the Stepping Stones to Victory will help you to work through your life challenges and move to the next level in your self-development.

DEBRA EXNER, *business and personal coach*

*V*ICTORIOUS WOMAN! IS COMPELLING, INSIGHTFUL, AND thought-provoking. In a straightforward, yet sensitive manner, Annmarie has captured the hearts and souls of the victorious women she profiled and has masterfully presented their poignant stories to inspire and empower the reader. *Victorious Woman!* is a must-read for anyone experiencing life changes and challenges. Through the Victorious Woman Model, Annmarie presents a practical approach to taking control of your life and creating your own personal victories.

KAREN LAWSON, PHD, CSP,
professional speaker, consultant, author, and
president, Lawson Consulting Group, Inc.

VICTORIOUS WOMAN!

Shaping Life's Challenges
Into Personal Victories

To Joy —
Love yourself
and live Victoriously!
Annmarie
Kelly

ANNMARIE KELLY

Optimal Living Press

Rosemont, Pennsylvania

Victorious Woman!

Grateful acknowledgment is made to the following for permission to reprint previously published material: Jana Stanfield and Jimmy Scott; Jana StanTunes/English Channel Music (ASCAP) for lines from "If I Were Brave." Copyright ©1999 Jana Stanfield/Jimmy Scott. www.JanaStanfield.com

Notes: *An asterisk indicates a name that has been changed to protect privacy throughout this written work. Victorious Woman™ and Victory Journal™ are trademarks owned by Annmarie Kelly. All rights reserved.

Order additional copies and bulk orders from:

Optimal Living Press
1062 Lancaster Avenue, Suite 15G
Rosemont, Pennsylvania 19010
(610) 918-0578   www.victoriouswoman.com

(discounts available for bulk purchase)

Library of Congress Cataloging-in-Publication Data:

Kelly, Annmarie.
    Victorious woman! : shaping life's challenges into personal victories /
    Annmarie Kelly
    p. cm.
    1. Change (Psychology). 2. Conduct of Life. 3. Success. 4. Happiness
    158'.1—dc21   2004101916
ISBN: 0-9746037-0-8

Printed in the United States of America

10 9 8 7 6 5 4 3 2 1

book design and production by
Whitline Ink Incorporated
(336) 367-6914 www.whitlineink.com

*Dedicated to each "Victorious Woman" within these pages,
each of whom made the decision to share her life in
a public way, with the intention of helping other women:*

Jean Otte
Maureen Ingelsby
Lilly Zook
Pattie Painter
Kathy Zingaro Clark
Alisa Lippincott Morkides
Nancy Hill
Toni Kershaw
Tekki Lomnicki

*May your story be the inspiration for many women to create
many victories. I am deeply grateful to each of you!*

CONTENTS

ACKNOWLEDGMENTS

THIS BOOK IS THE RESULT OF A LITTLE VOICE IN MY HEAD that would not stop gently nudging me to write and a series of events that forced me to listen.

For the women to whom this book is dedicated, thank you for dredging up and reliving the most difficult moments of your life. I am blessed beyond measure to have recorded those moments. I gratefully acknowledge your willingness and courage.

In addition, I extend my heartfelt thanks to:

Kate DiPronio, Deanne Bryce, and Bob Rosania, who not only extended their support through friendship but also with editorial input, sometimes on short notice.

The members of the ASTD Professional Publishing SIG, especially Andrea Sullivan and Theresa Hummel-Krallinger for reading the initial drafts and providing thoughtful but gentle critique and ever-positive encouragement.

My reassuring editor, Hillary Homzie, who cared not only about the content, but always thought about the women who would be reading my words and digesting the ideas. I appreciated her belief that I could write this book better and her stubborn insistence that I do it.

Jeanne Grayson and her dogmatic insistence on the Truth blended with unconditional love to get me on the path to healing and growth. My life is infinitely better for what I learned through her.

Gloria Williams who thought I could write and said the words that encouraged me to take the first steps toward that end.

Silver Melton who assisted me as I took the final steps...and reminded me to "BREATHE!"

My NDA Alums..."the friendships formed 'neath the gold and blue..." that still unite us.

A special thank you to my spouse, Joseph Eagle. You loved and supported me throughout the tedious process, believed I could finish this when I didn't, and you listened well enough to remind me of the words...even when I forgot them myself. I love you.

1

Seeds of Change

*H*OW ARE VICTORIES CREATED? ONE MOMENT AT A time, one decision at a time.

Victories occur when we opt to take a walk or go to the gym rather than mindlessly watch television. They also come about when we ground our teenagers for staying out too late because we want to be a good parent instead of their best friend. Victory is ours when we walk away from an abusive situation, even when fear is all we can feel.

Victory is also in the moment when we choose to speak up rather than let someone offend us or use us. Victory is especially in the split-second moments when we choose to replace feelings of anger or worry with positive and assuring thoughts, and praise for the parts of a job that we did well rather than a self-critical focus on what went wrong.

You may already have noticed that victory seldom unfolds in the midst of a big event. While we prepare for the wedding, move to our new house, or begin a prestigious new job, we are usually so caught up in emotions or the stress of the high priority tasks at hand that we seldom have time or energy to think about anything else. Those are the moments when we're more likely to be thinking about celebrating victory, not creating it. In actuality, victory comes about in the mundane moments of life when no one is looking. It comes about by taking one seemingly small action through which we turn our life *one more rotation* toward victory. No matter how small the step, we advance one more degree in our victorious design.

So, *what do women really do when faced with a challenge or difficulty?* If we are discussing victory objectively in casual conversation, we might glibly presume that all women would naturally choose the victory walk. However, when being squeezed in the vise of a challenging situation, sometimes our choices are not so obvious, and at other times, even the clearest of decisions can be difficult to make.

Like many women, I did not think a lot about victory, especially in relationship to my life. However, when I experienced a serious health challenge the idea of victory seemed patently important. Suddenly, I became incredibly curious about how women created victory in their lives.

During the winter after the 9/11 terrorist attacks, as everyone in my corner of the world tried to make sense of the tragedy, I faced a very personal predicament. My dilemma started during the holiday season when I experienced symptoms of a gynecological problem. Just after the new year began, I went to a doctor, who ordered a string of tests. One by one, he ruled out any STD, cysts, cervical cancer, or anything else that could be easily detected. Then the lab results revealed an elevated CA-125, sometimes an indicator of ovarian cancer. The doctor spoke in a matter-of-fact tone about the grim possibilities and sent me for an additional test.

As I thought about cancer, I wondered, "What does a women do to beat it? Is it something she thinks or something she does?" Maybe there's some kind of holistic cure, alternative treatment, or attitudinal magic that a cancer survivor uses to get well. It was at that moment my journey to define the Victorious Woman truly began.

While I waited for a phone call that would let me know the results of the latest lab work, I sat in my family room and tried to get comfortable in the rocking chair. Only moments later, I drifted into a light sleep. Two women from my past, both of whom had cancer but made vastly different choices, drifted into my thoughts. Annie was one of these women.

I'll never forget my time with her. A warm and funny yet poignantly sad woman, Annie learned she had cancer just as she turned sixty-two. Though there were no guarantees of a cure for her pancreatic cancer at that early stage, doctors told Annie and her family that the disease *could* be successfully treated. They believed that standard medical treatment would enable her to live *at least* a few more years.

Initially, everyone presumed Annie would begin therapy immediately. However, much to her family's shock and anger, she refused treatment.

I met Annie through Eileen, one of her four children. Eileen knew I practiced Reiki, a hands-on healing that uses energy to promote balance and wellness. Knowing that Annie had an interest in homeopathy and other non-traditional therapies, she asked me to give her mother a Reiki treatment.

My first day happened to be a crisp Saturday morning in late September. Annie chose that particular day and time because her spouse played golf and was out of the house. He did not believe in non-traditional medical treatment and taunted Annie because she did. He called everything from vitamin supplements to herbal remedies "that voodoo mumbo-jumbo." While he was playing eighteen holes, I could be in and out of the house without him ever knowing.

On that beautiful fall morning, as I drove down Annie's street, the grass seemed especially green and the white clouds practically popped out of the azure sky. As I parked my car in front of her house, I noticed the well-kept lawn and the yellow chrysanthe-mum-filled planters on either side of the door. When I rang the doorbell, I could hear the light, quick footsteps on the other side of the door. Annie opened the door and greeted me with a welcoming smile as she invited me inside. Before heading upstairs to her guest room where I would provide the Reiki treatment, she ushered me through the formal living room and into the kitchen. On my way, I noticed how the black and tan sofa blended perfectly with the Oriental rug and how the home seemed spotless and in meticulous order.

In the kitchen, I got a better sense of Annie as I looked at the fringed curtains, the porcelain puppy cookie jar, and the collector's plates proudly displayed on a shelf on the wall. She impressed me as a gracious woman who liked nice things. As she poured a glass of iced tea for me, through the curtained window I noticed a cardinal feasting at a bird feeder in the backyard. We sat at the kitchen table for a few moments and chatted. Annie told me she believed that her daughter really wanted her to accept standard medical help, and the Reiki would "do something" to change her mind. The determined woman laughed when she told me how angry her spouse and children were with her for not fighting her illness.

As if to challenge my intentions, Annie looked me straight in the eyes and said she had made her decision. She did not want to be treated for the cancer, and had no plans to change her mind for anyone. When I asked why, she cryptically cited "personal reasons." Her response made me feel sad and more than a little curious. She seemed to have it all: a nice house in a well-to-do neighborhood, four grown children, and a very comfortable lifestyle. Though I wanted to know more, I also knew it was too soon in our relationship for me to press further.

Beginning that morning, and for nearly three months, I visited Annie every Saturday morning for her Reiki treatment. As she got to know me better, Annie became more comfortable. At first Annie talked in generalities, but it wasn't long before she started talking about her deepest feelings; our sessions became more and more like confessions. Much of our talk focused on how Annie would conduct her life—if she chose to live. As I listened to her go over the pros and cons, she seemed to be using our time together to figure out what the benefits would be, *for her*, of living over dying. While I gently laid my hands on her face, head, shoulders, stomach, and back, I tried to maintain a detached, almost unobtrusive demeanor so that Annie could make the decision that would give her peace.

Each week it was as though Annie would take another part of her life out of a box, hold it up to the light and inspect it. She would reflect on her life as it was, and *as she wished it could have been*. We would talk about what she would like to do if she lived, almost as if she wanted to find something that excited her enough to want to fight the cancer.

As the weeks progressed, I discovered that one of Annie's greatest pleasures was to make bridal gowns— *no small task*! Just before her diagnosis, she agreed to make a very special wedding gown for a spring wedding, a gift for a warmly cherished niece. When she talked about the dress, her eyes lit up. In the course of conversation, I discovered that owning a bridal salon was one of Annie's dreams. If she lived, that's what she would want to do. I also learned that she believed she would never realize that dream. Her husband, an old-fashioned and domineering man, wouldn't have allowed it. From his perspective, Annie could sew whatever she wanted as long as it stayed a hobby and not something that took her away from caring for his needs. As a result, Annie believed her life would stay as it was, and nothing could change it.

With Annie's admission and acceptance, she revealed the great sadness of her life and her bleak view of the future. Though she created her own life, she chose to tailor it to meet the needs of everyone else. It satisfied her physically and financially but not mentally, emotionally, or spiritually. For her to live a worthwhile existence, Annie realized she would have to redesign her life, cut new patterns, and sew a different stitch.

Week by week, it became apparent to Annie that living longer would mean having to change in ways that did not please others. She feared that the alterations would generate more disapproval and rejection than she could handle. Whether it was true or not, Annie firmly believed that living happily would mean giving up everyone and everything she loved. She felt that she had little chance to live a life that satisfied *her*, rather than everyone else. The choice of death over the risk of change was the one decision Annie *could* control in a life that, according to her self-assessment, was otherwise decided by everyone else's wants, needs, whims, and agendas.

Every Saturday morning, I listened to Annie sorting out her life and affirming how much yielding to death felt peaceful and right while fighting to live did not. On the football field, only a few blocks away, I could hear the distant sounds of a high school marching band. Sometimes I would think about how happy and excited the teenagers must have been as they cheered their team to victory. I frequently thought about the contrast as I laid my hands on the head, face, and back of the woman who'd never see another football season.

As the autumn deepened, leaves outside her window changed from summer green to a mixture of yellow, red, and orange. I watched Annie change colors, too—from pink to yellow to the beginnings of a grayish tint.

Shortly before Thanksgiving, Annie discontinued the Reiki treatments. When she did, I felt an expansive range of emotions from anger and sadness to acceptance and happiness. In my heart, I knew what it meant. Annie had made her final decision.

For the next two months, Annie celebrated the holidays with her family. She worked on her niece's wedding gown, put her affairs in order, and met with special friends to have one last lunch and say goodbye.

In late February, Annie asked me to come back for treatments. Annie chose to die at home and when I went to her I was struck by how dark and depressed the once perfectly maintained house felt. By then, all I could do for her was help ease some of the pain. Though when I visited her I tried to be cheerful, all I could really feel was sad. Each time I wondered how much longer she had to live. I visited her for a few more weeks, seeing her for the last time on the day before she died. On that day, the pain seemed unimaginably great. Though she managed a little smile when I lightly teased her about how cute she looked in her nightgown, she knew she had a death look...and she wanted to go.

Days later, I attended the funeral services for Annie. The packed church offered standing room only. As I heard the eulogies, I could only think about all the heartrending, deep feelings Annie had shared with me. I became so upset over the memories that I left the church midway through the service. I returned to my car ready to drive home, but as I turned the key in the ignition, I began to cry. I do not know how long I sat in the driver's seat releasing my once unexpressed feelings, but when the tears subsided, I found solace knowing that Annie had found peace. As I drove out of the church parking lot, I felt satisfied that death gave Annie the freedom that she did not have in life.

A few months later, cancer also took the life of another woman I knew. I met Esther in 1989, the first time I attended a local writer's association. I did not know what to expect from the group, comprised mostly of older women, so I sat back and took in the proceedings. After introductions and business reports, one member wanted to talk about author Salman Rushdie. Recent news reports indicated that Rushdie's most recent book, *The Satanic Verses*, had been condemned by Orthodox Iranian leaders. Accusing the author of blasphemy against Islam, they issued a fatwa—essentially a death sentence—which forced Rushdie into hiding.

As a discussion got underway, the group focused on the first amendment rights of United States citizens. One woman, playing devil's advocate, defended the Iranian leaders' position. That was when Esther, whose spouse had defended U.S. freedoms in the Navy during World War II, jumped up from her seat. As her porcelain white skin turned bright red, she went on a tirade about the dangers of censorship. She warned the group that if it could happen in Iran, it could happen in the United States. Her fiery energy filled the room as she goaded others into taking part in the discourse.

Though I later came to know Esther as a generally kind and understanding woman and not one to actively seek controversy, I also learned that some subjects, like freedom of speech and patriotism, touched her deeply. When they did, she could get fired up in an instant—and everyone would know about it. Her passion impressed and inspired me.

After the meeting, I learned that we didn't live far from each other. Since Esther no longer drove, I offered to chauffeur her to future meetings. She accepted and each time we drove together, I had the pleasure of knowing her a little better.

Esther had a blunt manner that matched her sturdy carriage. She spoke with a directness that sometimes lacked tact. Not everyone liked her style, but with Esther you always knew where you stood.

Esther wore her pure white hair in a long braid that flowed down her back. Years of deep emotions, borne of a lifetime of experiences, seemed etched in her long, craggy face. Her blue eyes still twinkled when she talked about something that excited her, like her grandson's science project or the butterfly she observed while she waited for a bus. She loved poetry and read it often.

Esther had been a widow for many years by the time we met. She had given up her larger, single home in favor of a small but comfortable apartment. Though she had four children, any of whom she could have moved in with, she preferred to live by herself. Esther had a few good friends she spoke with regularly, and she also enjoyed the company of many acquaintances through membership in several writer's groups and book clubs.

When she wanted to go somewhere, if she could not get a ride with someone, she either walked or took public transportation. In fact, Esther used the utility so effortlessly that one would have thought she had her own private transportation service. With schedules at the ready, she knew just when and where she could hop on a bus or train to get where she wanted to go.

One of her regular trips included a weekly writing course at Temple University in Philadelphia. Though the distance from her home required several transfers between trains and buses, she eagerly made the trip because senior citizens attended free and could receive critiques of their work. Also, ever enthused by the challenge of writing, she thoroughly enjoyed the company of other authors and poets. She seldom missed a class.

Despite her advanced years, Esther had no intention of living a quiet or invisible retirement. She voraciously read newspapers and magazines, enjoying political news as much as the gossip columns and comics. Unlike some senior citizens who seem ever-nostalgic, Esther enjoyed knowing about the latest advances in science and medicine. She welcomed changing social mores, like couples living together before marriage. Whenever we talked, she seemed hearty and fearless. Marveling at her spiritedness, I could only imagine what a feisty person she must have been in her younger years.

Esther always had a canvas tote slung over her shoulder. I remember picking her up one day for a meeting and watching her as she walked from her apartment to the car. As I admired her perfect posture, relaxed not rigid, I laughed as I wondered how the heavy pouch didn't weigh her down. The bag usually contained an item or two of clothing, like a sweater and gloves. It also held at least a paperback book or two, several pens, and always a spiral-bound copybook—just in case she had a poetic inspiration. The books she read often reflected her love of the ocean.

Aside from an obvious love of family, Esther's greatest joys in life revolved around the sea. For years, on weekends and vacations, she and her spouse, Bill, enjoyed the eastern shore of Maryland with their children. In those days, they owned a small sailboat. Her memories of Bill and their nautical adventures made her smile, and sometimes brought tears to her eyes. She frequently wrote poetry about the sea, its delights, and her seafaring days with Bill.

When it came to writing, Esther put pen to paper daily. She would write, cross out, and rewrite until she felt satisfied. Esther would then transfer the handwritten words to print using an old typewriter that did not print all the letters evenly on a line. It gave a distinctive look to her work. Her children offered to buy her a word processor or a computer, but she declined. She had a successful system going and didn't want to mess with it!

Esther regularly submitted her work to magazines and occasionally one of her poems or short stories would be published in a local or national publication. One year she compiled her favorites into a small volume, made copies, and gave it to those she thought would appreciate it. I felt honored to be one of those who received a copy.

Unfortunately, Esther had a serious illness. She'd been ignoring abdominal pains for some time but eventually one of her daughters insisted she see a doctor. He ordered tests. We spoke for the last time while she waited for a ride to the hospital. Something in her voice told me she knew something more about her condition, but she did not share it with me. I respected her privacy, but I also had a feeling that I might not talk to her again.

The following week, Esther died from a cancer that began in her stomach but had spread throughout her body. Though she kept it quiet and never complained about aches and pains, she must have been ill and suffering for a long time. Yet she stayed strong and feisty to the end.

After her death, her daughter called the president of the writer's group who started a telephone chain to tell members the news. When I received the call, I felt shocked and saddened. I could barely wrap my mind around her death, let alone trying to understand that I would never see her again or hear her gravelly voice on the phone.

Reflecting on the lives of Annie and Esther, I marveled at the dichotomy between the two. Both were women of considerable talents. However, Annie chose to live in self-abnegation, a victim of familial and societal restraints. To me, she felt like the lovely ballerina found inside a jewelry box, only dancing when someone opened the box, and only in the same mechanical and familiar way. She was never free to leap outside the box to perform her own unfettered dance of joy.

On the other hand, the much older Esther chose to live with a sense of personal freedom, in spite of the cultural norms of her generation. Though she doted on her sons, daughters, and grandchildren, and thoroughly enjoyed friends and social events, she refused to be confined by them. She reminded me of a sailboat in the ocean that occasionally thrashed against a storm but usually drifted peacefully amid calm seas, always staying on a course of her own choosing.

When Annie and Esther died, I remember thinking about both of them and wondering what made the older woman continue to push ahead, and the younger woman choose to not even get into the game? How did one of them find it so easy to buck tradition while it overwhelmed the other? I thought about both of them for a long while, but then the daily considerations of my own life—spouse, aging mother, work, friends, household demands—gradually took over my thoughts and replaced my musings about the two women.

Now, as I sat waiting for the phone to ring that cold, dreary day in February, out of the blue and into my conscious thoughts, there they were again. If I had cancer, who would I be like... Annie or Esther?

As I anxiously passed the time, I thought about how much care I put into decorating the room in which I sat. I remembered how nervous my spouse and I felt when we selected the sage-colored paint for the walls, and how much we loved it now. I looked at vacation pictures hung on the wall, the inexpensive little candle lantern that filled its space so perfectly, and the doilies on the furniture, hand-crocheted by my mother for her hope chest before she married my father. Closing my eyes, I tried to meditate but could not calm my mind. "I've got to get myself up from this chair and out of this mood," I told myself. I stood up and went into the kitchen. I fixed myself a cup of aromatic Earl Grey tea and called my mother.

While I did not want to burden my mother with worry over my medical concerns, I *did* want some comfort. As we talked, I told her what had been happening during the previous few days. She gave me no sympathy. Instead, she told me to stop moping around, stop feeling sorry for myself, and get myself moving. I could barely believe my ears. Silently, I wondered if her advanced age prevented her from understanding what I was telling her or, since I was one of her caregivers, was she even less able to deal with the possibility of illness than I?

Finishing the call, I reflected on my mother's words. Though I felt they were cold, I also had to admit that she probably had a point about taking action—any action. However, the truth was, *I just didn't want to do anything.* I could tell something was definitely happening inside my body, but was it a life-threatening illness or something less serious? I felt weak, tired, depressed, and scared. In the middle of my own pity party, I looked for sympathy, not admonition or motivation.

In truth, I could have shifted myself out of self-pity. I could easily have gone to my office and done some work, made phone calls, or cleaned a desk drawer and a closet shelf—Lord knows my office could have used it. I didn't do any of those things. Instead, I plopped back in my chair and rocked back and forth, wishing the phone would ring.

As the waiting continued with each minute feeling like an hour, I started thinking about the "big picture" of my life. Looking at past pluses and minuses, I forced myself to think more positively. I acknowledged that, after surviving what could kindly be called an emotionally unsupportive family, I went on to achieve many personal victories. I thought about those of which I was proudest.

One of my biggest victories occurred during my mid-twenties

when I moved into my own apartment—and never again lived in my parents' house. For many people, that would not have been a big deal. Many of my peers moved out when they went away to college and never moved back with their parents. However, not only did I not go to college, my Italian-American parents presumed I would live with them until I got married. In fact, some outdated cultural expectation stipulated that a good daughter, who was a decent woman, only left her parent's home if she was in a wedding gown, a nun's habit...or a coffin. Anything else indicated a downward moral spiral.

Even worse than the idea that I was looking for trouble was the fact that my father reacted badly to my move. To him, my desire for independence signified a rejection of the life he provided for me rather than a sign of good parenting. Neither he nor my mother could understand how important it was for me to know I could support myself, or the confidence that would come from knowing that I could take care of myself.

Instead, my father told me I would move only over his dead body. We argued mightily and my mother responded scornfully when I talked about the move. My aunt called to tell me I would not make it; that eventually, I would fail and move back with my parents. Their lack of support magnified the normal uncertainties that accompany nearly everyone who makes that first step away from their childhood home. Adding to my fears, I barely scraped together enough money for the security deposit and first month's rent.

Still, undaunted by lack of money, Old World tradition, and parental resistance, and fiercely determined to live as my own person, I made moving arrangements. Fortunately, I had the support of friends and a couple of more "modern" relatives. Raiding their attics and basements, I gathered furniture and household items from the kind people who offered them. My parents were so angry that, right up until the day I moved, I didn't know if they would allow me to take any of my bedroom furniture. In the end, they did. But during those last couple of weeks at home, I often wondered if I'd be sleeping on the floor in my apartment.

On the day I moved, my brother and his friends helped. My father ignored me while he ate his breakfast. My mother stood at the bottom of the stairs crying. I had no idea what was involved with moving and I had prepared poorly. The move took all day.

Afterward, my father refused to talk to me and his anger lasted for nearly a year. While it hurt a great deal, the confidence I developed far surpassed the pain of parental rejection. I was right to move. It wasn't easy, but choosing to live independently was a big deal.

Though living on my own proved challenging, I didn't move back with my parents. In fact, I became the only woman in my family, at that time, who permanently moved out of her parents' home (and not in a wedding dress, nun's habit, or coffin). In the process, despite parental doubts, I learned that I could trust my own judgment. I would make mistakes, but I found that I could correct them on my own. If I made a mess of something, I could clean it up; more importantly, I learned how not to make so many messes. I developed into a responsible adult.

In addition to successfully maintaining my own living space, after several years I went a step further—I bought a house. In my family, a single woman buying her own house was also a first. My mother, however, felt disappointed. Buying a house did not trump getting married.

There were many other victories along the way, both personal and professional. When I eventually met and married my wonderful spouse, Joseph, we partnered to develop a successful business around his therapeutic massage practice. As the company grew, I left my job as a corporate training manager and went out on my own, providing workshops, presentations, and coaching. In May 2001, more than twenty-five years after I graduated from high school, I finally earned a Bachelor of Science degree from Neumann College, magna cum laude. The long-awaited victory was, and still is, one of the proudest days of my life. I doubt any graduate present that spring day could have been happier than I was when I walked onto the stage to accept my diploma.

Like most people, I achieved each major success, as well as the many less significant ones, by overcoming challenges involving things like money, time, energy, motivation, self-sabotage, support, and others. During my quests for victory, in spite of whatever difficulties I needed to overcome, I always found some spark of hope or was spurred on by seeing a light at the end of a tunnel—something that made me rise up in spirit, take action, and move forward.

That day, as I considered the possibility of a serious, maybe life-threatening illness, it was different. I felt weary of challenges and thought to myself, "*if* I have to fight this battle, maybe I just won't do it; maybe this time I will simply surrender."

Surrendering reminded me of Annie, and then Esther crossed my mind again. I wondered if I'd take the hand that life had dealt me but fold, as Annie did, or would I have Esther's dogged determination to keep doing what made her happy well into her eighties and in spite of illness. I wondered about the mental or emotional difference between these women, as well as the victory mindset of countless other women who were faced with difficulties but kept going even when they wanted to give up.

As the hours ticked away and I meandered around the family room, then the kitchen, then my office, I was still thinking about Annie and Esther...*and me*. My quest for answers intensified. I wondered what makes one woman settle for a mediocre, unfulfilling or unhealthy lifestyle while another pushes her way out of difficulty or harm and toward satisfaction and fulfillment. "What is the difference between the woman who overcomes life's challenges and creates a personal victory, and the woman who gives up or gives in? How does a woman keep going when the odds are against her?" I thought about these questions, but could think of no answers.

Eventually I asked myself the toughest questions of all, "How would I choose to continue to live my life, whatever the results of the medical tests? Moreover, what would I do if the doctor said the dreaded word: cancer?" Again, internal silence. I just didn't know the answer to that most important question. I did not know, but I decided to find out.

Over the next few days, the results indicated that my current condition was the latent result of a gynecological surgery. I needed treatment, but it was nothing I couldn't handle. My fears were calmed. In a few months, my health would be returning to normal. In truth, my body was out of danger, but my mind was not.

While I had always been a person of strong mind and will, this recent test of spirit alerted me to the fact that there was work to do. I wondered what I would have decided if I actually *had* to make my own life and death decision. I questioned myself about what would be "the one thing" that would give me the courage to choose life. What would be my motivation and provide the persistence to keep going? That I didn't know bothered me and it opened a proverbial Pandora's box.

With the lid off, my next thoughts were about women and the choices we make for our lives. I thought about how we often take up the role of victim, servant, or caregiver, believing we have no other choices. I watched a PBS-TV broadcast during which gynecologist and best-selling author Dr. Christiane Northrup discussed how much women run around doing things for everyone while ignoring messages and signals from our bodies; she asked her audience why we have to choose to die—*just to get some rest.* I also wondered why. I took some time to read inspirational books; I prayed for guidance. My health was getting back to normal, but I still felt something scratching on the inside of my mind.

The greater my need became for answers, the more I wanted easy answers. I made some glib presumption that the difference between victory and surrender probably boiled down to attitudes, behaviors, and communication. However, my reactions during my most recent challenge indicated that I could no longer live with pure speculation; it just wasn't enough for me anymore. If I ever again faced the possibility of a life-threatening challenge, I wanted to approach it as a stronger person. I needed definite answers that I could live with—literally and figuratively.

With a lot of big questions and no solid answers, I decided to find out first-hand how other women have done it. What kept them going toward victory when they wanted to give up? What brightened their spirit—was it a helping hand, a kind word, their religious belief, family, friends...or was it something else? When the situation was grave, what did a woman think and feel about herself, her life, and about others who were part of her story? What went on inside, in a woman's heart, mind, and soul that enabled her to overcome personal loss, fight cancer, get herself out of an abusive marriage, or any of the many unpleasant realities of life?

My quest led me to a variety of women with different challenges; some told of lifetime journeys while others told of specific events. Some faced incredible obstacles with extraordinary responses. For other women, victory meant meeting their everyday situations with courage and persistence. In each instance, a woman had a choice to be victorious instead of victimized.

As I listened, I quickly realized that most women could identify, as I did, with either the situation or the emotions of the Victorious Woman to whom I was listening. That was how this book evolved. The women you will read about have everyday lives filled with the challenges of home, work, relationships, or children. However, in ways great and small, each woman created a special kind of victory for herself.

In this book, you will read about women like Jean Otte whose earliest years were about fear and survival as much as about life. Throughout her life, Jean celebrated victories over one adversity after another—including her crash through the corporate glass ceiling to become her company's first woman executive. Her life is marked by happiness and tragedy—probably much the same as your life and mine. What makes Jean unique is how she took what she learned and, stepping out in faith, decided to create a way to mentor to hundreds of other women. *Where did she find the courage?*

You will also meet Maureen Ingelsby, who lived a reasonably unfettered life until the day her husband told her he had to "find himself"—leaving her suddenly alone to raise five children, all under the age of ten. *What did she think and feel as she figured out what to do? What steps did she take so that she could not only survive, but also flourish?*

Jean and Maureen each had a distinctive story. So did Pattie Painter and Nancy Hill. In fact, Victorious Woman after Victorious Woman had a unique experience. Yet early on in conversations, I began to notice commonalities among attitudes, specific patterns of thought and behavior, and certain characteristics that made the "victorious" difference for all of the women.

With that knowledge, my primary objective became to uncover the substance beneath the indomitable spirit of the Victorious Woman—that is, *the victorious spirit that is in each of us* and *all of us.*

My secondary objective is to help other women (you!) find the Victorious Woman inside, waiting to be summoned into action. With that in mind, at the end of each woman's story, you will find questions relating to the story, the victory, and you. Here's how to use them:

1. Think about the questions. Some may have quick answers but others will take more time. Prepare yourself for an exciting adventure in self-exploration. Sometimes you'll notice that the journey may not always feel comfortable, but neither is a trip to the summit of Mt. Everest. You are not climbing a mountain, but your personal victory is your Everest...*be ready for it!*

2. Buy a private journal and write down your answers to the questions. **Writing is key**. Until you take notes and see your thoughts and ideas in print, they are little more than guesses and illusions.

3. After recording your responses in the journal, reflect on your entries from time to time and challenge your thinking. Keep track of your own personal Victorious Woman journey.

4. Celebrate your victories! Set aside a portion of your journal just for recording the victories. While the rest of your journal will show the steps, this section is just for the outcome. When you feel down on yourself, reread your victory list.

In the final chapter, you'll find a summary of the Victorious Woman's most common characteristics. Using the highlights of each story, you will see a road map for victory. Of course, no two women are exactly alike and there are also characteristics that are specific to each woman's particular victory. Just the same, my intention is to formulate and present a fluid but working model of the Victorious Woman.

From a cultural vantage point, most women understand that many Victorious Woman behaviors, such as flawless focus and dogged determination, haven't usually been socially and culturally acceptable for a woman. I hope that reading this book will stir a woman's thoughts and create a conversation that raises the consciousness of men as well as women, both young and old. The impact of this dialog would be as important to fathers as to mothers, because both teach their sons and daughters about the strength of a woman. Through those exchanges, our individual and collective self-esteem can soar as we grow into our fullest power.

As you learn about each woman's victory and coach yourself through the end-of-chapter questions, I trust that you will find a thought that is meaningful to you, or a feeling that resonates with a place inside you. My greatest wish is that you learn something you can use to find courage and strength for a time when life knocks you down and you don't feel like getting up again.

It's my hope that the legacy of this book, coupled with the Victorious Woman Model and ensuing dialog, is one that challenges us to become our strongest and most praiseworthy self—

even when, *maybe especially when*, that self isn't the sweetest, most agreeable, cutest, or thinnest person in the neighborhood or on the job. With these sincere intentions, I invite you to share your own thoughts and stories by visiting www.victoriouswoman .com. Since its creation in 2003, this Web site has been a community where women can learn more about creating victory, sharing their victories with others, and find resources for victory-making. Many, many of us are more victorious than we, and the world, give us credit for being. This is a good time and the right place for each Victorious Woman to assert her victory!

2

Intimate Issues
Lillian Zook

A WOMAN LIVING WITH DOMESTIC ABUSE ISN'T LIKE-
ly to talk about it. She is even less likely to leave her situation because she probably has children, does not have money
of her own, and has few friends, if any. She is also likely to feel
that making the marriage work is her responsibility, so she
rationalizes abusive behavior and blames it on factors such as job
or family stress and she almost always faults herself.

Even worse, the abused woman knows that, while her life *may*
be in danger if she stays, it's definitely in peril if she goes. Statis-
tics indicate that sixty-five percent of intimate homicide victims
physically separated from the perpetrator prior to their death. The
statistic is frightening and may help explain the reason why so
many women stay in abusive relationships.

Lillian Zook tempted fate. She wanted to leave her abusive marriage, but fear and internal conflict thwarted her efforts. She did

leave several times, but each time she found herself back in the relationship and regretting it.

When Lilly left for the last time, she not only survived, she thrived. And while that would have been victorious enough, what she did for her children became her greatest victory.

At first look, the battle scars are not readily apparent. Yet the markers are there in the narrowing of her eyes and the hesitancy in her smile. The pain in her voice indicates just how rough the road has been.

In Lilly Zook's Puerto Rican family, she was the "good girl," the fourth of six children in an alcohol-affected family. With several years separating each child, her older two sisters and brother seemed almost like parents to her, as she sometimes did to her younger brother and sister.

Lilly's soft-spoken, artistic father worked as a welder in a local factory. In the summer months, he did landscaping as a side job. Passive in both his relationship and parenting styles, he frequently deferred to his more dominant mate. "He let her have her way," Lilly remembers.

Her mother suffered from a debilitating lung disease, an enlarged heart, and blood clots. She breathed only with help of an oxygen tank to which she stayed constantly connected. Embarrassed to be seen in public with the cylinder and tubes, she seldom left home, telling Lilly that she felt "like a dog on a leash."

Drinking acerbated her mother's health problems. She drank daily, often to excess, and usually to the point of becoming nasty. She also tended to be controlling. If she wanted something and did not get her way, Lilly says her mother could be demeaning. As a result, Lilly concedes that "whatever she said, I did. It didn't really matter. I think that's why she used to tell people I was her favorite, even though we seldom saw eye-to-eye. I just wouldn't argue with her, even if it was something I really wanted."

To this day, however her mother's actions may have been tempered by illness, an isolated lifestyle, or active alcoholism, Lilly believes love prompted the dominating behaviors. However, she also thinks her mother's motivation may have become somewhat distorted after years of disciplining her older sisters who "had already gone through their stuff."

By the time Lilly reached her teenage years, she already knew her mother did not want a repetition of hassles over academics, dances, boys, or any of the typical but risky situations that tempt young people. Lilly also understood that she could only have the right kind of mom-approved friends, strict curfews, etc. Because of her mother's insistent behaviors, sneaking out or pushing the envelope for more privileges seemed pointless to Lilly. She quietly laughs about how, "there was no fooling my mom...*and* what my mother said, *went!*"

In a life fraught with dysfunction, Lilly watched her parents live out their difficult lives day after day. She observed that, in a relationship spattered with frequent arguments, her parents did not seek counseling or guidance to help them deal more effectively with their differences or with the illness and alcohol that affected each day and every situation. In spite of their problems, they stayed together. From them she learned, "When you are married, you stayed married—no matter what."

During her teen years, Lilly spent most of her after-school time listening to the radio, watching television, and working a part-time job. Though she occasionally went to a dance or hung out with girlfriends, she felt equally content to stay at home. Whatever she did, her mother always knew Lilly's whereabouts. When Lilly wanted to do something or go someplace and her mother said she could not, Lilly enlisted the help of one of her sisters. If her mother *still* told her no, Lilly simply accepted it.

Though Lilly's passive behaviors seemed part of her personality, other factors contributed to her general submissiveness and timidity. Her mother had good intentions, but she depended heavily on her daughter. Throughout her teens, she functioned as her mother's caregiver. At just forty-seven years old, her mother died of complications from alcoholism. Lilly, only nineteen, took her mother's death very hard.

For many years Lilly lived in her mother's shadow. She depended so heavily on her mother's approval that she had not yet developed her own interests and had no real life direction. The socially immature young woman felt particularly lost and vulnerable without her mother, whose need for her daughter had been so absolute. Lilly had no goals or dreams of her own. She felt like a ship without a rudder, adrift in an ocean of sadness and grief. She missed her mother terribly.

During this confusing period, Lilly met the strong, smooth-talking Martin.* Suddenly, Lilly was experiencing loss and desire, death and hope, all at the same time. If not for this fateful intersection of emotions, Lilly might not have fallen for the seemingly sharp and suave man. But fall for Martin she did, instantly, and in a big way.

From the beginning of their relationship, Lilly saw Martin as a slightly older man who wore nice suits, looked good, and "knew stuff." Like her mother, Martin was strong-willed and dominant, and "he could convince you of anything...even that the tree out that window had dollar bills on it." She fell crazy in love with him right away. In fact, Martin so captivated Lilly that she wanted to be like him. Doing whatever Martin wanted her to do and say seemed natural and she quickly molded into Martin's image and likeness. One of her sisters warned Lilly to be careful to keep her own personality and not to "become Martin." The wise words fell on deaf ears. There was no talking to Lilly in love.

Before anyone could do anything to stop it, Lilly and Martin were married. Soon after their marriage, Martin found a house where he wanted them to live—just far enough away that Lilly could not easily see her family or friends. As she took on the role of wife, she began making a life for Martin and her. She took care of the household duties, and he handled the money and all the financial affairs. Lilly quickly learned that Martin didn't like being asked too many questions. In awe of his seeming intelligence, Martin gave Lilly the impression that he knew something about everything and she believed him.

What happened next is still not exactly clear to Lilly. First, Martin ran into some vague kind of problem with their landlord. Lilly did not know what it was, but one day Martin came home and told her that they lost the house. They fled the dwelling quickly, making only one trip and taking with them what they could fit into their station wagon. They relocated so fast that Lilly ended up leaving many things in the house, including precious items belonging to her deceased mother. She never again saw her mother's dishes, a cherished piece of furniture, the boxes of family pictures, or any of the other sentimental memorabilia that meant so much to Lilly.

The rapid retreat from their little home became spliced to a quick move into a roach-infested apartment. It became only the first of many such unexpected moves.

Though Lilly now admits she should have known early in their marriage that there was something wrong, she says, "I was naive. I *wanted* to trust people; he took advantage of that." Also, by the time they moved, Lilly knew she was pregnant. Believing she had the life of her unborn child to consider, she surrendered to Martin and a frighteningly uncertain fate.

Upheaval became a regular part of life for Lilly and Martin. When Martin came up with an idea or scheme, he had a reason; in fact, he had what seemed to be a plausible reason for everything he did, and Lilly consistently bought into his reasoning. So when he told Lilly not to call her family unless he was around, there was a reason. Repeating a pattern established in her relationship with her mother, Lilly went along with Martin and did what he wanted—and Martin wanted lots of things.

Lilly was well into the first of two pregnancies when Martin told Lilly to get a job. As always, he had his reasons. Though now she cannot fathom how they made any sense, somehow back then they did. At Martin's insistence, and only eight weeks from giving birth, Lilly went to work in a clothing factory outlet store. The manager felt sorry for the very pregnant young woman and let her work folding or hanging clothes.

Whatever money came into the house, Martin took control of it. If there was something Martin wanted to do, or wanted Lilly to do, she went along with it. Lilly did whatever Martin said. After all, he was the smart one and he always had his reasons; better not to think about it. Lilly went along to get along.

During those early years, Martin's mother and grandmother provided some comfort for Lilly. Martin's mother pampered Lilly whenever she visited. Lilly appreciated her mother-in-law, especially after the birth of her second child. With two children being only eleven months apart, her mother-in-law's presence helped Lilly feel calmed and reassured. Martin's grandmother was equally warm and kind. They made Lilly feel good. Yet even the pleasures of those relationships were confined to Martin's approval. No one could do anything for Lilly unless Martin allowed it. If anyone did, they quickly regretted their caring helpfulness.

During one of his mother's visits, she moved a piece of furniture to make it easier to walk around the dining room. When he returned home that evening, Martin saw what his mother had done and it set him off. He went on a tirade, tore the house apart, and chased his own mother down the street. Lilly experienced that behavior before, but only when directed toward her. It shocked his mother. She felt so rattled by her son's behavior that she never again returned to Lilly and Martin's house.

As Lilly lived her bizarre life, one might wonder what she was thinking. When asked, Lilly explained that early in the marriage she "thought it was normal for marriage to be rocky in the beginning." She believed that as time progressed, "X" would happen and their life would improve. The "X" factor was Martin's latest scheme or brilliant idea. When one of his plans failed to work out—it usually did not—and life didn't go Martin's way, he never accepted responsibility for any mistakes or problems. Worse yet, Martin kept Lilly convinced that she was the real reason for their predicaments. If a business deal fell through, he blamed Lilly. If they had no money for the rent that month, Lilly was held accountable for spending too much for food or diapers. If the car needed to be repaired, Lilly had something to do with it.

Lilly came to believe, "*I* was the problem. *I* was sick, and not trustworthy." She was convinced that something was wrong with her. She felt sorry for Martin because, after all, "all he was doing was just trying to deal with me with all my problems." Certain that everything was her fault, she concedes, "I was so scared... and there was no one to talk to...I just went into this place..." While in that depressed, embarrassed, and confused place, Lilly would not tell anyone what was happening, not even her family.

In truth, there were moments when Lilly questioned her life with Martin. One such time was a crazy night during Lilly's second pregnancy. They argued and Martin locked the pregnant Lilly out of the house. With nowhere to go, she slept in the car. After that, Lilly "had had enough" so she moved in with her sister. In retaliation, Martin got rid of everything in the house; Lilly lost the few personal possessions she had left.

Though her family tried keeping them apart, Martin pressed on Lilly relentlessly. "He kept calling and calling, and I felt bad. I thought 'maybe he's changed.'" However nonsensical it seemed, Lilly wanted to believe it. She and Martin got back together. Once again intact, the little family began all over again. This time they moved in with Martin's mother. In spite of the older woman's fearful concerns about her son's angry actions, Martin somehow convinced her that he had changed. He had not, and it quickly became apparent.

Over time, Martin became even more controlling and exceedingly verbally abusive. He and Lilly fought, but Martin always got his way. Whenever Lilly asserted herself, there was hell to pay, so she seldom did.

Lilly's story continued to twist and turn for some time. She told no one how bad it got. Her mother had always told her that "what happens in the house, stays in the house." So, though her family knew Lilly had problems, she never said a word.

Day-by-day and incident-by-incident, Lilly saw more reason to leave. But even as bad as it was, Lilly says she "was raised to believe that you stay together no matter what. My mom and dad stayed together...I had kids; I had to stay."

Life got worse before it got better. Lilly sunk from one low point to another. Part of Lilly's misery included a move to Puerto Rico that was designed to give the family a second chance to make a fresh start. Almost immediately upon their arrival, Martin wanted to return to the States. He badgered Lilly until she agreed to lie to their landlord and get them out of their lease. Only three months after they left, they returned home with no place to live. They found a homeless shelter, and for a while, all of them lived there.

While at the shelter, Martin applied for jobs. They moved in with one of Lilly's sisters and Martin found work as a nurse's aid. It seemed as though they were back on track—but it lasted only a few weeks.

Before long, Martin began coming home and immediately washing his face and hands. Lilly became suspicious. One night, she met him at the door and kissed him. She smelled the scent of another woman. The next day she went through all Martin's belongings and discovered receipts for flowers, jewelry, and hotel rooms. Furious, Lilly confronted him and kicked him out.

On one hand, the tide was turning. On the other hand, Lilly still had an ever-churning sea of challenges to navigate.

As the days passed, the marriage unraveled into its last phase. While separated, Martin begged Lilly for her forgiveness. When she refused, he threatened to kill himself if she did not go back with him. She still refused, but she called the local police. By the time they got to the hotel, Martin could not be found. At first Lilly feared that he followed through on his threat. However, she soon learned that he left the hotel and committed himself to the state mental hospital.

When he got out, Martin again begged Lilly to go back with him. Unbelievably, she gave him "one more chance" in an effort to save her marriage. By then, Lilly's life had spun totally out of control.

Even Lilly is amazed now that she continued to try to keep her marriage together under such consistently stressful and toxic conditions. At the time, however, Lilly remembers feeling that it was her duty to keep trying; it was what she thought she was supposed to do. However, unknown to her conscious self, something inside Lilly was changing for the better. A new awareness sprung from deep within Lilly and began to take hold of her thoughts and feelings. It began to surface in small ways, like when Martin told her something and she proved him wrong. Sometimes she watched him make simple mistakes that even her children recognized. Finally, Lilly no longer felt that she was the reason for all the problems. Though she didn't act on her new understanding right away, it was a big step toward Lilly's eventual victories.

Together again, they made one more "new start" in another state. First, they moved into a "crappy" hotel room, a place where the evidence of widespread drug use could be seen in the parking area, on grassy patches, and behind their building. Through the grapevine, Lilly learned that Martin was among the drug users. Though she suspected it in the past, Lilly always feared talking to him about it. Now she wondered how long he had been doing drugs. Was it recent or had it been all along? Maybe he was even dealing. She speculated about the answers, but kept her thoughts to herself.

Martin quickly got a job selling meats and delivering them to houses. At first, the work went well and the family moved into a nice apartment.

Lilly soon learned that though the melody seemed new, it had the same old words. Martin continued his psychological battering, as well as his infidelity and irresponsible behaviors. He told Lilly that nobody wanted her. Even worse, he turned his brusque and erratic actions toward their children. When he became angry with them, his face turned red and became contorted, his eyes widened and appeared to pop out, and from his angry voice bubbled a stream of verbal abuse. She began wondering if the sweet girl and boy she loved so much would learn Martin's ways and eventually turn out like their abusive and condemning father.

The idea that her children could carry the pattern of abuse into their future frightened Lilly. All along she did whatever she thought would be best for herself and her children. Year after year, she thought hanging in and staying married provided it. After a while, however, she questioned her own judgment. In the end, she found she had nothing left to give. For Lilly, it was the end of the line.

During those difficult years of drama, and in spite of all that happened during her disturbing and chaotic marriage, Lilly matured and grew within herself. No longer the lost kid who missed the strong presence of her mother, she grew tired of the lies and the constant upheaval. She no longer thought Martin had all the brains in the family, and began to realize that she wasn't as dumb as Martin led her to believe.

The young mom, not yet out of her twenties, made a profound decision. She would fight for more than just survival. The more her discontent grew, the greater Lilly's desire became for a better life for herself and her children. As the desire increased, Lilly made a decision. She would do what she needed to do to make that happen. At first she didn't know how or when, but she knew she could change her life. Over time her decision calcified; having a better life became her main focus. Still, as in many cases of domestic abuse, it would take a couple more years and even more turbulence before coming to fruition. However, Lilly's resolve strengthened; it was just a matter of *one last push*.

That push came one night, after another episode in which Martin threatened Lilly. Her resolve finally peaked and to herself she said, "No! There's got to be a better way." Though she gave the appearance of continuing to stay with Martin, she saw their relationship heading nowhere but to the dump. Lilly's pain reformulated itself into the purposefulness, resolve, and determination that would soon set her free. This time would be different from all the others because this time she had a plan. Day-by-day Lilly prepared herself mentally, emotionally, and physically to take control, for herself and for her two young children.

Since Martin meted out money to Lilly only when she needed it for the family, she began taking money from Martin's wallet while he slept. She stashed money away, hiding it wherever she could; she managed to gather a few hundred dollars. Next, with the help of her in-laws, Lilly located the nearest shelter for victims of domestic abuse. Remarkably, the safe haven ended up being just down the road from Lilly's apartment. Everything fell into place, ready for her to break away from the abusive life she endured with Martin.

Lilly's moment of truth came after an argument during which Martin threatened to hit her and then followed through on the threat, punching and hitting her on the head with his fist. Next, Lilly heard him rummaging through the kitchen drawers. Fearing he might return with a knife, she "went running past the kitchen, running past Martin, and running out the door." She called the police first, then called Martin's mother. Martin took off in his truck, and took the children with him. The police chased Martin, but lost him on a back road. Fearing the safety of her children, Lilly went home and waited alone.

A little while later, Martin returned with the children. He acted as though nothing had happened. The excitement of the police chase seemed to have calmed him down. So following his lead, Lilly also appeared calm. As far as Martin could tell, everything returned to normal. He seemed satisfied that he got away with his craziness once again—or so he thought. Lilly knew differently. Lilly was done with Martin and ready to make her move. Lilly went to bed, but she didn't sleep that night; she stayed alert, and waited.

The next day, before leaving for work, Martin threatened Lilly once again, telling her, "If you thought you went through hell, you haven't seen nothing yet. If you aren't here when I get home, I'll show you what hell is about."

Martin went to work and Lilly called his mother and sister. She told them the previous night's escapades provided her with "the last straw." She told them she decided to leave for good and asked them to get her and the children. Then she packed a suitcase with items that she would need, including legal documents (birth certificates, social security cards, etc.) and clothes. In another suitcase, she packed whatever meats were in the freezer. Then, as though releasing pent-up anger, Lilly tore apart their house, including Martin's clothes. Finally, she left—for the last time.

When her in-laws came, they took Lilly and her children to the newly-discovered domestic abuse shelter. It was the beginning of Lilly's new life. After a short time, she left the first shelter and transferred to one in her home state and nearer to her family. All the while, Martin looked everywhere for Lilly and the children, questioning his mother, her sister, her friends, everyone.

Lilly stayed at the second shelter for two weeks and then transferred to A Woman's Place, another facility closer to her home. She stayed there for an additional six weeks. Next, Lilly moved to her sister's house.

It did not take Martin long to find Lilly there. When she refused to have anything to do with him, he began a series of both psychotic behaviors and illegal actions. He robbed a house and stole a gun. He smashed Lilly's car, left, then returned to smash her car some more. Someone in the neighborhood finally called the police and they arrested Martin.

With Martin in jail, Lilly thought, "Now is the beginning of what I have to do for me and the kids." Around that time, one of the support agencies that helped Lilly suggested she become involved with the Economic Self-Sufficiency Program provided by the Opportunity Council, a local community action agency. She made the call.

Through that program, she received counseling and support. More importantly, everyone in the program, from her counselor, Carol, to the office and clerical staff, encouraged Lilly to take one positive step after the other. She took courses and learned clerical skills, software programs, and other office work. As Lilly explains, "It was like baby steps. It was stuff I'd never done before."

As a result of her efforts, Lilly got a job in a manufacturing plant. The man who hired her liked her, and he helped her along by giving her more responsibility. Lilly discovered how important it was "for him to have that confidence in me" because it made her feel more confident in herself. It was the first of many times when Lilly would feel stronger and more motivated by the confidence others had in her.

Confidence was a new feeling for Lilly; it made all the difference in how she saw herself and her ability. She moved from the factory to the office and began doing data entry work. Next, she was promoted and, in time, she was earning nearly fourteen dollars an hour plus health care and benefits. Lilly felt great because, for the first time in her life, she "was making good money." She had a decent job and an apartment. She bought a small car. She felt good. The better she felt about herself, the more confidently Lilly was able to take additional control of her life.

Unfortunately, corporate changes in the manufacturing plant caused Lilly to be laid off. For some time, Lilly says, life went "up and down and up and down...it was scary." In spite of changes around her and her frequent fears, Lilly stayed in counseling. Undaunted, she continued to improve her skills, as well as her confidence. Looking back, Lilly laughs, "I did things I never thought I could do. I surprised myself!" Finally, she found another job, which created some degree of stability in her life. For the first time she tasted the sweetness of success.

Regrettably, Martin stayed in the picture. When he got out of jail, he insisted on seeing his children. Against Lilly's wishes, Martin sought and received court-appointed visitations. Though Lilly "went around in circles" about it, she concluded that she had to put her feelings aside and go with what the courts said. Rather than continuing to resist, Lilly hoped that in jail Martin "learned his lesson." She finally determined that "like it or not, he's going to be involved; it is what it is." The judge allowed Martin to have the children on alternate weekends.

On visitation weekends, Lilly dropped the children off at their father's home. She cringed at the dirty and disorganized look of the place. Also, Martin had a live-in relationship with an older woman. Witnessing how Martin treated her, Lilly worried about what the children would see and hear.

In addition, when her daughter and son stayed with their father, they never knew what to expect. Martin said he "found God" in prison, and often spent long hours reading the Bible to them. Sometimes he woke them up in the middle of the night so they could confess their sins. Between what she saw and the stories her children told her, Lilly sensed that visitation weekends grew increasingly more peculiar. Knowing how easily Martin could become angry and lose control, she felt concerned about putting her children in what could easily become a dangerous situation.

Over time, Lilly began noticing changes in her children. After their weekends with Martin, they usually returned home "wired and difficult to control." They had trouble getting back into the school week and began doing poorly in their academics. While both children seemed more edgy, her son especially began demonstrating troubling behaviors, including losing his temper and acting out with the other children.

As her concern intensified, Lilly did some serious soul searching. The visitations clearly had a negative effect on the children. At the same time, she dreaded any confrontation with Martin. Slowly, Lilly came to an uncompromising decision to stop the visitations, "even if it meant that I could get in trouble."

Lilly got up the courage to call Martin and told him that she would no longer bring the children to his place on the weekend. Incensed, Martin threatened to have the children taken away from her. When Lilly refused to change her mind, he took action. They both retained attorneys and went back to court.

Then she made a life-altering decision. The only way to put a stop to Martin's questionable activities in front of her children would be to seek sole custody. Lilly knew the giant step meant engaging in a lengthy legal battle with Martin. She also knew the accompanying attorney's fees would be substantial. Earning just slightly more than minimum wage, Lilly knew she'd be required to make lots of sacrifices.

Fearful but bold, Lilly pressed ahead and while the children's weekend visitations with Martin continued, she went to court ready for the fight of her life. The tension between Martin and Lilly escalated with each passing month.

On the homefront, Lilly's daughter and son did not yet have the maturity to grasp the full impact of the court case, including mounting legal fees. With youthful lack of understanding, they complained when they could not have pizza for dinner or eat out at the local fast food joint. In spite of their protests, Lilly knew their discomfort would be short-term. She pushed ahead.

The battle for custody dragged on month after month. By order of the court, each family member had to submit to psychological testing and attend counseling. Lilly went first, then the children, and finally Martin.

During his sessions, the ever-clever Martin managed to conceal his raging outbursts. On his best behavior, he also convinced counselors to question Lilly's charges of psychological battering. The court ordered Lilly and Martin to be counseled together.

Angered but compliant, Lilly tolerated the judicial process, though she found it frightening, disturbing, and tedious. During one session, however, something unexpected happened and Lilly caught a break! After being asked a series of questions, Martin stood up and began pacing. Lilly, all too familiar with his behavior, knew what would happen next. In a terrifying explosion, he lost control and launched into a verbal attack. Using one expletive after another, he told the therapist to shut up, leave him alone, and get out of his business.

When Martin left, the counselor admitted the shocking but eye-opening dose of reality validated Lilly's claims of abuse. The wheels of justice sometimes move slowly but, in the end, the incident would affect the court's decision and make a critical difference in Lilly's case.

Staying focused and motivated was Lilly's greatest challenge in the midst of court, her children, bills, and work. Yet instead of giving up, week after week, Lilly grew stronger. Feeling increasingly less afraid of being controlled by Martin, her confidence and self-esteem blossomed.

While Lilly continued to fight Martin through her attorney, the legal fees mounted. When totaled, the fees were nearly nine thousand dollars. Lilly watched as the hard earned money in her bank account dwindled to nothing and she slid into debt.

At last, the day arrived for the judge to make a final decision. Lilly went to court. She could feel the shaky nervousness growing like a flame in the pit of her stomach and spreading through her whole body. She sat on the hard wooden seat while she waited for her case to be announced. She prayed.

Finally, she heard the judge's ruling. In a long-awaited but happy decision, the judge awarded Lilly sole custody of her son and daughter. Martin would be permitted supervised-only visitation rights.

Lilly felt joyous! She could barely wait to tell her children the good news.

In the following months, she watched as their grades improved and their normal personalities again surfaced. Though still bearing the scars of their earlier life, the children gradually began to settle down.

Though all along she still battled shyness and fear, Lilly proudly explains what kept her going, "I have two beautiful kids. Everything I do, I do for my kids *and I feel good about it.*"

Looking back, Lilly sees how her lack of self-worth contributed to her abuse. Even after she left and filed for divorce, she had so little belief in herself that she easily could have just given up. At one point, she felt so ill-equipped to provide for her children that she considered putting them up for adoption, believing someone else could provide a better life for them. The thought of it, however, depressed her. Lilly simply acknowledges, "I couldn't do it. I love them too much." Instead, Lilly chose to make more of herself and her life, even though it meant experiencing the scariness of pushing herself outside of her comfort zone.

Believing her life had meaning in the world, especially for her children, Lilly started a progression of positive changes in her life. She stopped being the quiet "good girl" she once was. She asserts herself more and she exclaims, "I'm done having people walk on me. I had it for so long when I felt so bad...I thought that was the way it had to be—that [life] was the way it was, and I just had to take it." Now, she does something she could never do in the past. She has boundaries.

Though she still has to improve her people skills and become a smoother and more effective communicator, Lilly is learning to tell folks "no" when she feels she's being pushed into something she doesn't want to do. She is no longer afraid to tell others what she likes and doesn't like.

Something that Lilly believes has helped her build confidence is "learning how to read people." She watches a person's behaviors to see if there is a match between what a person says and what a person does. While she admits it is still more difficult for her to read men than women, she's working on it.

While Lilly looks at her life and proudly states, "I like myself for what I've accomplished," she also believes there is room for improvement. "I don't know when you reach the point of being satisfied. I haven't gotten to that point." Yet she believes she is on the right track and aspires to a better life. Most importantly, she now knows that no matter what happens, she confidently affirms, "*I can protect myself.*"

Walking her victory path one step at a time, she often "feels scared at times when it comes to doing certain things." Yet she acknowledges that she is light years wiser than the young girl who married the controlling Martin. Not only does she value the skills that enable her to stand up for and protect herself and her children, she now believes she can do more than merely survive. She knows that when she makes the effort, she learns new skills that help her advance her life. For Lilly, *knowing is power.* And she continues to move forward, one step at a time.

Lilly believes victory begins with attitude and belief. When it comes to domestic abuse, whether it is mental, physical, or both, Lilly says that a woman must understand that "nothing is worth staying, everything is worth going." Through her own difficult experiences and personal fears, she learned that "if a woman is scared of what could happen and tells herself, 'I'm not going to be able to do this', it won't ever get better. You have to try...and try again."

If a woman is in an abusive situation and has family, Lilly suggests that she go to them. If she cannot confide in them, she *must* find someone she can trust. It is something Lilly wishes she had done sooner. For years, Martin's threatening and demeaning viewpoint became her only window to the world—and herself. She says she saw and did things she shouldn't have, admitting, "I was in places I shouldn't have been. I was tormented...things he asked me to do, things he did to me, things nobody knows about..." Too embarrassed to tell anyone, even her own family, she became dependent on Martin in every way.

Only when Lilly began telling others, both her own sisters as well as Martin's mother and sister, did she receive the external validation that helped shift her thinking and emotionally prepare her to leave. Without it, the cycle of abuse might have continued indefinitely.

In addition to talking to others, Lilly suggests that a woman find one of the many programs designed especially for women in difficult or abusive situations. In her case, Lilly received great support from the Self-Sufficiency Program. As she talked about Carol and the other counselors, she wondered aloud, "Wow... *what would it be like without them?* I didn't think I could do it. I was scared." She had the motivation, and the program provided the support that enabled her to follow through and succeed.

In 2002, Lilly graduated from the program that helped her get her start. As a result of her victories, she earned the Worthington Award, an award given to an outstanding woman in the program. On the day Lilly received the award, her children and her family attended the special event. During the ceremony, the presenter told Lilly's story to the audience, which included her two teenage children. For the first time they were at an age when they could appreciate the seriousness of what happened. Afterward, at a celebration dinner, her children took her aside. They humbly, and in their own way, expressed their gratitude and appreciation. Lilly was touched and fervently believes that "their words will ring in my ears for the rest of my life."

When she looks to the future, Lilly wants to be, do, and have more. During her passage from the meek and passive teenager she once was to the strong woman she is today, Lilly says that she found "another side of me that I didn't know I had." As she reflects upon the younger Lilly, she realizes that not only did she stay isolated, but also that much of her thinking used to be negative. She works on looking on the more positive side of life, at the good in the world and the positive possibilities for the future. She improves daily. She is not perfect, and does not always do everything right, but she continues to do her best.

She struggles regularly with the problems of being the single parent of teenagers. Keeping them on track is a roller coaster ride. Yet her children continue to be a motivating force. She says, "The reason I work so hard, even when I think I can't do it, is that I truly don't want my kids to go down the road I went down."

Along with Lilly's victory, however, came a very different outlook. She no longer allows anything or anyone to get her bogged down. She does not smoke or do drugs. While a social drinker, she does not allow alcohol in her house. Recently, she gave her boyfriend an ultimatum to stop drinking or they would end their relationship. He chose alcohol and Lilly told him to leave. "I'm not doing this [toxic relationship]," she told him. "If you are the kind of person I don't want to be around, I don't *have* to [be with you]." Looking at dating relationships with more mature, self-respecting eyes, Lilly affirms, "I don't have to be with a guy to make my life work. I know now *I have a choice.*"

In 2003, Lilly achieved one of her major goals. She became

the proud owner of her own home. It's a mobile home, complete with a mortgage. No more shuffling around, living in apartments or subsidized housing. Her area is a decent one and she has good neighbors.

Though awarded child support by the courts, the financial assistance from Martin isn't consistent, and Lilly doesn't depend on it. She works in a local restaurant and, a short time ago, received a promotion to assistant manager. She has plans to take more computer courses and upgrade her skills to procure an office job with better pay and broader benefits.

Looking back and knowing where she has been, Lilly is amazed and grateful that she has gotten this far. She continues an uphill fight for financial stability and independence, and she conquers one obstacle after another. Lilly has clearly developed what she needs to stay on her new road, and she is taking her children with her. They can all experience her victorious journey with pride.

STEPPING STONES
TO VICTORY

1. Do you know the "red flags" for domestic abuse? Can you see them in your own relationship? Or do you recognize them in the relationship of a loved one? If you know or suspect you are in an unhealthy domestic situation, learn what you can from domestic abuse hotlines, agencies, and the Internet.

   Contact the National Domestic Violence Hotline at 1-800-799-SAFE (7233), 1-800-787-3224 (TTY), or www.ndvh.org. They will help you to strategize a plan for leaving your abusive situation, or if you choose to stay, will work on a safety plan with you. In addition, you will receive referrals to shelters in your area, counseling, and low cost legal help.

2. Most women stay in domestic abuse situations because they:

   - have at least one dependent child;
   - are not employed outside the home;
   - have no property that is solely theirs;
   - lack access to cash or bank accounts;
   - fear being charged with desertion resulting in loss of their children and joint assets;
   - may face a decline in the standard of living (personally as well as the children).

   Do any of these fit you and your situation? How can you get out of an abusive dependence or protect yourself from falling into this kind of dependency? Lilly's victory came in "baby steps." In your Victory Journal write down three "baby steps" you can take to create some financial independence and some personal power. Take one of those steps today, take the next one tomorrow, the third one next week. Record your results.

3. Education, or lack of education, hampers the opportunity and earning power of many women. Is there some form of education you need to do to improve your ability to get a better job? In your Victory Journal, devise a plan for getting the education you need. Include how you will get the money and make the time for classes.

4. Lilly says she went into a place of depression, embarrassment, and confusion. She didn't tell anyone. If you were in trouble, whom could you trust? Where could you go? If you do not have a trusted family member to turn to, who is there for you? If you don't have someone/someplace now, take action to find a person, place, or agency that can help. In your Victory Journal, write the name, location, and phone numbers of the people or services you need. Use them for quick reference.

5. Are you raising your children without a healthy warning system? Lilly was so dependent on her mother's guidance that, when her mother wasn't available, she didn't have a personal protection system of her own. Now Lilly has learned how to "read people" better and can protect herself. What can you do to teach your children how to read others, as well as read situations better? Gavin de Becker's book, *The Gift of Fear*, is an excellent resource. Knowledge is power and personal power leads to personal victory.

6. Lilly says that learning how to "read people" is an important new skill for protecting herself. Do you know how to read people? What are some of the resources you can use to develop this skill?

7. Many women don't know how to say no to a boyfriend, spouse, children, and others in their lives. There are many books and CDs about creating boundaries and developing assertive communication skills. These resources can help a woman to learn

how to say no, as well as how to ask others for what she needs. Find a book, audio/video program, or class that focuses on assertive communication skills for women. If you cannot find those, find an assertive woman whose communication techniques are ones that you would like to model.

Once you have located an education source, then:

a. Take one technique, such as telling people you have to consider their request before answering. Get comfortable with saying it to yourself and then practice it with others until it becomes a natural response.

b. When it does, try another technique.

c. Get someone to practice with and who will help monitor your progress.

8. Being "filled up" is important to a woman's self-esteem, yet many women are consistently running on low or empty. What are three healthy things you can do on a daily basis to help you stay filled up? Example: Read something light and fun for 15 minutes each day; take a weekly "don't bother me" bubble bath; hire a high school student to help you for an hour or two each week.

3

Family Matters

Maureen Ingelsby

U NTIL THAT NIGHT, THE THURSDAY AFTER CHRISTMAS
1983, Maureen thought she had it all: a kind, handsome
husband with a well-paying job, five healthy and happy children,
enjoyable friends, a lovely home, and pleasant neighbors. When
she came home from work that night, she found the children in
bed and John sitting on a chair in the living room. He looked
oddly nervous, his uneasiness showing in the strained expression
on his face. She asked him what was wrong.

John told her he was leaving.

At first, Maureen wanted to put his words into some kind of
context. "Are you going to your parents'?" she asked.

"No," John responded, "I'm leaving...*you.*"

She stared at him in stunned silence. Then, as she turned her
head in confusion, she noticed the suitcases in the family room.
Only moments later, before Maureen could fully process what

was happening, John picked up his bags and walked out the front door into the cold December night.

Maureen rummaged around in her memory for some clue that might have prepared her for what had just happened. She thought John had been "acting funky" for a few days. But he had just formed a new part-time business and worked late nights to get it off the ground. Maureen chalked up John's somewhat odd behavior to business-related stress. Not only did they not discuss splitting up, he was not even home enough to have a significant argument. Suddenly, with no advance warning, she stood alone in the center hall trying to make sense of it all.

Until that moment in time, no one would have said Maureen had a tough life. An only child with a middle class upbringing, she enjoyed a well-cared for and happy life. Her father was well-respected in his career as the manager for a regional restaurant chain. Her mother, a vivacious woman in a traditional stay-at-home role, cared for Maureen's aging and sickly grandparents.

As a girl, while attending local parochial schools, Maureen earned consistently high marks and pursued many extra-curricular activities. In high school, she played in the orchestra and wrote news stories for the school newspaper. She also performed in three musical productions at a local all-boys school. Through her efforts Maureen discovered how going the extra mile and giving *just a little more* went a long way toward excellence. Maureen recalls how she "wanted to be different" and admits that she "always wanted to do a little bit more because I thought it was to my advantage."

Maureen continued her winning performance while attending West Chester State Teacher's College. She played in the orchestra and was a charter member of the Delta Zeta Sorority. In addition, Maureen also wrote for the school newspaper, covering many Vietnam-era sit-ins for the college.

Though serious about her studies, Maureen found plenty of time to socialize. While she made new friends in college, she also still hung around with her hometown crowd. Within her group,

Maureen enjoyed the company of all the guys. She found one of them, Bob Ingelsby, particularly interesting. A decent guy, Bob became good friends with Maureen and she had a lot of fun with him. After they began dating, she liked him even more.

Both Bob and Maureen were ready for a serious relationship and began discussing marriage. As an only child, Maureen told Bob about her dream of having "lots of kids with Irish names." Bob, on the other hand, was the second oldest of seven children and grew up with plenty of family responsibility. He didn't share Maureen's vision. He wanted to be with Maureen, get married, and buy a house. After a while, he wanted to have a couple of kids with more conventional names.

The more they talked about it, the more they realized that they wanted different things from life. Their dating relationship fizzled, but they remained friends for many years.

Maureen graduated from college and quickly secured a position teaching elementary school, beginning the September after graduation. That August, shortly before school started, Maureen attended a wedding with her parents. Her father's secretary married one of their neighbor's sons. At the reception she bumped into John, brother of the groom. Though Maureen and John knew each other growing up, he was a few years older. Through the years, they attended different schools and each had their own set of friends. During Maureen's college years, John joined the Navy and the two never crossed paths. Suddenly, meeting again as adults, the sparks flew. Quickly the couple became an item.

While Maureen began a teaching career and John continued his military service, the two dated. As the world changed from autumn's golden warmth to holiday sparkle, the couple fell in love. Maureen cared enough for John to consider the relationship serious. In addition, they shared the same desire to have a lot of children. John loved kids and his eagerness to have a family won Maureen over.

Shortly after Christmas, John received orders for a tour of duty in the Mediterranean and left quickly. In March, he sent an engagement ring and proposal instructions to his father. At a Saint Patrick's Day party, much to Maureen's surprise, John's father gave Maureen his son's ring and asked Maureen to marry John. Maureen accepted this unique proposal. In a subsequent phone call, they planned a wedding date for later that year, and the long-distance engagement began.

In June, with wedding arrangements in the forefront of her mind, Maureen wrapped up her fourth-grade teaching assignment. She prepared for the wedding, writing to John regularly about the latest developments. The couple exchanged letters of excited anticipation as they planned for the nuptials and Maureen's subsequent move abroad. They looked forward to being together again and starting their new life.

Only days before the wedding John arrived home on military leave. Within a week, Maureen and John married, enjoyed a short honeymoon, said their goodbyes to parents, and left for the island of Cyprus. The next year, they welcomed daughter Meghan into their lives.

The following year John completed his military service. The couple returned home, already expecting their second child. John accepted a banking job in a neighboring state. They set up housekeeping in a small apartment, then bought a house, which they moved into as the baby arrived.

During the final stages of Maureen's pregnancy, her doctor told the couple something was wrong with the baby. Without the benefit of current technology, the doctor could provide only minimal information. The couple worried about the health of their new baby, but hoped for the best.

During this time, Maureen and John moved into their new home. Afterward, Maureen's doctors induced her labor. Sadly, daughter Heather was born with anencephaly, a congenital malformation of the brain resulting in small or missing brain hemispheres. Infants with this condition are usually either stillborn or die within a few days. When the doctors told Maureen and John, they were filled with grief.

Maureen visited the hospital daily after returning home, holding and rocking the tiny baby, giving her all the love she could. Heather lived for just one week before dying of meningitis.

Afterward, Maureen threw herself into housekeeping and caring for Meghan. Within the year, Maureen was pregnant again. In the spring of 1976, Ryan was born. Seamus came into the world the following year.

Maureen's parents decided to sell their house a short time later. Seeing it as a great opportunity, John and Maureen happily purchased the modest three-bedroom suburban home. Once settled in the new home, the couple celebrated the births of Timothy and Rory. Finally, by 1982, Maureen had her big family with the Irish names.

At some point in those first years, citing that he was the breadwinner, John decided that he'd handle all the finances. Looking back, she remembers how much work it was to care for five young children, and it felt as though she didn't always have her own mind. In relinquishing the finances to John, though contrary to her take-charge temperament, Maureen believes she did the right thing. John handled the finances, and Maureen assumed duties involving the well-being of the children.

The children became the primary focus of the couple's life. Maureen was a homeroom mom and John served as a Boy Scout leader. To help make ends meet, Maureen found a part-time job with Weight Watchers. She worked only a couple of nights and Saturday mornings, times when John could be with the children. The small salary helped stretch the budget and provided a few extras for the young family.

In Maureen's perception, the couple had a good marriage. In her view, Maureen and John both worked hard, co-creating the life they dreamed together.

In addition, Maureen also thought of John as the most stable son in his family. Though his brothers were nice enough, the older one liked to drink and party while the younger, more likeable brother lacked common sense. Both had troubled marriages and, during the first few months of 1983, both brothers left their spouses. Throughout the year as she watched the pain her sisters-in-law experienced, Maureen considered herself "the lucky one who was still happily married." She remembers being grateful that she was married to "the sane one" in the family.

That was, until several months later, on that cold December night. As she sat alone on that Thursday night, watching the tiny lights twinkling on the Christmas tree, she realized ruefully that she faced the same fate as the others. Trying to understand his unexpected and irrational behavior, she wondered about John's mental state. She frantically searched her mind, asking herself, *How could this have happened?* When there were no answers, she questioned, *Why me?*

By the life-changing Christmas of 1983, Maureen had just turned thirty-three and her five children ranged in age from nine to one. It seemed almost inconceivable that mere days before, she'd been thinking about New Year's and how they would welcome it together. Now, looking at the remnants of unwrapped gifts still under the tree, she wasn't sure she even wanted to greet the next day!

On Friday, as she tried to make some sense of her situation, Maureen didn't know what to do next. She told no one, not even her children. Her head pounded as she tried to go about her routine, pretending that nothing was wrong, acting as though John was just out of town for a few days. Her body went through its everyday routine, but her mind searched incessantly for signs or clues...something—anything—she must have missed.

That weekend, Maureen received a mail offer for a credit card. Looking in her wallet, she realized she had little cash. With no credit cards in her own name, she knew she needed something to help bridge the money gap when the children needed clothes, shoes, and whatever else. With all accounts in John's name, having a credit card in *her* name suddenly became a most important item. She didn't think twice about the offer and applied for the card immediately. It was the first of many unexpected blessings.

Throughout that weekend, Maureen meandered around the house, hour after hour, telling herself, "I'm just going to have to take this on." She knew it was true, but *what was she going to do? How could she take care of five children* now? Her part-time job with Weight Watchers was to provide extras, not support a family. She only ran a couple of weekly classes in her local area. The income was nothing on which a family could even begin to live.

On Saturday, she called her estranged sisters-in-law, knowing they would understand. Next, she waited for John to tell their children himself, but he did not. Though he called the house to talk to them, he said nothing about leaving permanently. As the weekend drew to a close, she finally told her children. However, they were young and were used to their father being away on business, so they could not fully understand what Maureen told them. It would take time for the meaning to sink into reality.

By late Sunday night, Maureen found herself lying in bed, crying for hours in the privacy of her room. Then she says, "I was hit like a bolt of lightening. I said to myself, 'I can either lie down beside this, or I can pick myself up and move on.' I didn't know what I would do; I just knew I wasn't going to ask for pity. I'd do whatever it took!" It was Maureen's moment of truth.

In that defining moment, she forced herself to consider options. Determined not to wallow in self-pity, Maureen recognized that she alone had control over her own life. Rather than waste time feeling sorry for something she couldn't change, she would take charge and become the ruler of her kingdom. She would find a way to make life work for her family.

The more she thought about it, the more ideas materialized. She knew she could go back to teaching, so for now, that would be her path. Boldly, she made up her mind to greet the new year with determination, a plan, and a hopeful sense of confidence. It was a courageous decision that would soon be tested.

Though John called Maureen through the week, their conversation focused more on the children than on their relationship. On the weekend, John came over and took the kids out. When they came home, her children told Maureen about their day... and about the woman who went along with them. That was when Maureen learned that there was a girlfriend. In fact, the woman was John's secretary and the one who was helping him set up his new business, and the same person for whom Maureen bought a Christmas present only weeks earlier. Maureen never suspected she was buying a gift for her husband's mistress, and John had never given her a clue.

He also didn't bother discussing common household expenses, such as utilities. Without her knowledge, John called each company and told them he would no longer be responsible for the bills. In turn, each company—heat, electric, water, phone—called and told Maureen that the service had to be put into her name or it would be shut off. Once again, she was stunned. "I didn't know where my next meal was coming from, and now I had to take on the utilities. I hadn't even started working yet." Feeling the sting of such a blow, Maureen wondered how the same man who once professed his love for her and their children could now be so heartless?

Still reeling from John's actions, Maureen's determination to be self-sufficient became an all-out mission. After all, the bill collectors didn't dole out pity. They didn't care that her five children needed heat, electricity, water, and food. On the contrary, instead of assistance, they offered a cold, dark house. The harsh reality pushed her to her true turning point. Welcome 1984!

As the new year unraveled, Maureen proceeded as planned. She found another part-time job, this one as a nursery school teacher at the local Baptist church. It wasn't her first choice, but it was available immediately. Though she knew she could earn more money as a substitute teacher, she was without an on-call babysitter, which restricted her availability and gave her limited options.

With her three oldest children already in school, she took the part-time position and started immediately. She took her two youngest children with her, putting them in different classes. Two part-time jobs didn't provide a lot of income, but as a first step in the right direction, it worked.

While at that job, Maureen learned of a Catholic school that was looking for a kindergarten teacher. The very next day, she went to the new school and met the principal. She asked for the job and got it. A neighborhood woman agreed to watch her two little ones and, with that, Maureen took another step forward. Though it was also not a high-paying job, it catapulted Maureen into much needed full-time employment.

Another unexpected blessing occurred soon thereafter. Her teaching position provided a salary, but no benefits (a common practice in Catholic schools at the time). Father Dempsey, the church's curmudgeon pastor, graciously and secretly provided health insurance for Maureen's children. Given her meager wages, the health insurance benefit eased some of her financial burden. At last, a full-time job with benefits. In addition, she continued to work at her part-time job with Weight Watchers. Maureen saw progress.

Juggling a plate so full that it often overflowed, step by step the determined mother put her new life together. In retrospect, she affirms her evolution and proclaims, "After I made the decision to go forward, I never felt I couldn't."

Yet with two jobs and five young children in the house, "topsy-turvy" best described her home life. Though she yearned for the organized chaos of her old at-home mom job, her outside work afforded Maureen a space for focus—and her mind always clued-in to moving forward.

In her scarce quiet moments, Maureen wondered silently how she would make it all work. She clearly felt the stress, and she remembers *always* feeling tired. Still, she recalls, "I was always talking to myself and telling myself it would be fine. *We'd* be fine." During that year, Gloria Gaynor's "I Will Survive" became a chart-topping hit song—and Maureen's theme song!

Time passed and the couple filed for divorce. In the settlement, Maureen kept the family home. Though she expected it,

Maureen counted her blessings. Her children didn't have to move from their normal, familiar environment. One less change, one more blessing.

Though the courts finalized the divorce, Maureen regularly went to court for non-payment of child support. John slipped into a pattern of making payments only when the courts gave him no other way out, which seldom happened. Though she continued to fight, disputes dragged on month after month. She paid hefty attorney's fees, yet she still didn't have any support money.

Maureen eventually came to think that the lawyer wasted too much time and cost too much money. Figuring she couldn't do any worse, Maureen fired her lawyer and began representing herself. One year folded into another while Maureen received virtually no financial help from John. Adding insult to injury, John's efforts to spend time with his children were about as reliable as his support payments.

In spite of the upheaval in their lives, the children did fairly well in school. In addition, they became active in school activities and sports. With her flexible jobs, Maureen could attend games as well as other after-school and weekend activities. With her children so close in age, she often attended several events each week; during some sport seasons, it was every day. More than once Maureen recalls having two children playing for different teams at the same time. She remembers driving back and forth to different fields, trying to time her maneuvers so she would catch both sons playing! Without a doubt, Maureen jokes about how it was "a little crazy," yet she was determined to make her life work for her and her children—and work well.

During this time, Maureen's father died. Now widowed, her mother moved in with Maureen and provided a much needed helping hand. Mother and daughter pooled their resources. Her mother watched Maureen's youngest son, Rory, until he was old enough for school. Maureen counted on her mother to be there when the older children got home from school, and on the nights when Maureen was at her part-time job. While it was sometimes more than her mother bargained for, she liked the activity and the energy of her grandchildren.

In addition to her mother's help, Maureen acknowledges, "As an only child, I was used to being around older people and I had a network of older adults." This kindly group of seniors, as well as some neighbors, would sometimes watch her children. Also, a couple of times each year someone anonymously sent small amounts of money to Maureen. The gifts helped pay for holiday gifts, school activities, and clothes. Maureen always felt blessed by the generosity. Not until years later did she discover that her kind benefactor was a distant cousin. She appreciated the assistance then, and still says a silent "thank you" when she thinks about it.

Maureen says that her life had plenty of highs and lows— enough to make an outsider wonder *what kept her going?* "I stayed motivated because of the children," Maureen explains. "I wanted to keep things on an even keel for them." Once she got past the initial shock of John's desertion, Maureen says she didn't get inside her own head nor did she spend a lot of time thinking about the how or why of her life. Instead, she "just did it." She kept going because, as best as she could tell, "things were moving along all right."

Although her income was low during those years, Maureen did not allow money to be either a stimulus or a deterrent. "It's funny," Maureen muses. "I guess I should have been motivated by money, but I always felt that we could live within our means as long as we were all together and healthy." Leaning on this philosophy, Maureen's goal was to consistently move forward with her children; she continued to focus on that goal—no matter what, year after year.

Though teaching was the career that helped her get on her feet, eventually it showed signs of being counterproductive within her family. As her children advanced into upper grades, their homework and school projects took additional time and energy. She noticed that the work she did with her own children often echoed the work of her day job. However, with her own children, she did the activities with much less patience. She confesses, "I was good to everyone else's kids, but could sometimes be nasty with my own at the end of the day." Maureen realized the time had come to leave the classroom for a new, child-free job. While she was pondering her next move, Weight Watchers offered her the opportunity for a promotion to a full-time position and she eagerly accepted it. The new job did not pay considerably more, but it afforded Maureen greater flexibility and more variety. Perhaps most importantly, the work included adult contact and conversation during the workday.

Looking back, Maureen recalls her life as something akin to split screen mode. Not wanting to sugarcoat the past, Maureen remembers the everyday, hectic challenges she faced. Rather than pretend that life was all "sweetness and light," Maureen laughs about how life then was "one baseball game at a time, a birthday party at a time, and one crisis at a time." Yet when she thinks about it, she marvels at what she and her children accomplished together.

Maureen believes her positive thoughts coupled with stubborn determination provided the keys to her victory during this challenging period. Both consciously and unconsciously, she remained steadfast in her thinking. "I *never* second-guessed myself. I just trudged through with never a thought that I wouldn't—or couldn't—succeed. I didn't ever look at the big picture." Her attitudes and beliefs permeated her reality and in spite of Maureen's challenges, she says, "I never *felt* that I had it tough. I had family and friends who cared, a belief in God who took care of us all the time, and a belief in my kids and I, that we could do this together." And so she, *and they,* did. Maureen *had survived* and she created a *victory for herself and her children.*

As a single parent, Maureen focused mainly on her responsibilities to her family. Wanting her children to have a strong religious background, she took them to church regularly. She became more active in her congregation and often sang for weddings and funerals. Maureen enjoyed singing, and the extra income was welcome. She also joined a single parent's group, which offered great and inexpensive activities for the children, as well as discount tickets for special events. She seldom dated; in fact, dating was almost the very last thing on Maureen's mind. Even if she had the time, she thought, "What person would take on a woman with five kids?"

Maureen's children grew from tots to teenagers. They became tall and lanky high school kids who worked after-school jobs in addition to their school-related activities. One by one, they started talking about teenage topics like dating, driving, and graduating high school.

In the midst of all the bustle, one day Maureen had an unexpected phone call from her former sweetheart. Bob Ingelsby, the college boyfriend who didn't want a big family, had never married. When Maureen's picture appeared in the local paper for a church-related event, Bob's mother saved it for him. Learning that Maureen was single, his mother encouraged Bob to call.

Though happy to hear from Bob, Maureen set the record straight during that first phone call. She emphatically explained to Bob, "I have two jobs and five kids...I don't date." He replied, "I'm not asking you." Just the same, they reestablished a talking relationship. A few weeks later, Bob called again. This time he did ask Maureen out, not for an "official date" but for an afternoon walk in the renowned Longwood Gardens followed by a casual dinner. She agreed.

Before their meeting, Maureen instructed the children—especially the younger ones—to watch their manners. Someone had told Maureen that Bob had gained a lot of weight since their college days, so she especially warned them not to make an issue about Bob's size. That night, when Bob came to her front door, she was surprised to see that he was fit and trim. While it was true that he put on some pounds in previous years, he no longer carried the extra weight. Naturally, she didn't have time to inform her children. When Bob entered, he found her five children sitting politely on the living room sofa, lined up by age. Expecting a bigger man, one of the younger boys blurted, "But Mommy, he's not fat!" Good-natured Bob took it in stride, but it made for an interesting first meeting between Bob and the brood.

For some reason, Maureen presumed their rendezvous would be a one-time event. But while walking around the beautiful horticultural estate, Maureen noticed their relationship had much the same easy quality it had back in their college days.

Their relationship quickly developed. Though it was very different from the one of their carefree academic days, the dissimilarity was solidly positive. Gone were questions around having a big family. Instead, Maureen and Bob had frequent, serious conversations about raising her children and getting them through school.

Since the traumatic Christmas season of 1983, Maureen had lived a lifetime of small victories. While she had no fear of being abandoned again and she continued to be comfortable with Bob, she was also in no rush to get remarried.

As their relationship developed, she saw the same good man, trustworthy and dependable, that she knew from their younger years. As their dating became courtship, they seriously discussed their future. Wanting to be realistic, they agreed that two major challenges lay ahead.

First of all, Bob was a long-time bachelor who lived alone, and liked it. Not only would he have to adjust to marriage (his first), but also adapt to living with a spouse, five children, and a mother-in-law.

Secondly, with her children nearing young adulthood, Maureen's small house already barely fit the seven people who lived there. With Bob, marriage meant selling the house she lived in most of her life and buying a bigger, more expensive one.

As they dated, Bob wondered if he could make such a great adjustment. At the same time, Maureen wondered how she could bear to sell the house that had a lifetime of memories and was the place that embodied her victory over abandonment.

In addition, neither Bob nor Maureen wanted to relinquish control of their finances. Maureen's past experiences with John and the family finances prompted her concerns. Futhermore, Bob lived too many years as a bachelor to be readily comfortable with suddenly pooling his money with Maureen. Each understanding the other's needs, their maturity lent itself to practicality. They decided to divide the financial responsibilities and maintain separate bank accounts. It is a practice they continue to this day.

The kind of conversation they shared about money typified the quality of all their conversations. They continued honestly discussing obstacles and developed an attitude borne of Maureen's positive approach, Bob's love for Maureen, and their loving desire to be together. Slowly they made the necessary emotional and logistical adjustments, including buying a bigger house.

Two years after that first phone call, Bob and Maureen married. Maureen felt she found a true partner with whom to share a new life together. She recalls those early days of marriage with a special feeling. Everything was new again. She and her new spouse had great chemistry. In addition, Maureen enjoyed being together again with Bob's large family, now expanded to include spouses, nieces, and nephews.

For the first time, Maureen felt as though all the bad years simply evaporated into the ethers, and only the good times remained. In the same situation, others might feel they earned the right to put their life in neutral and just coast. Not Maureen. As the hands-on part of parenting diminished, a new career waited.

It began after the newly-formed family moved into a larger house. They bought a more expensive home than they planned, and then spent more money decorating it. One day, Bob seemed seriously concerned about the family finances. Used to having lots of money in the bank, he told Maureen he thought he might have to get a part-time job. Since Bob was helping to support her children, she felt it was only fair that if he felt he had to get a part-time job, so should she.

When she thought about what she could do, she remembered

someone suggesting that she might be a good real estate agent. Maureen decided to try it on a part-time basis. She enrolled in and completed the necessary real estate courses, got her license, and joined a firm. In 1992, she completed her basic training and began. She credits her first real estate manager and mentor, Larry Etherton, for creating a cheerleading type of environment. He encouraged Maureen to take risks and do her best work, for her own good.

Maureen applied herself to her new venture the same way she did to her other challenges, using hard work and positive energy. She built her reputation slowly but surely, one customer and one referral at a time. In 1993, she did so well that she left Weight Watchers and became a full-time real estate agent. Through classes and conferences, she continued to learn. Her performance improved and business grew. In 2001, Maureen was named the top Century 21 sales agent in the eastern Pennsylvania region. She continues to be one of the top three agents in the area. In September 2002, *Realtor Magazine* named Maureen as one of the "Top 300" realtors in the country. In addition, she twice received the coveted PAR Excellence Award from the Pennsylvania Association of Realtors, presented to realtors who exhibit a high standard of professionalism. She appeared in a *Philadelphia Magazine* article entitled "Realtors You Can Trust."

Though she revels in her current professional success, Maureen feels that the greatest victory of her life was guiding herself and her family successfully through those difficult earlier years.

Today, parenting is a different role. Her children are grown and on their own. She thinks proudly of how each child worked their way through school, every one paying a share of their tuition. When she talks about them, she does so with pride for the successes they have achieved. The older children all did well in college and went on to management positions in different fields. The youngest still attends college, carries a full course load and, at the same time, works full-time in the accounting office of a local food market.

Maureen feels she can be philosophical about the past as she looks to the future. Upon reflection, she supposes, "It could have all gone sour." She knows there could have been conflicts and rivalries that split the children apart or problems with school or police. "There were none!" Maureen says. In spite of what *could have been*, she proudly affirms what *was*. "We banded together," she beams. "Now, when family, friends, or strangers tell me what great kids I have, I know I have arrived."

While Maureen is certainly in a better place today than she was in the early eighties, she hasn't forgotten the kindnesses she received during her gutsy struggle to maintain her life and the lives of her children. Still involved with her high school alma mater, Maureen created a "guardian angel" program to honor the cousin who anonymously sent money during those difficult years. In appreciation for the help she received, she annually funds the tuition for one child whose family has fallen on difficult times. In doing so, Maureen believes she is honoring those who gave time, energy, and gifts in her time of need. Grateful still, she does not know how she would've made it through some of her darkest moments, except for the goodness of those who gave her a ray of hope. In appreciative acknowledgment of her numerous contributions, Prendergast High School awarded their Legacy Award to Maureen in 2003.

These days Maureen feels that "the tough times are over. Now I can do things for me, for and with my husband, and for my ninety-year-old Mom who lives with us." She loves the work she does and looks forward to continuing success. Maureen happily anticipates weddings, grandchildren, and travel time with Bob.

When she thinks of other women facing similar situations, Maureen emphasizes, "You can survive—you can do *more* than survive—if you put your mind to it and trust that others will help out when they see your determination."

As Maureen reflects on her eventful life, she exudes the confidence and satisfaction of someone who faced dark days and emerged victorious. "I sure hope life stays good to me. If there are any challenges in my future, I guess I'll just deal. I know that I know how!"

Maureen passes along her personal suggestions for achieving your own victories:

↝ **Move proactively.**

Get involved; push yourself into the forefront instead of lingering in the back row, waiting for something to happen. She advises that you make something happen for yourself, and the first step is to make yourself positively known to others. She doesn't think that looking at the big picture is important, "except to make the picture a goal." Maureen emphasizes how critical it is to consistently *move forward*. Regardless how small the movement, or how difficult, she tells women to "take the baby steps—one day (or even just one hour) at a time."

↝ **Avoid feeling sorry for yourself.**

"You stagnate when you wallow. It's a waste of time and energy." If considering how hard it is for you, Maureen suggests realizing that "others have it rough, just in a different way."

↝ **Create alliances.**

Maureen believes in connecting with others. Initially, her network supported her by lending a helping hand. Later she appreciated the benefits of being a part of a larger group, such as her company's real estate franchise. She feels strongly about the power of networking. Maureen's alliances put her in the right place, at the right time, with the right people, when an opportunity presented itself. It made a difference in her life.

↝ **Look for opportunities.**

Whenever Maureen saw an opening or recognized a break, she seized the moment. For example, she was teaching part-time at a Baptist church when she heard about a full-time teaching job at a Catholic school during a morning recess. Within a day, she approached the principal, asked for the job, and got it. If she wasn't looking for something better, wasn't alert to opportunities, or procrastinated, someone else may have gotten the job.

☛ Keep your focus and priorities straight; ignore opinions of others.

When Maureen took her daughter and four sons to church, she remembered that someone told her that children behave better when they sit in the front pew. So that's where she and her children sat each Sunday. Years later, someone told her they admired this, considering her circumstances (specifically, in 1983, divorced Catholics found much less acceptance in their church). She was surprised by the comment about her circumstances. She hadn't thought about what people might say about her private life and she muses, "It didn't even occur to me not to do what I was doing." She only knew that sitting up front was a way for her children to behave in church and better participate in the services. Maureen feels that as long as whatever she is doing isn't hurting someone else, she does what she wants and what she believes is right.

☛ Strive to work with excellence.

Find out what you need to do to succeed and do just a little bit more. And, Maureen declares, *"presume your success."*

☛ Go for it.

Maureen relied on herself, her abilities, and her people skills. Even during the down times, she trusted that if she took one step, the next would follow. She's competitive, mostly against her personal best. How does she do it? "I just take something and I go for it, especially when it is something that not everyone else does." She tells other women, "There are no limits. There are no boundaries. Just *go for it*, do a little extra, and you'll be rewarded. *Don't let anyone tell you that you can't.*"

STEPPING STONES
TO VICTORY

1. Maureen maintains that self-pity is an energy drain. When was the last time you felt sorry for yourself? In your Victory Journal, write down *what you said to yourself* that prevented you from taking a step forward. Look at what you wrote. Now ask yourself: What self-talk, what specific words or phrases, can better support you? Write them down and use them the next time you begin to feel sorry for yourself.

2. In the situations you described above, think about the *specific behaviors you used* to sabotage your efforts, e.g., giving up your goal, doing a poor job, making yourself late for an important appointment, snapping at a key support person, overeating/drinking/doing drugs.

   Draw two columns on a page in your Victory Journal. In the left column, write down whatever self-sabotaging behaviors you used. In the right column, next to each sabotaging behavior, write two positive counteractions—actions you can put in place now—that would prevent you from giving in to those behaviors in the future.

EXAMPLE:

Sabotaging Behavior	Counteractions
☞ I overeat.	a. I'll plan my day's menu in advance; and I'll only eat what I write down.
	b. I'll carry healthy "emergency food" with me in case I begin to give in or feel ready to give up.

3. Now that you have a plan in place, how will you know when to begin using those behaviors in a crisis? Using the same two-column method, write down your personal warning signs, the attitudes, thoughts, and behaviors that signal the beginning of a downhill spiral. Do you tell yourself it isn't worth it? Do you oversleep or eat, watch too much television, get depressed or angry? Once you get specific, look at your indicators. Write down what actions you will take when you notice one of those warning signs, e.g., enlist the help of a trusted friend or get a personal coach.

EXAMPLE:

<u>Warning Sign</u>	<u>Counteractions</u>
☞ I oversleep.	a. If I oversleep just once, I'll call two friends. I'll ask them to call me each day for a week. One will call me fifteen minutes before my alarm and the other can call fifteen minutes after my alarm goes off.
	b. I'll keep the phone, and my alarm clock, far enough away from my bed that I must get out of bed to answer the phone and turn off the alarm.

4. Maureen says that to get ahead, think of one place where you can do just a little bit more than everyone else. How can you "go the extra mile" to make yourself stand out—positively—from the crowd, your co-workers, or other peers? Record this in your journal. Choose a specific date to complete the "extra-mile" activity. Afterward, don't forget to write down your results. How did going the extra-mile lead you closer to victory?

4

Starting Over
Kathleen Zingaro Clark

FROM THE DAY KATHLEEN ZINGARO CLARK GRADUATED high school, she put her energies toward her career. Raised with a strong work ethic, she entered the business world just as the feminist movement got underway. Diligence, dedication, and ever-increasing competence enabled her to soar professionally, but Kathy's savvy did not extend to her personal life. A long-time, live-in relationship ended after six years. Barely a year later, she decided to marry an old flame, a teenage boyfriend turned adult best friend. Unfortunately, instead of getting the happily-ever-after she desired, she got conned. The toxic marriage ended quickly, and the short union left her suddenly broke, without a home, emotionally numb, and looking for a job.

After enjoying a professional life filled with hard-won successes, a failed marriage stopped Kathy dead in her tracks. The career pioneer found herself starting over with nothing but her emotionally devastated self. Once back on her feet, the quiet and unpretentious Kathy concluded, "You can be victimized, but you don't have to remain a victim."

Self-preservation led her charge toward victory. It enabled her to overcome profound emotional distress and a financial trouncing that might have destroyed a less grounded individual. Then her work-ethic values shaped the game plan as she picked up the pieces and Kathy reassembled her life.

Growing up in an urban rowhouse, Kathy's parents provided well for their four children. Her parents, second and third generation Italian-Americans, gave Kathy and her three siblings a strong parental message: work hard and do well. Always encouraging their children to "do better," they lived by their words and taught through example.

Kathy's father, a hard-working family man, seemed to be able to do nearly anything around the house from making a piece of furniture to fixing a plumbing problem. In addition to his regular job, her father worked part-time as a musician. Playing keyboard, accordion, and clarinet, he earned extra money on the weekends by performing at weddings and parties.

Meanwhile Kathy's mother "would take nothing she didn't like sitting down. She had high expectations, demanded what she wanted, and knew how to get her needs met." As Kathy grew up, her mother deftly managed the income her father earned so that it provided a small but nicely decorated home, an occasional vacation in Europe, and put aside savings for a desired new house.

Along with hard work, her parents also taught their children, "If you are going to do something, do it right." They expected excellence from Kathy and her siblings in everything from doing household chores and earning good grades in school to behaving properly in public.

Just outside her home, Kathy learned other lessons. Living near a busy highway, she and dozens of children found a playground in the shared driveway that connected the back sides of two long strings of houses. In the spring and summer, they rode bikes or played dodge ball. Halloween prompted the creation of a "spook house" which became an annual moneymaker for the more creative kids in their ranks. In the winter, they waited for snow, school cancellations, and the fun of making snow caves. Kathy remembers how, at any given time, there would be ten to twenty kids out back; she could always find someone there and never felt lonely.

Looking back at those days, Kathy thinks the driveway provided an excellent "training ground for developing social skills" where she looked at both boys and girls as friends. Kathy "became especially comfortable socializing and relating platonically [to men]." In fact, in later adult conversations with non-city bred friends, Kathy remembers she felt, "surprised to learn how uncommon it was to know someone of the opposite sex as 'just a friend.'"

Kathy also found a strong influence in the women who populated her life. In addition to her own kindly grandmother, she learned a lot by watching the women in the neighborhood. Kathy recalls them as "pretty vocal...clear about what they expected and what they wanted." They regularly gathered in the same common driveway as their children, and chatted while they hung laundry or as they watched their children riding bikes or playing in their small, inflatable pools. They looked out for each other's children as if they were their own.

Through the years she watched the women run their households, manage finances, and be fiercely protective of their families. Seldom did Kathy witness anything she would have called subordination or abusive behavior. Instead, they commanded respect from their spouses and children as well as the rest of the neighborhood. All the women mirrored the same strength and determination Kathy saw in her mother. As she grew into adulthood, Kathy took a little of each woman with her. However, one woman in particular had the greatest impact on Kathy.

The very caring and strong "Aunt" Flor worked with Kathy's father. She stood out as both the only one without children and the only full-time "working woman." While Aunt Flor spent time with the whole family, she often invited Kathy over during summer vacation. Kathy enjoyed the "only child" kind of attention Aunt Flor gave her during those long, lazy days. The two sat and talked over afternoon tea, and Kathy saw life from a different perspective. Through the years, she observed the older woman commit her time and energy as a volunteer for both church and community projects. As she watched the woman she admired successfully organize and manage many volunteer events, Kathy learned about mentoring and leadership.

As Kathy entered her teens, her parents purchased a "much-desired single house in the suburbs." Kathy's own sense of leadership and independence came about when she did not share her parent's enthusiasm for the bigger and better suburban home. Though it signified progress to them, the move meant leaving old and new friends and a boyfriend. The high school sophomore had no desire to leave her established social environment. Doggedly determined, she convinced her parents to allow her to spend the school weeks with her grandmother, who lived nearby and went along with Kathy's appeal. She recognizes that this arrangement became her first steps toward independence and says, "Probably eighty percent of my high school years were spent somewhere other than the new single home my parents so proudly provided for us."

Immediately after graduation, Kathy found a job as a clerk in an accounting department of a large company. Though the seventeen-year-old liked the work, she felt pulled toward a career in architectural design.

When she told her parents that she wanted to go to college, they did not appreciate her ambition. Typical of their generation, they believed a woman's place was in the home and wanted her to get married and have children. They placed little value on their daughter having a higher education, and a career appealed to them even less.

Still, when Kathy arranged an appointment with a college

counselor, they begrudgingly agreed to talk to him. As the meeting progressed, her parents asked probing questions about the long-term outlook for Kathy's potential career. Much to her consternation, the man told the questioning trio about the challenging coursework and how, even if she graduated, "the men simply wouldn't work with a woman."

After the meeting, her parents told Kathy to forget college because they "had no intention of paying good money to send her to school for nothing." As far as they were concerned, the meeting closed the door on any further discussion regarding higher education.

Furious over the results of the meeting, Kathy refused to believe the man's dismissive forecast. Wanting to find out if the counselor's claims had any legitimacy, she decided to check with her company's designers. She recalls "fairly stomping my way up the stairs to the (all male) engineering group." She told them about the counseling session and the counselor's negative viewpoint. Thinking of the men as her friends, she trusted their experience. Expecting a denunciation, she asked the men for their opinions. To her great dismay, one by one they corroborated his story and emphatically supported his allegation. They advised her to "forget it." Dejected and disillusioned, the teenager left the department and took what seemed like a never-ending walk down the stairs and back to her suitable-for-females-only clerical job.

Damaged but not shattered, Kathy shifted her focus and concentrated on the more readily available pursuits of travel and independence. She spent long and happy hours talking with her sister and girlfriends about her dreams to travel abroad as well as her plans to get her own apartment. She backed up her talk with action. She diligently put away money from each paycheck and watched it grow. The chatter about faraway places and personal independence excited and motivated Kathy, while her increasing bank account gave her a sense of accomplishment.

Before long, her travel plans materialized. Kathy and a friend made a dream come true when they visited England. They had a great time, seeing all the places they planned for and talked about for so long. With wide-eyed excitement, the teenagers visited Buckingham Palace, Trafalgar Square, and countless museums. Not only did she come home with a lifetime of memories, she returned with a great sense of satisfaction and confidence.

Convinced she could take care of herself, she moved on to her next goal. Kathy and a friend began apartment hunting. Soon they found a little place just over the river and in the next state. Both girls loved it, quickly signed the lease, and planned to move six weeks later.

Only a couple of weeks before the much-anticipated move, Kathy had a serious auto accident. Her injuries produced seventeen facial fractures. To ensure proper healing, her doctors gave her forty stitches around her eyes and wired her jaw shut.

Knowing the recuperation process would span more than three months, Kathy's parents presumed their daughter would give up the apartment idea. Much to their consternation, Kathy considered her shattered face and the accompanying pain a minor inconvenience. On the designated date, the young women moved into their new apartment as planned.

Though Kathy moved a short thirty minutes away from her parents, mentally she might as well have moved to another country. At age nineteen, Kathy found herself self-sufficient, independent, and increasingly more confident in her ability to take care of herself and achieve her goals.

Work improved as well. Throughout the seven years that Kathy stayed at her first company, she assumed increasingly more difficult administrative responsibilities. She did well and progressed to a semi-management position. Also during her tenure, she befriended Dan*, one of the engineering department's designers. Their acquaintance grew into friendship over drinks and good conversations at after-work socials. Accustomed to having male friends, Kathy never thought much about having lunch with the married Dan and their co-workers. Dan "had an edge," a sarcastic wit that made everyone laugh. Fun to be around, he seemed to be able to fit into every situation by adapting his behavior, yet he maintained a sense of independence. Kathy liked him.

Through his later divorce and remarriage, and Kathy's own dating life, they remained friends. In fact, while both were unattached, they even dated briefly. However, Kathy had upwardly mobile plans. A serious relationship, one that could lead to marriage, had no place in her life. Still, Dan became someone Kathy felt she could trust.

Several years passed. Kathy developed good rapport with the company president who recognized Kathy's hard-work and loyalty. He later left the company and purchased two manufacturing plants. Knowing Kathy's track record, the executive asked her to manage the personnel for his new company. Though she would be considered one of the top three corporate officers, Kathy had little idea what the position would entail. Just the same, she recognized that the "opportunity in front of me would have been foolish to pass up." Happy to advance her career, Kathy accepted and quickly plunged herself into the tasks of her new employment. Just twenty-four years old, Kathy took over a department that oversaw the work life of more than five hundred people.

As she began to create the department and her role in it, she had a lot of support but little help from the man at the helm. For the most part, Kathy had to figure out how to hire, train, and retain competent people and effectively staff the two fledgling companies.

Kathy quickly grasped the enormity of her challenge. "It was trial by fire," she recalls. Not only did she have to make sure that laws met compliance, she also had to keep the facility staffed, convert old managers to a new philosophy, effectively deal with two unions, and develop her department in a way that would serve the needs of the business. Conceptually, Kathy knew what she had to do; practically, she had no idea what specific tasks would help her reach those goals.

Looking for resources to help her, she attended a seminar. A chance meeting at the class resulted in an invitation to join the

Society for Human Resource Management (SHRM), an international professional organization. She quickly became active in the group and "aggressively pursued every avenue" for professional growth, from meetings to volunteer leadership positions. Her involvement helped her develop her knowledge base and hone her skills. In addition, it provided Kathy with a "circle of colleagues, friends, and mentors" who supported her growth for the next ten years. With their help and guidance, she learned both what she needed to do, and how to do it.

The management position turned out to be a great stepping stone for Kathy. More importantly, the timing proved serendipitous. Corporate America began paying more and more attention to the needs of workers and wanted people who could effectively address their concerns. "Before I entered the field," Kathy explains, "my function had been jokingly referred to as the 'dumping ground' for managers who couldn't make it anywhere else in the organization. Now, it was quickly becoming one that required a myriad of skills and capabilities and a new perspective on the people side [of business]."

Within a few years and wanting to take her career to greater heights, Kathy sought and secured a coveted position with one of the premier employers in the community. The new role gave her new opportunities to advance her skills. Working in a larger organization gave her access to greater resources and a larger staff. Using them to the fullest, she revamped the human resources function. Under Kathy's direction, the department shifted from a paper-pushing entity to one that contributed to the bottom line. By offering more to employees, the company attracted a better and more qualified workforce.

In addition to her internal work, representing her employer, Kathy got involved in the surrounding community. She joined the Business and Industry Association, launched innovative projects, and became active in charitable and business-education projects.

For seven years, she guided the company through great times of change and growth both internally and in her field. Upon reflection, Kathy notes, "It was not only to my benefit to come into the field at the time I did, but to be able to bring to this new job a fresh outlook. Paper wasn't my business, people were."

As the profession grew, Kathy served as president of her local SHRM organization. During her tenure, the chapter, for the first time in its thirty-year history, won the Superior Merit Award. She also established a student SHRM chapter at the local college. In addition, she started a much-needed SHRM chapter in another part of the state. Next, Kathy created a newsletter addressing government-related concerns for human resource professionals and then became the legislative liaison between the state and national SHRM organizations.

Each project, both for her company and for SHRM, became successful and showcased her skills as a leader. Kathy developed a reputation as a focused woman of action, someone who could get things done. She also began championing other women, encouraging them to seek management positions as well as providing support and assistance along the way.

Outside of work, Kathy developed a well-rounded life. Always engaged and usually busy, she flea-marketed on the weekends and fell in love with the experience of backpacking. She spent many weekends and holidays hiking parks and trails up and down the East Coast, satisfying her interest in travel and connecting her with friends.

Along the way, she began seeing Kevin*, one of the corporation's highly successful rising stars. He became her significant other, and with Kevin, Kathy bought her first home. A few years later, the couple bought another, bigger house in a better neighborhood.

Though her parents would have preferred that she get married, have children, and truly settle down with a wedding ring on her finger, Kathy felt happy with her living arrangements. Marriage never found its way to the top of her priority list. "There was too much living to do," Kathy laughs.

Work-wise, however, Kathy followed her parents' teachings by working hard and consistently doing better. In addition, while she made her way through difficult challenges and professional growth spurts, Kathy continued talking regularly with her old work buddy Dan. Both moved on from their first jobs, and Dan moved to another state with his spouse and children. Though they no longer worked together, Kathy often sought Dan's input and support about her job. She often shared details of her life with him the same way she did with her girlfriends. He did the same with Kathy. They seldom actually met, but enjoyed infrequent but happy camaraderie as phone cronies. Through professional ups and downs, Kathy's domestic partnership with Kevin, and Dan's two marriages and divorces, they remained friends.

Though they maintained a platonic relationship, Kathy felt she could be herself with Dan and she says they "had a closeness that was unusual to have with someone of the opposite sex. We weren't just friends, but *the best of friends*." Dan became someone she could count on for support and understanding, as well as someone with whom she could laugh off stress. For Kathy, typically being both the only female in management and also the youngest executive, her conversations with Dan became an invaluable support and often felt to her like "a break in the battle."

Some of those work-related challenges came during periods of time when Kathy experienced what she calls a "subtle undermining and lack of support" from her male colleagues. Like many other women who climbed the corporate ladder, she learned that "the boys knew how to play the game of keeping someone, usually a woman, at a disadvantage through exclusion." When thinking about those maddening days, Kathy remembers, "They didn't make it easy. I'd be left out of meetings or discussions, not kept up-to-date on important issues, and didn't receive return phone calls." Even when she did speak, Kathy often felt invisible. The men clearly conveyed the message that the value and relevance of her input paled in comparison to theirs. Confounded by their close-minded attitude, Kathy recalls how "instead of fostering a partnership and working for the common good, they stuck together and kept the 'girl' out." She concedes, "It was an irritating stick-together mentality that often defied reason and caused me to clench my teeth more often than I care to remember."

The years moved on and she got past the opposition, managed her tasks, and accomplished her goals. In the meantime, Kathy honed valuable skills and developed an impressive resume. By the time Kathy turned thirty, her accomplishments became worthy enough to be listed in several Who's Who publications. Within her company and through the local SHRM chapter, Kathy pursued ongoing professional development programs. She attained a professional designation in the field and managed to remain on the cutting edge within her industry. A blend of self-preservation and personal values became her mantra for success, and it worked for her.

Yet, as many women who broke through all-male corporate ranks can attest, Kathy found that new responsibilities and greater professional commitments left her with little time and energy for her personal life. For years, her lifestyle posed no problem. Kathy considered herself "a well-organized woman with a game plan." Early on she decided that marriage would have to wait until her thirties or even later, and she vowed not to get married "until I *knew* it would last forever." In addition, Kathy prided herself on being "savvy, astute, and above making mistakes with my life... an anomaly, a person who rose above a half-dozen odds."

In surveying her life to that point, Kathy knew she could feel proud. After all, she says, "I was only a generation or two removed from immigrant status, had been self-supporting since my teens, and was raised with neither encouragement to have a career nor career aspirations. Yet I had not only survived, I had thrived."

In her early thirties, Kathy and Kevin ended their relationship. Though saddened, she had no regrets. Kathy describes the relationship as "mutually beneficial to both of us at that point in our lives—we cared deeply about each other, but it was just never going to end up in marriage." They sold the house and Kathy banked her share of the proceeds.

During the break-up, Dan unexpectedly came back into her life. He called Kathy to touch base and wanted to get together. The two met for a friendly reunion. The meeting led to a date and then to courtship. They rekindled the old romance that they had, thirteen years earlier, played with and discarded.

Soon but quite naturally, after years of "just friendship," the relationship progressed quickly. Yet Kathy felt comfortable with the rapid development with the man she had known for more than a decade. She also found that, even after all those years, Dan could still impress her with "the brilliance of his mind and his creativity." In addition, Kathy thought she "knew the good and the bad...and could live with all of it."

They enjoyed a whirlwind, fairy tale romance that dazzled her with "promises of life with my friend-turned-love." Soon they decided to marry and Kathy remembers thinking she would be marrying her best friend. "It couldn't have been better," she recalls wistfully.

The couple invited friends and family to a unique outdoor celebration in the country. Beside a waterfall, with Irish fiddlers playing in the background, the couple exchanged vows. The wedding would turn out to be "the best part of the marriage." As they said their "I do's," Kathy would never have guessed how bizarre the union would become.

After their honeymoon, the newlyweds moved temporarily into a rented colonial-style house in a small but quaint town. Kathy put the money from the sale of her house into joint savings, earmarked for the future. They seemed to be having an idyllic experience.

Around the same time, her company went through a change of executive management. Something about the new officer made Kathy feel uneasy. He seemed to be creating havoc and quickly lost the support of key people. Concerned that the situation may turn sour, and already feeling ready to make a change, Kathy thought about going out on her own.

While she considered the feasibility of starting a consulting practice, she and Dan talked about how they would handle their new life during the transition period. After nearly sixteen years of traditional work, she talked excitedly about making the change to self-employment, a less structured work mode and greater opportunity to infuse more creativity into her work. She set aside a year's income, put out her feelers, and found potential work. Dan, whose own newly-formed business appeared to be doing very well, encouraged her in every way. Kathy felt so secure about her new support system that she welcomed the chance to spread her professional wings in new directions.

When Kathy finally made the jump into her own business, opportunities came to fruition and she found consulting projects to work on right away. Looking back, Kathy thinks the experience ranks as the best one of her career. Creatively on fire, she felt refreshed and rejuvenated by new and different challenges.

Within a short time, however, Kathy made some startling discoveries. One day, as she rummaged through some paperwork, she learned that Dan's business did nowhere as well as he consistently boasted it did; instead, it turned out to be pretty shaky. The deceit became only the first of Kathy's unsettling revelations.

She started noticing a type of behavior she had not considered earlier, although in retrospect, she thinks she should have. All along she knew he had great passion for his work and social gatherings but could be lax about details and doing other, more everyday things like getting home on time and returning phone calls. As friends, Kathy could laugh off Dan's irresponsibility. As partners, however, she had to live with his off-handed behaviors—and they no longer felt funny.

By the couple's first anniversary, Dan still dazzled Kathy, but no longer in a good way. Day after day, she uncovered a level of dysfunction in Dan that she did not understand and for which she had no frame of reference. Even today, Kathy speaks with astonishment when she describes the "never-ending stream of lies and deception" that marked her marriage to Dan. "There were many things I should have explored before agreeing to be his life partner," she admits sadly. "I took far too much for granted. Because I'd known him for so long, I thought I 'knew' him. I didn't."

One Saturday, as Kathy walked down the stairs and into the living room, Dan came over to her and gave her a quick kiss. Telling her he had to go to the store, he jumped into his car and left. When he did not return within the hour, Kathy got suspicious. By nightfall, when he failed to return and did not call, she became frantic. After anxiously thumbing through her phone book, she began calling the people and places where she thought he might have gone.

When she called some of Dan's family members, she learned for the first time that he had a long-standing problem with alcohol. She remembered from those early working days that Dan could party, but she never thought of his drinking as an addiction. His sister admitted that sometimes Dan "just went off the deep end." She told Kathy that when the couple started dating, Dan seemed "so happy" and so "totally different" that his family all thought he changed for her. They wanted to believe that his love for Kathy made him stop his excessive drinking, and that he put his "bad behaviors" behind him.

Hearing for the first time what everyone in Dan's family knew all along, Kathy felt betrayed. Not letting her in on the "family secret" compromised her life. How could they not have realized how devastating it would be when she found out—as she just had? *Kathy was furious.*

When Dan returned Sunday night, he acted as though nothing happened. When she asked where he was and what he did during his absence, he ignored her. No matter what she said or how hard she tried, she could get nothing from him.

The incident marked the beginning of the worst time of her life. Dan's behavior went from bad to worse. He disappeared several times, always returning with the same nonchalance. He refused to answer questions about his work or their money. When she learned of possible gambling, he denied it. In spite of constant inquiries, Dan offered no explanation for the outrageous bills that appeared unexpectedly, for purchases made before and during the marriage. When she blamed alcohol, he refused to admit that his drinking had anything to do with his aberrations.

The more she talked to Dan's family and his business partners, the more she learned about his lack of integrity and reliability. It seemed that for a long time he could keep up a "best self" act with Kathy, but in other parts of his life, others enjoyed no such false impression. She wondered how she could have been so blind to the truth, especially for so many years before she married him.

With her own illusions shattered, Kathy knew she had a huge problem on her hands. She hid the truth from no one. As her life spun out of control, she made distressed and heart-wrenching calls to her parents, siblings, and other family members, both Dan's as well as her own. She met friends in small coffee shops where, sitting at tiny round tables amid eclectic décor, she sought their advice.

At the same time, she continued trying to get her business started. During those crazy months, she found an amazing ability to compartmentalize. Though she wonders now how she did it, she says that in those days she could "kick into gear with business partners and colleagues as if it was the only thing of importance." Business and life each had their own space, and Kathy maintained both well.

At home, however, she became increasingly angry and frustrated. She felt even more outraged by the degree of disrespect Dan exhibited toward her. In addition to his disappearing acts and his denial, their bank account dwindled. They argued frequently over both his behaviors and their money. At different times, one or the other would walk out in the middle of an argument. Kathy wrote "venomous letters," which Dan either laughed at or ignored. She insisted they seek counseling and Dan agreed. Kathy made the appointment and went, but Dan never got there.

One day, she met a friend for lunch. Shielded by the noise of the crowded bistro, she quietly discussed her problems with her trusted friend. The woman said something to Kathy that struck a chord. They were talking about values and differences. Her friend spoke bluntly. She told Kathy that Dan *would never* live in Kathy's world and that Kathy *could never* live in his. In Kathy's experience, a relationship's foundation had to be trust, honesty, and integrity. She believed in living up to responsibilities, and business almost always came before pleasure. The painful observation made Kathy realize that she and Dan would never see eye-to-eye about the values that Kathy held most sacred.

For the first time, her friend's hard words made Kathy realize that all along she had been seeing *only what she wanted* rather than seeing *what really was*. She came to understand that "too many years had gone by and the person I knew at twenty-one was not who I married."

Finally, believing she had nothing left to hang onto, Kathy packed Dan's clothes into his suitcases and left them on the porch. When he saw the bags, he went inside and they talked. No matter what Dan said, Kathy refused to believe him. With their marriage irreparably damaged and Kathy physically and emotionally drained, the relationship ended. Dan disappeared.

Practicalities pressed on Kathy. The lease on the house, originally a transitional home, had thirty days left until it expired. Before, during, and after the marriage, Dan incurred thousands of dollars of debt. No longer around to hide the bills from Kathy, she began dreading the daily mail in which more arrived.

Until then, she always dealt with difficulty in a logical and pragmatic manner, and moved on with her life. Until then, nothing ever froze Kathy. The end of her marriage left her motionless. The woman who always had a game plan, had nothing. "It was the worst thing that had ever happened in my life," Kathy confessed quietly. "To have trust betrayed...crushed my spirit beyond words...it was very painful." And personal destruction proved to be only part of the tragedy.

By the time Kathy ended the eighteen-month union, she had no energy, no house, little money, and no income. Throughout their marriage their combined earnings and savings, *everything*, went into joint accounts. Dan went through *nearly every penny* in checking and savings, including the proceeds from the sale of Kathy's house. Only a few months went by from the first time Kathy realized there was a problem until all the money disappeared. With absolutely no explanation from Dan, it evaporated into thin air like steam from a teakettle.

Kathy's head reeled from the financial devastation. When the dust of her life settled, she could barely believe it herself. "It had been like an explosion. [I] suddenly found myself without a husband, a job, an income, medical insurance, or money in the bank. I had given up my home when I married and now was stuck in what was to have been a transitional rental. The lease was about to expire. Thousands of dollars of bills needed to be paid. My opportunity for a new, independent career was shot to hell. The situation was so overwhelming, I felt smothered just thinking about it."

Though priding herself on being an independent woman, she was experiencing a new low. Feeling overwhelmed, some women would have retreated into victim oblivion. Kathy took another tract. Initially, she sought counseling to deal with the emotional trauma. Then she accepted help.

One of her brothers, who lived back in her home state, offered her room and board. She had not lived with any family member since her teens. Though she liked her brother and his family greatly, the idea of sharing the same living space with him, his spouse, and their small child held little appeal to her. However, she humbly and thankfully accepted. She told her brother and sister-in-law she would stay only until she got back on her feet. She stuck to her word.

Kathy moved her life into one bedroom in her brother's house and began putting it back together. "I had certain standards about how I wanted to live. I was never one to believe that you marry into [money, success]...that that's how you got it. I had learned to do for myself." With determination, Kathy decided *not* to be a victim of her sinister life circumstances.

Needing a steady income, she put away her small business ambitions and sought full-time employment. Using all the transferable skills she had from leadership and management, organizational development, and human resources, she compiled multiple resumes for several different fields. She landed a job as the director of public relations for a non-profit agency. There she developed more communications expertise.

Kathy might have stayed there, but another company received her human resources resume. The multi-billion dollar, international company made her the proverbial offer she could not refuse. She says they wanted to "double my salary, give me a portfolio of benefits, and the opportunity to start up their first U.S. facility." Aside from the dollar-value of their proposal, the security felt especially attractive. She accepted their offer.

Within a year, Kathy paid off marriage-related debts, moved out of her brother's house, and reestablished herself as an independent woman. Through it all, she came to "a number of new understandings about life." First and foremost, she learned that no matter what happens, "you can always start over." In fact, she found that not only can you begin again, *you can do better.*

Throughout her nightmare experience, Kathy never got to the point of not having enough money to buy proper job interview attire. However, as a teenager, she had a male friend who found himself in that kind of "catch-22" situation. As hellish as her difficulties seemed, when she thought about it, Kathy realized her situation could have been worse. One day, as she read about a national program that found professional apparel for low-income women seeking employment, she had an idea to do the same. She passed the idea on to people who could make it happen, and the Lehigh Valley CareerLink created "Career Closet." Kathy worked with the program's executive director in framing its policies.

Reflecting on her marriage, she learned that "people intent on hiding things are able to do so for a considerable period of time." By the same token, Kathy adamantly insists that no one has to be a victim forever. Something bad can happen, but you can fight back and win.

While she gratefully accepted help and support from others, and discovered how much better most people are than we often realize, she also understood, "In the end, you *have to* rely on yourself. The only one who can *really* save you, even in your worst times, is *you*."

After getting back on her feet, Kathy continued moving forward, propelled by her work ethic, deeply held values and strong-willed personality. She left the job with the major corporation to accept a senior executive position with a mid-size manufacturing company. In the era of the "glass ceiling," she admits garnering the position proved to be quite an accomplishment. Grateful for the support from the company's owners, she proudly boasts, "As a vice-president, I've been able to facilitate changes in organizational management...I've been able to harness best practices and ideas that enriched the lives of employees and their families, ultimately and most probably affecting generations." Her skills guided the company into being a model employer known for progressive employee relations programs and innovative initiatives. Her enterprising endeavors helped her company earn a "Best Place to Work" award in her state, an award presented by the Governor.

Clearly, the VIPs noticed what Kathy did in the workplace. They were not alone. One of her co-workers also paid attention.

Roger, an attractive, salt-of-the-earth kind of man, first got Kathy's attention when he applied for a job at her company. Involved in his hiring process, she checked out his references and found out they all held him in high esteem. Kathy hired him as a manager at the company. Later on, as she got to know and like Roger, she tried to fix him up with a couple of the single women she knew. After a few tries, Roger told Kathy that he had only one dating interest—*her*.

Surprised but flattered, Kathy readjusted her thinking to see Roger in a new light. While still co-workers, Kathy noticed that

Roger had a "what you see is what you get" kind of personality. Knowing him as a relationship-builder within the company, she thought of him as a good and decent person. Roger did nothing to influence others, but made an impression by simply being himself. She liked that about him.

When Roger asked Kathy for a date, she accepted. Once alone and away from the company, Kathy found that Roger came from a background similar to her own, raised with similar values and ethics. She says that trust—or lack of it—never entered her mind. Totally opposite from the independent and chameleon-like Dan, Roger's behaviors stayed consistent. She noticed he changed for no one and she saw his positive behaviors as "an outpouring of his good character." Also, Roger demonstrated his integrity, which Kathy says "is more than any ten people put together." Both as a co-worker and a boyfriend, he never let Kathy down. Over time Kathy noticed they placed the same importance on trust, honesty, and loyalty.

Five years after the marital disaster with Dan, Kathy felt ready to take a chance on marriage with Roger. When he proposed, Kathy had no qualms about saying yes.

Kathy and Roger set up housekeeping in a beautiful home in Bucks County, Pennsylvania, "one of the most beautiful places in the country." She loves her home and its country atmosphere.

Now married over ten years, Kathy knows she made a good decision. She talks about her spouse with glowing compliments, professing that he is "a gem." She admires how he is "secure in himself, supportive of me, and capable of having a real partnership." When it comes to their life together, Kathy admits they occasionally have some conflicts, but also says, "We know how to work through our issues, of which there are remarkably few. We both recognize life can be hard and is often hard work, so for us, marriage is in part about making life easier for each other where we can."

Continuously active statewide and in her community, Kathy Clark has cultivated an impressive and seemingly endless list of professional and volunteer accomplishments. They include Kathy's appointment by the Governor to her state's Workforce Investment Board. She maintains her membership with the Society of Human Resources, the organization that was so helpful to her earlier in her career, and is an accredited Human Resource Professional. In addition, she volunteers in her community and still finds time to support other women.

Aunt Flor, one of Kathy's early role models is still in Kathy's life. In her nineties and living in a retirement community, Aunt Flor is mentally astute and as physically active as possible. Kathy still visits so they can enjoy good conversation and each other's company.

With all of her professional accomplishments, Kathy often wonders how much women have progressed in the work place. She still notices "subtle sabotage" toward women with power, and observes that after all this time, "we're still the outsiders."

Today, Kathy continues to move forward, both professionally and personally. She steadfastly believes that nothing is impossible, and no goal is past the time of its achievement. Kathy insists that she, along with every other woman, can decide what she wants and then pursue it with expectation. Even today, though she is "at the point of being well-established," Kathy asserts, "I never stop thinking about what I'm going to do tomorrow if things change or I want to make a change." Kathy continues to peer into the future and asks herself, "What's next?"

From a deeply personal perspective, she believes a happy marriage to Roger is proof that she—and you—can overcome financial and emotional devastation, even when they happen at the same time.

In addition, Kathy now understands the two great mistakes that contributed to her ruinous union with Dan. First, she ignored their differences, especially about what they valued. Unlike Kathy, Dan liked to party, spend money, and keep odd work hours. She naively believed their love for each other would conquer their differences. By the time Kathy met Roger, she clearly understood that shared values are key, especially about how to spend money, what situations take priority in the relationship, and the shared understanding of the significance of the marriage partnership.

Secondly, she did not make the same mistake of presumption. As much as she trusted Roger, she asked direct questions as a part of a natural exploration of interests and values. Though she knew him for several years, she took nothing for granted (as she had with Dan), and sought factual and emotional congruency between what Roger said and what he did. She paid attention to the truth and carefully made judgments on *what she actually saw* versus what she might have *wanted to see*.

Looking back, whether making her way in the world, creating professional success, or overcoming a devastatingly dysfunctional marriage, Kathy Clark demonstrated how self-preservation takes you part of the way, and living by solid, uncompromising values sees you through to victory. "External influences and temporary setbacks aside, we control our own destiny....*that* is really what being victorious is all about."

STEPPING STONES
TO VICTORY

1. Have you ever stayed with a partner who you knew, in your heart, wasn't good for you? If you did, answer the following questions in your Victory Journal:

    a. What made you stay?

    b. If you are still with him now, why?

    c. If you have moved on, how did you do it?

2. If you stayed in a toxic relationship more than once, can you identify a pattern of self-deception?

3. One of the reasons that Kathy got so entangled in the relationship with Dan was that she didn't look at him as he really was. She was willing to see what she wanted to see. Have you ever practiced the same type of self-deception with men?

    a. If so, how did you do it? For example, did you ignore red flag moments or warning sign behaviors, like excessive drinking, uncontrolled anger, lying, or possessiveness?

        ☞ What did you say and/or do that allowed you to deceive yourself into staying with someone who was "trouble"?

    b. Did you ever notice an internal warning signal? For some women, it is like a sinking feeling in their stomach. For others, it's a little voice that reveals the truth.

        ☞ What was it for you?
        ☞ What did you say to yourself to convince yourself it was nothing to worry about?

4. What was it in you that allowed you to look the other way when it was in your best interest to pay attention to warning-type behaviors? Was it a fear of being alone? A need to be needed? If you don't know, ask yourself the question, then quiet your mind and listen in silence for the answer.

5. What can you do to change the outcome with someone else? Think of not only romantic relationships, but also of work and friendship relationships.

   a. Write down the items you believe you can change.

   b. What will you do when those situations occur?

      ❧ What trigger words and feelings will you look for?
      ❧ What actions will you take to prevent an unpleasant outcome?

   c. If you lose some ground and make a mistake, what will your recovery plan be?

      ❧ Will you be willing to listen to yourself or another, trusted person?
      ❧ Do you have a support network in place?
      ❧ Will you see a therapist?
      ❧ What else can help you protect yourself by preventing self-deception?

6. Food for thought: Kathy leaned heavily on the work ethic and values she learned in childhood. If you are raising children, are you teaching them the kind of values that will enable them to create victories?

5

Loving Boundaries

Toni Kershaw

WHAT WOULD YOU DO IF YOUR NEEDS CONFLICT-ed with the needs of your child? If you are like many mothers, most likely, you put the needs of your child first. It seems like a normal and natural thing to do, something most mothers do all the time. Fathers often do the same.

But imagine what might happen when both mother *and* child have physical problems that could mean life or death for both of them. Is there any justification for a mother to choose herself first, drawing the line between herself and her child?

Toni Kershaw found herself in just such a circumstance. When both she and a teenage daughter found themselves battling food-related health issues, Toni struggled to find a balance between caring and self-care. Though it took many gut-wrenching months, she sought and discovered a healthy place where her mind and heart converged so she could make the right decision.

A pleasant and soft-spoken woman, Toni is the kind of person who looks at life with a glass-half-full viewpoint. Barely five feet tall, her stature and mild demeanor hide a quiet determination. However, preferring that her life run smoothly, she strived to be liked and often seeks the approval of those around her.

Toni grew up with three older brothers, two of whom played team sports. Her father, a strapping and robust man who loved all sports, influenced his only daughter to get involved in athletics at a young age. While her parents encouraged her to do her best both athletically and scholastically, Toni displayed talent in sports, especially in field hockey and lacrosse. In high school she performed well enough to play varsity defense on both teams during all four years.

During the winter months, when her teams were in the off-season, the athletic director taught Toni how to care for sports injuries. At the time she displayed a talent for doing it, and now wishes she took the learning further. However, her father did not believe in sending girls to college. In his mind, it was a waste of money. After all, girls just got married and had children, a job for which they did not need a college education. Without encouragement to attend college, furthering her education became a low priority.

Toni also had a boyfriend and being with Tim took the top spot in her life. A good-looking kid, he could be sweet and charming. Most importantly, Tim loved Toni and she had the same feelings for him.

Like many teenage lovers, the couple wanted to begin their life together as soon as possible. After her 1977 graduation, while friends shopped for college clothes, Toni put together her trousseau. A September wedding followed the June graduation.

From the beginning, Toni and Tim agreed their household would be an old-fashioned one. They decided that once their children came along, the couple would step into traditional roles. Tim would be the breadwinner while Toni stayed at home running the household and raising the children. That was the plan.

The following year Toni became pregnant with their first child. Excited to start her family, she looked forward to quitting her job and staying home with the baby. Toni believed motherhood was her vocation. Being the best mom she could be was her primary goal.

Daughter Marcie was born when Toni was just twenty years old. By age twenty-nine, her brood also included Tim Jr., Kristie, and Ashley. With four young children, her days were often hectic and challenging, but she managed. Her family was everything Toni wanted.

From the time her children were very young, Toni involved them in sports. They started with swimming lessons. All the children enjoyed swimming so much that each of them joined teams and swam competitively. Later, as they found their different passions, the youngsters also got involved in other sports: lacrosse, field hockey, soccer, softball, basketball, wrestling, cross-country, and track and field. Good at their chosen sports, their children liked the challenge and took pride in winning. Through their various schools and organizations, in and around their locale, the children became well known for their athletic prowess.

Scholastically, the small flock also did well. As students, they carried above-average grades. Several made the honor roll and achieved National Honor Society ranking. Toni liked being part of their successes, proudly disclosing, "They are all high achievers...we have so many trophies, plaques, and statues."

In addition to her full-time job as spouse and mother, Toni often worked part-time jobs to help make ends meet financially. When the children were younger and all at home, Toni provided daycare for other mothers. Later she had a series of office assistant jobs with local companies. Then, shortly after her youngest child went to first grade, Toni got a full-time job at the nearby university.

No matter what outside work Toni did, she remained steadfastly active in her children's progress. She attended practices and meets after school and on weekends. Because the wide range of activities spanned all seasons, sporting events filled Toni's calendar throughout the year.

In order to be available for sports, Toni usually left work early. Grateful for the approval of her understanding boss, Toni made up for lost work by splitting vacation time into hours and using them day by day. Once she left work, Toni switched gears. After-school hours consisted of mad dashes from one child's school to another, picking them up and, as designated driver for several teams, taking them to scrimmages and games both at home and away. She also coached soccer and lacrosse. In addition to active participation, Toni often volunteered for a variety of behind-the-scenes support activities.

Each day after completing her sports booster and coaching activities, Toni shifted back into her mom tasks, serving dinner and helping the children with homework. Once the family settled in for the night, she began her volunteer service. Sometimes assignments required more time than others and became like a second full-time job. Many times, while everyone else was in bed, Toni continued working. Too often, with tired and bleary-eyes, Toni looked at the clock above the kitchen sink, usually surprised to find the hands approaching midnight. Putting the work away for the night, she shuffled off to bed, only to begin all over again at the break of dawn.

Keeping with their original agreement, Tim did not usually get too involved in the daily family happenings. Through family edicts and personal demands, Tim clearly ruled the roost. His work as a truck driver left him physically tired at the end of the workday. When he came home, he wanted to eat, enjoy some family time, relax, and end his day. Though usually amiable, he could also be quick-tempered when his needs were not met. His strict parenting style frequently clashed with Toni's somewhat more easygoing approach.

Though less hands-on with sports than Toni, when Tim could get to games, he loved being there. He could be as excited about winning a game as the players.

Always concerned with finances, Tim monitored the family's spending. While proud of his four healthy and active children, the high cost of all the sporting activities got his attention. While he approved of the expense, Tim tended to push the children, wanting them to do well enough to make the expenditure worth the monetary sacrifice. When they did not play well, they heard about it from their father. It was a double-edged sword: the children were happy to have their dad watch them, but sometimes felt pressured and nervous about a subsequent critique.

When it came to food, on-the-run refreshments and overeating became an issue for Toni. With her crazy schedule, she frequently nibbled goodies while running out the door, driving in the car, between games, and sitting in the bleachers. Work/school night dinners featured whatever was quick and easy to make, not necessarily healthy and balanced. On the weekends, especially for Sunday dinner, Toni cooked a big, family-style meal. Leftovers tempted her and seemed to call her from inside the refrigerator. Family video nights were great occasions for comfort food and goodies like pizza, popcorn, and chocolate chip cookies.

While the way they ate did not affect the weight of her spouse or her children, gradually Toni's weight climbed. Of course, like most other women, Toni dieted. Occasionally she joined Weight Watchers or some other popular weight program. Most programs worked for a while, but when they got too tough to stick with, she usually quit.

Sometimes Toni just could not follow the requisites of a diet. Figuring out and preparing balanced meals often demanded more time and energy than she usually made for herself. Also, most diets offered too little food or too few desirable choices, and Toni would feel deprived.

Other times, money provided a good excuse to leave. If she wasn't following the program faithfully, or was not getting quick results, she easily felt guilty about using the money. This became especially true if Tim complained about how much money her diet was costing the family.

In addition to trying diets, Toni sometimes got on an exercise kick. Once, using her health care plan's financial incentive as motivation, she joined a gym. Though she liked working out and she felt good doing it, the reimbursement required that she exercise three times a week. Making time in an already tightly organized schedule proved too great a challenge, and eventually caused more stress than benefit. Once the initial year was complete, and she got her money back, she did not return for a second year.

After many years of recurring weight struggles, Toni gave up. She stopped worrying about being thin. There just wasn't enough time, money, incentive, or support to keep fighting what seemed like a losing battle. Telling herself she was young and in good health, she chose to believe that an extra ten or twenty pounds was no big deal.

Then, in the summer of 1998, Toni was force-fed a strong dose of reality. Her mother underwent triple bypass surgery *and* had a stroke. In the role of caregiver, Toni's already busy schedule grew even more hectic. With additional demands on her, Toni gained weight. Though her mother recovered from the surgery, Toni began considering her own health. She and her mother had a similar build, and both carried extra weight. As she heard snippets of medical reports in the media, she wondered about the connection between body type, fat, and health. Not for long, though. In her ultra busy life, there was much to do. She tucked her concerns in the back of her mind, and continued with her life.

The very next summer, her typically strong and fit father suffered a debilitating stroke that left him paralyzed. In the following months, she watched her formerly vigorous parent go through a pain-filled convalescence and rehabilitation. In a gym-like but clinical rehabilitation space, surrounded by machines and therapists, Toni watched her weakened father struggle to relearn even the simplest of movements. It proved to be a difficult experience for Toni. She never saw her father so weak. Only months before, she didn't even consider her father's condition a possibility. Now it frightened her to the core.

Toni knew that since *both* her parents suffered from heart disease, her risk for the same fate increased. Thoughts of poor future health filled her mind. Turning forty with nearly as many pounds overweight, she had to do something to turn the tide. If she did not, Toni knew she could easily be on a collision course for permanent disability and even death. After all, coronary heart disease claims the life of 250,000 women each year, making it the number-one killer of women. Fearfully, Toni gave herself a stern lecture. "I've got to start taking care of myself," she mandated, and she vowed she would do something for herself.

Yet like many women who tell themselves the same thing, the time and space for self-care always took second place. Toni did make an effort to focus on her own needs, with initiatives such as going to Weight Watchers or the gym, but nothing stuck. With constant stress and everyone's never-ending demands on her time, Toni concedes that in spite of great intentions, she "never really *did* anything." One bad feeling fed into another, and the failed efforts began to affect Toni's self-esteem and emotional well-being as well as her health.

A third warning arrived in the form of shooting pains in her arm. Frightened enough to seek medical attention, Toni submitted to a full physical examination and a stress test. Looking at her results, the doctor told Toni that her heart seemed fine and the pains were stress-related. Heaving a sigh of relief, she waited for a plan of action. Sadly, her doctor's only advice was to *"do something"* about the stress. She felt lost and angry. Already convinced that her "life was like a 'before' ad for mood-enhancing drugs," she knew something had to be done...*but what?*

Toni felt as though she was "on her own" again. This time, however, she seriously looked for something that fit with her schedule. She wanted a plan she could live with and make a part of her life. It was the beginning of a turning point...but she was still a long way from victory.

One day at work, a co-worker told Toni about a new weight loss program. Since Toni already thought her colleague looked thinner and wondered how she did it, she asked questions. Unlike most programs, Toni learned this one focused on behaviors instead of food. As she listened, understanding that good heart health included losing weight and exercising, Toni wondered if maybe behavior modification offered the missing piece.

The new group met weekly in a familiar area location, and best of all, *the program was free!* It sounded tailor-made for Toni. She decided to give it a try.

From the beginning, Toni recognized stark contrasts from this and every other diet she ever tried. To begin with, she could not just join. She had to complete an application, be accepted into the program, and then wait for a new cluster to begin.

Toni submitted her application in early August. A couple of weeks later, a program leader called and told Toni she could join in September. As the university where she worked began its new school year and her children moved into new grades and onto new teams, Toni embarked on a new mission of her own. Mostly seeking better health, Toni had no idea what a life-changing adventure awaited her.

As Toni waited out the balance of summer, she noticed something different about her sixteen-year-old daughter Kristie. One day, as Kristie walked through the kitchen, it struck Toni that her daughter looked unusually lean. As athletic as Toni's other children, Kristie played several sports. Her passion, however, was swimming. Over the years, as a result of the rigorous demands of the sport, the petite Kristie developed the kind of tight, shapely, muscular build common to many swimmers.

In those last weeks of summer, Toni's mothering instinct registered a red flag. Thinking it could be too much swimming, or just a part of normal growth, Toni didn't want to overreact. Still, she wondered how concerned she should be. Toni made a mental note to watch her daughter more closely.

On the first Thursday of September, as she attended the induction meeting for the new weight loss program at an old, one-room schoolhouse, Toni thought the air seemed filled with the hopefulness of new beginnings. As she soaked in the sights and smells of the historic building, Toni contrasted the new program with other ones she attended in previous years.

"It isn't a diet," announced Lynn, the person in charge. She passionately told the newbies that first night, "This is a lifestyle change." On that foundation, Lynn told the new participants that they had to make a solid commitment to the program. The program required strict adherence to the rules, including mandatory weekly meetings, maintaining a food diary, and a required monthly weight loss. Unexpected absences weren't allowed, precluding any "I don't feel like going tonight" laziness.

Adding to the diet difference, at the first meeting Toni never even saw a scale; weigh-ins did not begin until Week Two. As they went around the table with introductions, Toni took a good look at the people she would be meeting each week. Their desired weight loss and motivations varied. One woman wanted to be thin for a wedding, and another wanted to get off blood pressure medicine, and still another could not have a necessary surgery until she lost some weight.

Lynn continued explaining the program. Toni discovered that, if terminated, the participant could never return. While weight loss became the scorecard, clearly the program focused on individual behaviors.

As Toni looks back on that first meeting, she remembers how the "never again" edict was the greatest contrast to other programs, as well as a shock. She thought, "Wow, these people are *really* serious!" Something about the do-or-die strategy brought back the hopeful competitive spirit of her athletic days. Toni left the first meeting with a strong commitment to succeed. She had a game plan and she had to follow it...*or else!*

During the following week, after each meal, Toni kept track of her eating behaviors. She recorded what, when, and where she ate, as well as how she felt, and other behavior-related reactions to food. Sitting at her kitchen table, she sometimes found herself staring out the window over the sink while she tried to tap into her food-feelings. She noticed how in previous diets she seldom thought about whether she was happy, sad, angry, or anything else. In fact, until now, Toni realized she seldom considered hunger at all, at any time. Mealtime focused on family matters, or what she had to do after dinner, or what the next day required of her. When it came to snacking, food offered instant gratification, not mindful ingesting.

At her second meeting, when it was her turn, Toni stepped on and off the black weighing machine. She cringed. The scale registered an extra forty pounds, and Toni's greatest health risk ever. While previous health alerts felt like warnings, this one felt like a two-by-four between the eyes. Toni decided to stick with the program, no matter what. Although she thought the incredible strictness was a bit much, Toni also believed it was her lifeline and she grabbed for it. She felt nervous, excited...and motivated.

During the first month, as required, Toni kept a food diary. The accounting required her to look at what she ate, and it became an eye-opening experience. As though putting her eating habits under a microscope for the first time, Toni saw what she actually put into her mouth each day. She developed a new awareness of just how much she ate. More importantly, she discovered how often she ate without thinking.

Changing life-long patterns proved no easy task. Toni began shifting from on-the-fly eating to planning meals and snacks in advance and started making better food choices. She surprised herself when she realized the healthier foods satisfied her more.

By the end of the first month, Toni felt she learned more about herself than she expected. When she stepped on the scale, it indicated a twelve-pound weight loss. She felt successful and even more motivated than when she began.

Throughout the second month, Toni settled into the program. As she thought more about unconscious eating, Toni began making emotional connections with the foods she ate. She saw patterns emerge and recognized that different stresses created specific cravings for comfort foods and fat or calorie-laden goodies.

The more Toni learned about how food helped her dissipate anger or feel relaxed, safe, and peaceful, the more the program made sense. It seemed easier to follow. By the end of October, Toni was a total of fourteen pounds lighter.

Unfortunately, so was her daughter. While weight loss signified better health for Toni, for her now too-thin daughter it was a frightening red flag. The earlier warning signal of the summer months now amplified into a fire alarm. In spite of Kristie's protests, Toni made a doctor's appointment for her daughter. When she refused to go, Toni promised her a new dress for an upcoming dance. In the end, Kristie reluctantly agreed.

When the doctor saw the young woman, she recognized a serious problem. She told Toni she suspected bulimia and/or anorexia. Until then, Toni knew little about either. Within days, she got a fast and frightening education, including how ten percent of bulimics are teenagers. Toni soon learned that both are emotional conditions and both could result in death. Anorexia Nervosa is characterized by severe and unhealthy weight loss caused by self-starvation and prolonged periods of exercise. Bulimia Nervosa includes a secretive binge eating and purging pattern that is often accompanied by negative feelings, low self-esteem, depression, and mood swings.

Though Kristie denied it (another common symptom of the disease) and gave logical reasons for her weight loss, the doctor insisted on seeing her weekly. Angrily, the young woman kept her appointments; within just two weeks, Kristie's scale showed another five pound loss.

Her doctor told Toni to take action and gave her options. Still in shock, she and Tim could hardly make sense of their daughter's illness. Kristie dropped out of sports and became despondent. Her eating disorder affected the whole family, which quickly found itself in emotional pandemonium.

By Thanksgiving, while Toni healthfully dropped another two pounds, Kristie lost even more weight from her small frame. She became clinically anorexic.

Toni panicked. She and Tim discussed the options. Something had to be done right away. There was no time to lose. With the help of their physician, Toni and Tim had Kristie admitted to The Renfrew Center, a nationally recognized institute for the treatment of eating disorders. Renfrew was the best center of its kind in the area, and their insurance covered most of the cost. Kristie began treatment in the cold days of early December.

As they attended those first sessions, the family tried to make sense of Kristie's illness. Individually and collectively, they wondered how their smart, well-adjusted daughter and sister could be giving in to this devastating disease.

As they explored the possibilities, all eyes fell on Toni. Though Kristie's bulimia began in late summer, the effects didn't become significantly noticeable until the fall, shortly after Toni's program began. For the family, the behavior modification group was the easiest, most tangible, and most immediate explanation. They seemed to determine that Toni's daily writing, diligent focus on healthier food, new behaviors, and ensuing weight loss must be the culprit—after all, *what else could it be?* One by one, her spouse and her three other children lashed out at Toni, insisting that she quit the program.

Until then, always in an effort to be the peacemaker and mediator, Toni usually gave in to the requests of her family. As she thought about their demands, Toni knew that if she quit now, she'd surely suffer ill health in the future. Just as heart disease took from her parents, it would surely rob Toni of a healthy, activity filled life now and later. No matter what her family thought of her weight loss, Toni's achievement represented life itself.

While she made the right decision, saying "no" under pressure made Toni feel nervous. She seldom acted so out of character, but Toni refused to yield to the collective family demand. The program guided her in doing the right thing, in a prudent way, for all the right reasons. With sensible eating and regular exercise, Toni believed she'd reach a healthy weight and keep it off.

It was different for her daughter. While Toni's new behaviors promoted good health, Kristie's eating disorder promised to ruin hers. No rational person could or would associate wellness with the accompanying anti-social behaviors. She became more withdrawn and rejected all of her friends. From them Toni learned that Kristie walked the halls at school looking at the floor so she would not have to talk to anyone. When they called Kristie at home, she would not talk to them.

As Toni recalls those cold winter days, the memories evoke a sadness that darkens her face and clouds her expression. "Life got worse before it got better," she remembers somberly.

If an outsider looked without emotion, a striking similarity became glaringly obvious. Mother and daughter held the same coin, but the silvery token displayed opposite faces for the women. While both expressed comparable emotional issues around food, each chose different manifestations, demonstrating different goals and motivations.

As Kristie's treatment began, the women were about to be pushed to their limits. Soon the two women would be propelled into their own worlds of self-discovery.

Like Toni's own program, The Renfrew Center had strict rules. Admitted as an inpatient, Kristie stayed at the institute for several weeks and the center required the family to attend therapy sessions.

On a good day with no traffic, Renfrew was an hour away from home. During the Christmas season, the couple left work and traveled from the suburbs into the city. Busy shoppers added to the already crowded rush hour traffic. With their relationship strained to its limit, toxic tension permeated the car like a thick fog during the arduous daily drive.

Sometimes they had to attend two sessions a day, one before dinner and another afterward. They could not eat dinner with their daughter because the center monitored Kristie's meals.

While the family members each managed Renfrew's requirements, Toni also managed her own strict program. Feeling she could be nearing a breaking point, Toni appealed to the program leaders to excuse her from weekly meetings. Though they sympathized with Toni, they were unbending. In order to stay in the program, Toni would have to make the weekly meetings, still turn in her weekly food diary, and meet the required monthly weight loss goal.

When faced with dueling priorities, it was not like Toni to choose herself. In the past, her personal priorities were the first items to go. Not this time. She wouldn't give up on herself anymore than she would give up on her daughter. It was one of several positive, self-care decisions she would make during Kristie's recovery. It was also the beginning of a breakthrough for Toni. Her brave determination would quickly be tested.

On Toni's own meeting nights, she traveled to Renfrew but left at the dinner break. She made her way back to the suburbs through the extra-heavy rush hour traffic and attended her meeting. When it ended, she got back in her car and drove another hour to Renfrew for the second therapy session.

Kristie's weeks as an inpatient were among the most stressful of Toni's life. Many days, as she drove to or from Renfrew in the darkness of short winter days, Toni would stare at the red taillights on the cars ahead, wondering about Kristie's future. As she listened to radio commercials about diet drugs, she wondered if her daughter would get well or become a frightening statistic.

During those weeks, she felt emotionally, mentally, and physically exhausted. In her old behaviors, her natural response was to eat. Comfort foods like cookies and potato chips appealed to Toni the most. Yet if she gave into her cravings, she experienced a weight gain. She did not want to be kicked out of her program; therefore, the conundrum forced Toni to put her newly forming, non-eating stress behaviors to the test.

Day after day, and sometimes minute to minute, she struggled. Yet in spite of the challenges, Toni persisted. Though she made some mistakes, most of the time Toni succeeded in replacing junk eating with better food choices and/or her new, more supportive activities.

Weeks passed. On Christmas Eve, Renfrew released Kristie into an outpatient program. Permitted to spend some time with her family, that night Toni and Tim took Kristie home.

If ever there was a time when Toni wanted to medicate her emotions with food, that was the day. Usually one of the happiest family times, a holiday that left her with joyous memories, that Christmas stands out in Toni's mind as one of the most difficult and saddest events ever.

Trying to keep the holiday "normal" for the rest of the family, she served the customary holiday meals complete with everyone's favorite side dishes, cookies, and several different kinds of pies. While everyone ate, Toni watched to make sure Kristie consumed enough food...and kept it down. At the same time, Toni waged her own mental and behavioral tug of war. The pain Toni felt for her daughter's battle clashed with her own struggle to stick with *her* program. Two women, two unyielding programs, two choices: give in or keep fighting.

Throughout the night, it hurt Toni to watch Kristie grapple with her eating disorder. She ached as she felt the tension in her house. Troubles surfaced between Toni and Tim, between them and the children, and between *everyone* and Kristie. Relief marked the end of the day.

As the holidays progressed into New Year's Eve, Kristie moved into the next phase of her treatment: a daily, full-day program. Toni chose to keep fighting, managing to lose her required few pounds by December's end. She felt optimistic that her daughter would choose the same. Up from her lowest weight of eighty-two pounds, Kristie entered the new stage at ninety-six pounds—still too low, but definitely going in the right direction.

For the next few months, Toni took Kristie to the new treatment facility at seven each morning. On workdays, Toni dropped Kristie off, made the hour-long drive to work, and then left her job early to pick Kristie up at four in the afternoon. Toni counted heavily on the understanding of her boss, who permitted Toni to use vacation days to accommodate the lost work hours.

Each day the long drives seemed even longer because Kristie shut her mother out. She seemed so angry, Toni thought, *about everything.* Though Toni tried talking to Kristie, she treaded lightly, fearing she might say something to make matters worse. During those months, only Kristie's music pierced the heavy silence of the drive time.

Phase Two ended in the spring and Kristie returned to her classes. The next portion of the treatment presented yet another logistical challenge for Toni. Three days a week, Toni picked Kristie up at school and took her to a five-to-nine meeting at the center. Two days a week, she stayed at the center and waited. On Toni's meeting day, however, she drove Kristie to the center. Then, through rush hour traffic, she made the hour-long drive to weigh in and get her weekly dose of support.

Though Toni faced a daily emotional conflict between easy eating and healthy food, she continued to have small but consistent weight losses. At the same time, Kristie's weight fluctuated. Sometimes she gained and sometimes she lost, usually as a result of the stress of balancing school, meetings, homework, and food. Slowly, however, she gained back most of the anorexic weight loss. She began to look like her former self.

As the pages of the calendar turned, Toni continued to focus on the good steps she took for herself. During the past stressful months, the people she met at the weekly meeting supported her and became her emotional lifeline. Though she spoke sparingly about Kristie, the situation, or how she felt, Toni departed each meeting feeling stronger. She felt affirmed by Lynn, other meeting leaders, and participants alike.

Toni's twenty-plus pound weight loss soon became obvious. Few people knew how hard Toni worked to realize her goal. Instead, at least at home, it seemed as if nearly everyone lobbed considerable criticism at her for staying in the program during Kristie's treatment. It was about to get worse.

When Kristie's after-school program was over, her therapists recommended ongoing counseling. Following their advice, Toni searched through the lists provided by the family's insurance company. She took Kristie to a few, but none of them worked out, mostly because they did not connect with Kristie. Though frustrated with the failed attempts to get the proper counseling for her daughter, Toni persisted and finally located a therapist who seemed right for Kristie. Unfortunately, insurance wouldn't pay for or subsidize the sessions. Although the therapist fought the insurance company for payment, most of her fee was paid out-of-pocket. The financial burden of Kristie's latest treatment added to the family stress.

At first, only Kristie attended the weekly meetings. Later the therapist saw Toni, Tim, and then the whole family. In family therapy, the psychologist focused on Toni's weight control program. Supporting the family's disapproval, the therapist told Toni that she thought the weight loss and accompanying behaviors, like keeping a food diary, confused Kristie. She wanted Toni to quit, telling Toni that her program distracted Kristie.

It was one thing when her family wanted her to leave the program, and another when a licensed therapist recommended it. Wracked with guilt, Toni again faced the difficult choice between her health and her daughter's health. Toni wanted her daughter to be well. At the same time, Toni feared that without the support she received from those in her program, she would go back to old behaviors. She worried about gaining back the lost weight, and then ending up either dead or disabled.

For months it seemed as though there could be no compromising, no happy medium. As though she had a dirty little secret, Toni kept her food diary, but did it almost sneakily. Increasingly, Toni found it difficult to focus on her own needs.

At her weekly meetings, the scale became almost like a barometer of Toni's emotional dilemma. Toni noticed a pattern in her weight. It seemed as though a lower weight mirrored a balanced and in-control week while a higher weight matched a difficult week. Her body weight fluctuated with Toni's commitment, as though it waited to find out if she would continue or quit.

For a while, Toni confesses, "battling guilt and a sense of re-sponsibility for [Kristie's] illness" became an all-consuming is-sue. The only place Toni felt truly supported was at the weekly behavior modification meetings. Though still somewhat reticent, the more progress she made, the more often she spoke at the meetings. The group listened and tried to understand her strug-gle. Week after week they offered Toni suggestions for creating stronger behaviors during the upcoming week. In truth, most of the ideas were not viable in Toni's situation. Just the same, she always walked away from a meeting feeling positively reinforced.

In spite of her successful efforts, Toni began to think about giving up. She grew tired of the constant struggle with weight, food, behaviors...but most of all, with the guilt. It was as though her now thirty pound weight loss converted itself into an alba-tross. Visibly thinner, some made Toni feel that her victory was not a sign of good health but a discernible manifestation of bad mothering. With so much pressure for her to quit, it certainly seemed to be the easier choice.

Each day, Toni waged an emotional battle among her spiritu-al self, the mother within, and the world. Still, when it came down to Toni's personal bottom line, a healthy weight meant a healthy life. Over the past year, in the face of such turmoil, she fought to do well and stay in the program. Whatever the strug-gle and however upset her family and others were about it, Toni felt good about her own success. Yet as much as she wanted to keep going, she hated the daily barrage of guilt. Toni felt her emo-tional resolve weakening.

One night she nervously placed a call to team leader Lynn. Speaking in the hushed voice of one not wanting to be heard by others, Toni laid out her difficult position to the other woman. A voice of reason for Toni, Lynn listened. She reminded Toni that her personal goal was about a strategy for saving her life, not simply about being thin and pretty. The longer they talked, the clearer it became to Lynn how fiercely Toni felt pulled in all direc-tions. Presenting a straightforward solution with the conviction of someone who had been there, she advised Toni, "*You* have to take control. You have to take control *of yourself*."

Though it was a message Toni heard often at meetings, that night Lynn's advice struck a nerve. The words reverberated in her head for days. Pressure, guilt, and the normal frustrations of her weight program were mounting. How could she get control when it seemed as though everything was against her? Toni appreciated the advice, but she didn't think it applied to her situation.

The next morning, her internal battle continued as she struggled to fit in some exercise before going to work. Emotionally worn out and frustrated, Toni told herself, "I just can't do this anymore." She decided to quit the program. Yet instead of feeling as though a burden lifted off her shoulders, Toni felt disappointed. Throughout the day she questioned her choice.

As Toni walked through the halls of the university, soaking in the youthful energy of the college campus, she questioned herself repeatedly. As the workday drew to a close, she felt a force rising up within her. Would quitting the weight program really help Kristie? What lessons did she teach Kristie by giving in to the pressures of those around her? In her heart, and in spite of what everyone else wanted to think, Toni knew her weight loss did not create Kristie's problems. As she turned questions and ideas over in her head, Toni asked herself what action sent the strongest message to her struggling daughter.

Suddenly, as she thought about her questions, Toni made a startling discovery. Through all the past months, Toni listened to negative feedback from everyone. Everyone, that is, but Kristie. Toni realized she never had a discussion about her program with her daughter. In truth, since her daughter's diagnosis, Toni saw her as "a beautiful and fragile glass rose." Except for mundane or trivial banter, meaningful conversation took place only in therapy, with the therapist present. Even then, she avoided any talk about food and food-related behaviors.

For months on end and amid all the blame and guilt people dumped on Toni, she felt paranoid and worried that anything she might say to her daughter might undo any of the treatment's benefits...until now. All this time Toni lived with the disapproval of everyone around her, yet never consulted the person most directly affected.

"You have to take control," Toni heard Lynn saying to her. *You. Control.* These were the operative words. Was Toni in control of herself, or was she allowing everyone around her to be in charge of her own life? The longer Toni thought about it, she wondered how she could best help her daughter. If Toni could not work through the connection with food, emotions, and behaviors that Kristie battled—the same behaviors that made Toni obese and her daughter anorexic—how much good did she really do for her daughter?

Rather than quit the program as planned, Toni reevaluated her progress. Yes, she was thinner. No, she did not starve herself or follow some crazy fad diet. Yes, she succeeded by changing her lifestyle. These days she made better food choices. She packed food for lunch and after-school events. She added exercise and now included running in her daily routine.

At the next meeting at the old, red-brick schoolhouse, Toni reflected on the program and the many things she learned as a member. Toni *had* changed, and not just her food choices. Previously soft-spoken and often ready to acquiesce to others, Toni learned to assert herself more. She didn't give in when she really wanted something. These days she said "no" to people, situations, and foods that would sabotage her efforts. The new behaviors got easier each time.

As she mulled over the positive changes in her mind, she listened to some of the newer members. Remembering how difficult the program was at the beginning, Toni identified with their challenges. Suddenly she realized that she no longer faced many of those same challenges. Unlike the early days, staying on track was the norm now, not the exception. *Control.* She *was* in control—*of herself.* Yes! Once aware that she actually integrated many positive changes in her life, she discovered how much she liked the feeling. Realizing it was like a breath of fresh air. In fact, that moment was the best Toni felt about herself—*ever!* As she heard others talk about how they would handle the next week's challenges, she recognized how much healthier she became since that first September meeting. Not just in her body either, but in her mind and spirit as well.

By the end of the meeting, Toni reached a new conclusion. She recommitted to staying in the program. This time her decision *did* have the feeling that it was "right." She wanted to keep doing this program for herself. Not only did she feel good about herself, she recognized how, during this most challenging time, the small group represented the only "sane place" in Toni's life.

When she went home that night, Toni told Kristie she wanted to talk with her. She did not know how she would find the right words, but she had to try. It was after eight o'clock when the mother and daughter sat down at the kitchen table. In spite of her trepidation, Toni spoke from her heart. She told Kristie what she was feeling, how pressured she felt, and how much she wanted to be the best mother for Kristie. She also told her daughter how important her weight loss program was to her.

When she was finished talking, Kristie asked a lot of questions. She wanted to know more about Toni's emotional connection to food, what her plan was, and how she got and stayed motivated. She also inquired about the program "rules" and why they were so rigid.

After each question, Toni responded as honestly and openly as she could. As she did, she saw understanding spread across Kristie's face. For the first time, her daughter recognized how important the program was for Toni. As they talked, and for the first time in many months, her daughter seemed to relax into the safety of her mother's love and understanding.

Before long, Kristie opened up to Toni about herself and how she felt. She told Toni things that she'd held back, even in therapy. She identified with her mother's struggles with emotional eating. She talked about how her illness affected the family, and how upset she felt about the family's denial regarding the nature of her illness. By the end of the night, tired but satisfied, both mother and daughter saw how they were both battling the same emotional issues, just in different ways.

Later, when she thought about their talk, Toni realized that each woman held the key to her own victory. She felt that talking directly to Kristie turned the key and opened the door. Feeling better about her daughter, and feeling good about their conversation, Toni renewed her commitment to herself and her personal goals. It was the first time in her life that, when faced with serious opposition to her goals, Toni chose herself. It was a courageous step, one that supported Toni's victory in every way, in every corner of her life.

At the next therapy session, Toni told the therapist about her decision. The therapist did not approve. This time, however, Toni no longer felt bad. She was past the point of being guilted out of doing something good for herself. As therapy continued through the months, Kristie opened up more. It became clear to everyone that her eating disorder didn't come about because of Toni and her weight loss. Instead, other issues both private and personal, surfaced. Some involved her own teenage problems and reactions to teenage situations while others were more family-related.

Once Toni's weight was no longer a topic for discussion, she ceased being the family scapegoat for Kristie's problem. Instead, family members began to deal with Kristie in their own way, dealing with their own problems and perceptions within the family dynamics. As the therapy evolved, it forced each person to focus on themselves, their perceptions, and their individual family responsibilities.

In the end, Toni no longer felt fully accountable for everyone's unhappiness. She accepted that she could only control her own feelings and her own happiness. In addition, part of Toni's victory came from understanding that everyone had his or her own family issues. Though every problem was initially centralized and focused on Toni, too many family matters had been ignored too long. Now they had to be addressed, discussed, and resolved.

In retrospect, Toni feels good that she didn't cave in to external pressures and she's glad she didn't give up something so important to her. Toni considers this the first time that she made a decision and stayed with it. For some women, that may seem minor. For Toni, and for millions of women like her, sticking to the decision to make self-care a priority is a *major* victory.

Since that difficult year, both Toni and Kristie stayed with their programs and created their own victories. Toni reached her goal weight and moved into the maintenance stage. Likewise, Kristie is back to her healthy weight and getting stronger.

These days, unlike days of old, Toni now includes herself and her needs in her priorities. In addition, she plans meals in advance. When she knows dinner is going to be away, she includes travel food and takes snacks. When traveling with Kristie, they plan their meals together. These days, Toni seldom eats fast foods. However, she makes better selections when eating at a quickie restaurant. The meals she cooks are healthier, a change that benefits the whole family. She doesn't bake at all now, leaving it up to her children to bake their favorite goodies if they want them. Each day Toni takes time for herself, usually in the form of exercise, and focuses on healthy rather than emotional eating.

In time, Kristie got back to athletics. Like her mother, she began running. She started with cross-country and loved it. Later, she excelled in that sport as she previously had in other sports, eventually securing a place in the statewide competition.

Though Kristie is still working through her eating disorder, Toni feels she is out of the quicksand, but not yet one hundred percent out of danger. Acknowledging her daughter's progress, Toni believes Kristie is well on her way to her eventual victory.

Toni is still involved in sports with the rest of her children. With three children still active, she regularly attends her share of practices and games. Toni continues to run several days a week. When asked if she and Kristie run together, Toni laughs, "No, she's too fast for me. I can't keep up."

Happy to be on the other side of her challenge, Toni says things have changed in the Kershaw household. Many issues surfaced as a result of family therapy, and the sessions brought up concerns between Toni and Tim, the couple and their children, and from one child to another. Talking together resolved many matters; others are still being resolved. It is a slow process, but improving.

Through Toni's growth in the process, she is stronger. In the past, she did everything for everyone. Toni now delegates more responsibility to her family. She has greater expectations for Tim and his household involvement. Their children, now all young adults, do their own laundry, pick up after themselves, and participate in other household chores. Her new "house rules" don't always meet with the approval and acceptance of her children. In the old days, lack of agreement bothered Toni. Now she no longer feels guilty when they bicker and moan, but chalks it up to family growth.

Toni's goals are for each child to be more self-sufficient and independent. "Things happen for a reason," she believes. "[Kristie's illness] tore the family apart, but also brought us closer together. [The children] are more supportive of each other today. In fact, they are better people because they have an understanding about other people and other people's feelings." According to a happy Toni, they seem to be getting the message.

Toni still feels that her first job, her first calling, was and is her family. However, when she reflects on her past mothering behaviors, she thinks that being the "all purpose" mom did not serve her children's growth—or her own—particularly well. With loving but overzealous intentions, she willingly became everyone's "go to" girl. Overdoing and overcaring, Toni thinks she was too in control of everyone else's lives, and not enough in control of her own. While she smoothed over problems and accommodated everyone else's agendas, the true Toni got lost. She made time for her family, but robbed herself of time for personal growth.

Now Toni approaches life with her newfound "I count too" attitude. As a result, she feels more like her true self. She jokes at how she is a forty-something "late bloomer" who is finally learning how to be more assertive. Toni is more likely to verbalize her feelings instead of internalizing them, and that's surely a healthy change for her. Though still timid about conflict, she addresses it, and is improving daily.

While Toni lost weight, she gained greater control over her own life, which led to more self-confidence. Her victory is not so much about the pounds lost as it is about the life she gained. As she gave up her Toni-as-supermom persona, she found a strength that she did not know she had. As she gains momentum, she is more likely to tell her family what her own needs are, and they are more willing to listen and accommodate those needs. As they get older, she looks forward to more "me time" for hobbies and travel.

When someone looks at Toni's fit body, they are not looking at the result of a diet plan. Instead, they are viewing a healthy woman whose body reflects the victory of internal growth.

Toni offers a piece of advice to other moms who have fallen into the same pattern, with or without the excess weight. She recommends that the image of the long-suffering mom is not particularly virtuous. Sacrificing too much is as bad as doing too little. To the overcaring mom, Toni urges, "Life is never how you plan it. Stay focused on the things that matter the most, and surround yourself with good people that help you see that most important person...yourself!"

STEPPING STONES TO VICTORY

1. When you say "no" to family or friends, how often do they say or do things that cause you to feel guilty? What do you do? If you give in and do what they want, how does it make you feel? In your Victory Journal, record one new behavior that will help you live a better and personally more fulfilling life.

   In your journal, draw three columns. List five situations when you can use this behavior. Keep track by writing it down. In the first column, list the five situations. In the second column, write what you've done in the past. Next to that behavior, in a third column, write your new behavior.

EXAMPLE:

Behavior: *Saying "no" to last minute requests.*

Situation	Past Response	New Behavior
Son waits until the last minute to request that I drive him someplace, presuming I'll drop everything and do it.	I agree, rearranging my schedule and altering my plans to accommodate his lack of planning.	I don't agree and tell my son that if he'd given adequate notice, I would have honored his request. I inform him that I have plans and would gladly drive him in the future with twenty-four hours notice.

2. Many women do not allow time for themselves. Even just thirty minutes a day seems like a lot—but it really isn't. Also, many women claim if they had that extra time, they aren't

sure they would know what to do. Are you one of those women? What do you do for yourself alone that fills you up and makes you feel satisfied?

    a. For the next week, keep track in your Victory Journal of how long you have to yourself each day and what you do. If you want more time, strategize how you will find that time. What will you rearrange to make time for yourself, who will you say "no" to, and how will you do it?

    b. Next, make a list of twenty things you'll do with your free time. Will you read a book, take up a craft such as scrapbooking or knitting, meditate, walk alone, make a cup of tea and call an old friend, listen to your favorite CD...or something else?

    c. Practice implementing your strategy for one month. Star your calendar on every day that you keep your "me time" appointment. If it still isn't a habit after the first month, practice for another month. Continue practicing until you, and those around you, know that you take time for yourself each day.

3. Do you have personal goals? In your Victory Journal, make a list of one hundred things you would like to do before you die. Write down everything, no matter how outrageous some items may seem. One woman who did this listed the world's eight greatest art museums and decided that she would visit them all. She did not make it a top priority and, in fact, thought it was a pipe dream. During the next few years, she changed jobs, traveled more, and found herself in several of the museum's cities. At last count, she only had two more to visit and felt thrilled about her accomplishment.

6

A House Is Not a Home
Nancy Hill

NANCY HILL WAS DYING. SHE KNEW IT. THOUGH OB-
viously weak from the debilitating sickness that was rav-
aging her body, she sat comfortably in the bedroom of her beautiful home. Everything was neat and clean including the powder
blue chenille robe that she wore.

On this particular day, two of her three sons were with her,
doing what they could for the woman who had done so much for
them; a third son was arriving shortly. The small stack of books
next to her chair included a well-read Bible. Her tired eyes shone
with the peace that surpasses all understanding. This was the final chapter for the courageous woman with the gentle demeanor
whose subtle but powerful victory began many years ago.

Nancy came from a rural, farming background. She was born
in Virginia in 1925, the fifth of twelve children. She lived "in the
hollow" in a small, one-story house on the grounds of a large

farm. Her parents worked for the owners: Nancy's father worked the land while her mother cleaned the owner's house.

Nancy was a mere child when The Great Depression descended on the country. Between the country's miserable economic conditions and so many mouths to feed, her parents prayed for *just enough* money to take care of their family. They managed to scrape by but usually just barely.

With a dozen children, one child or another always needed something or had to be supervised, creating a somewhat chaotic household. Every child, oldest to youngest, had a job, and Nancy's parents charged her with keeping the house clean. With so many in one little house, Nancy had a never-ending list of chores.

As she grew into womanhood, Nancy graduated from high school and moved east where she secured a job doing housework. While living in the military town of Norfolk, she met and married Chief Petty Officer Charles Crutchfield, a man ten years her senior with three children. Soon the new family moved north to McKeesport, a small, industrial town about fifteen miles outside of Pittsburgh, Pennsylvania.

Nancy quickly began organizing the household. A quiet and timid person, her life revolved around what her husband wanted. Having lived with a similarly autocratic father, in the beginning Nancy presumed that compliance was simply a normal way of life. However, running the household according to the dictates of her controlling husband did not seem to make her happy or secure the way a home should do.

Nancy soon realized that a house is not necessarily a home. This distinction became critically important for Nancy because she wanted to make her house a peaceful home. In time, the idea of having a home and not just a house would take root in Nancy and become a driving force in her life. But not just yet...

Not long into their marriage, Nancy had her first child—and her first real tragedy. When the baby was only six months old, he died of pneumonia. Over the next few years, Nancy had three more children, all sons.

Nancy hadn't accumulated many material possessions before getting married, and she didn't expect too much while living in McKeesport. That is, not until she met Sadie, an older woman who lived up the street. Still a young mother when she met Sadie, and hours away from the comfort of her own mother, Nancy and Sadie became fast friends.

In Nancy's day, car travel and phone calls were not as inexpensive or commonplace as they are today. Because Nancy could not visit with her own mother, Sadie took Nancy under her wing. A woman of strong middle class values who expected a lot from herself, Sadie showed the young mother a way of living that filled her with a new respect for herself, as well as a fresh vision for her life and her children's future. She encouraged Nancy to believe that no matter the situation, if she didn't like it, she could always make it better. When Nancy's house, clothes, and overall surroundings appeared impoverished or shabby, Sadie instructed her not to allow them to dictate who she was. Sadie motivated Nancy to rise above her situation, choose the priorities that would define her life, and improve her environment accordingly. Sadie stirred something in Nancy as the wise woman passed along her belief that "you can make a home out of an old shack." She persuaded Nancy to look at what she had in her house, find ways to spruce it up and make it her true home. When Nancy followed the sage advice, the older woman applauded her protégé's efforts.

Over time, Nancy says that Sadie's values "became a part of my life—to make something out of nothing, and the value of high quality housekeeping." With Sadie's mentoring guidance, Nancy came to see greater possibilities for her life. In turn, Nancy's vision came to include expecting a lot from her children. Eventually, Sadie also became like a second grandmother to Nancy's children.

In addition to the support of Sadie's friendship, Nancy also had the comfort and assurances of her religion. She had great faith, and lived her faith. Nancy counted both her friendship with Sadie and her church community among her greatest blessings.

Unfortunately, her family life wasn't as uncomplicated. Over the years, the man she married insisted more and more on having his own way. The outside world saw him as a likeable man, the kind of man who was good to everyone—except his spouse. He drank, and as his alcoholism progressed, he became increasingly abusive. Nancy became more and more frightened for herself and her children. But it wasn't only her safety that worried Nancy. In peering into the future, Nancy feared that her sons would suffer from their father's abuse, or that they would learn to be abusive, or worst of all, *both*. She had to protect herself and her children, no matter the cost.

In the 1950s, a woman seldom left her marriage. Though it did happen, countless women of Nancy's day remained in abusive marriages. Citing some of the same reasons today's woman continues to live in an abusive marriage, the women of the fifties and sixties feared being alone and did not feel they could raise their children by themselves.

Unlike those women, Nancy decided that staying came at too high a price for both herself and her children. Living in a house that she could not call a home was just not enough for Nancy. She believed she could have something better. She made a decision. She would find a way to get out of her situation and into a better one.

All things considered, given the attitude of the day toward single mothers and working women, she made an exceptionally courageous decision. Leaving a marriage and supporting three children alone would be a risky move for any woman. Given the opportunities afforded to an African-American woman like Nancy, the risk seemed even greater.

Yet undaunted and walking in faith, shortly after the birth of her third child Nancy began making plans to leave her husband. She had no strategy at first, but her vision was clear. She believed she could, and in fact *would*, do better. Nancy focused on believing that a home should be a place of peace and love. She would make a home for her children, and do better than ever before.

She believed that God would make a way for something better to happen.

As her plan began to unfold, Nancy took the first critical steps of preparing herself financially. Her husband kept a tight rein on her spending, wanting to know how much she spent and where. Nancy had to find ways to get around him and save some money.

One of Nancy's methods included shopping with a friend who had a larger family, and who spent more money on groceries than Nancy did. When they finished shopping, Nancy would switch grocery receipts with the friend. She would give the more expensive grocery receipt to her husband; it satisfied him. Then Nancy would keep the difference between the actual receipt and the one her husband saw. She stashed the money in a safe place so she would have it when she was ready to use it; it grew into her victory fund.

In whatever spare time she may have had, Nancy read novels that reinforced her belief that there could be something more for her and her children. The novels substantiated Sadie's influence and inspired Nancy to think differently about herself. She came to realize that she wasn't just a woman, wife, and mother, but that she was a lady. Thinking of herself that way raised her self-esteem and helped her stay focused on her goals.

Once the children started school, Nancy began cleaning houses. In addition, Nancy taught herself to sew and began taking in sewing from people. She used her jobs as another way to save money without her spouse knowing about it. Being paid in cash, Nancy would surreptitiously keep a portion of the money for herself, while turning over the rest to her waiting husband.

As well as saving money and building her confidence, Nancy used the time to rally her forces. Her married stepson witnessed the spousal abuse, in one instance even taking a gun away from his father. One day he told Nancy that whenever she was ready, he would help her to leave.

While Nancy continued planning, her father died. A few years later, Nancy's mother met and married a good and kind man who lived only a few hours away from Nancy. Nancy knew her mother's new home would be the safe haven to which she could take her children.

Nancy waited nearly six years to make her move. She delayed only as long as it took for all the boys to be in school, reasoning that with the children in school, she could work full-time to support her family.

At last, everything fell into place. The day after her youngest son finished his last day of kindergarten, she called her stepson and told him she was ready to go. The next morning, a beautiful Sunday in June, Nancy made her move. After her spouse left for work, she told her children to quickly pack their things.

When Nancy's stepson arrived, they were ready and he drove them to her mother's house. The stay with Nancy's mother gave all of them the needed time to regroup and afforded Nancy the time to make connections for her next step.

Nancy designed the move to her mother's house to be a temporary one. Through the summer Nancy registered her children for school while lining up several housecleaning jobs in the McKeesport area where she had worked in the past. She also managed, with the assistance of a kind judge for whom she previously worked, to arrange housing. In fact, the judge used his influence to help move Nancy to the top of the list for project housing. Subsequently in the fall, Nancy and her sons moved to the city of Pittsburgh.

The projects of the late '50s and early '60s were filled with working class families and not a bad place to live; but unlike her nicer McKeesport house, it was public housing and considered welfare. While the small family could live there on her wages, Nancy felt it was a painful step down. In spite of any negative feelings she might have harbored about the location, she determined she would turn the house into *a home*.

As she began her new life as a single mother, Nancy faced the same fears that many women must confront when starting over. Though not one to shy away from work, she still experienced her share of difficulties. Just getting to work turned out to be a challenge in the beginning. Having lived in more integrated areas most of her life, she found that living in a segregated area for the first time presented new challenges. Fearful of city crimes and muggings, she admitted, "It was very frightening the first time I got on the bus in Pittsburgh to go to work." Yet Nancy gradually got over her fears and "became more determined and stronger" to do what she needed to do.

In time, the judge who helped Nancy find housing also facilitated the procedure for her divorce; her spouse did not contest it. Additional aid came from some of her customers in the form of leftovers she could take home, or hand-me-down clothing and household goods. Though always appreciative for the assistance, Nancy also found it humbling.

The job of cleaning houses also had its ups and downs. While Nancy had her regularly scheduled customers, sometimes a customer would call and tell her not to come to work for a day, or even several days, thus leaving Nancy without expected income. And though awarded child support through the courts, her former husband didn't always send it. Support payments became a moot point when, a few years after the divorce, he became ill and stopped working; he died while the children were teenagers.

If she had no work and no income, however brief the time, Nancy would apply for welfare. However, there was often a gap between the time she filed for welfare and when the check arrived. Sometimes it took weeks for a check to come and Nancy and her boys had to make do with the little they had. The family seldom had an easy time making ends meet, and for many years they lived hand-to-mouth, and from day to day.

Nevertheless, no matter what happened, Nancy continued to stay focused on her goals and centered in her faith. She continued to stay in touch with the ever-encouraging Sadie, who occasionally provided some financial assistance as well as emotional support. Each day Nancy persistently followed Sadie's guidance to "work with what she had and look for ways to make it better."

One day at a time and step-by-step, Nancy gradually made progress. She advanced into the better life she desired for herself and her children. She faced the fact that raising three boys in the projects by herself would require a gargantuan effort accompanied by strict discipline. She prayed, and regardless how shy and frightened she was, Nancy consistently took actions that demonstrated her faith in God. As a result of her strong consciousness, Nancy developed standards of living and household systems designed to create a peaceful home for herself and her sons, laid a solid foundation for her boys' future, and taught them life skills and values.

Starting with the physical environment of the home, Nancy mandated that the house would be neat and clean at all times. Each child would share in that responsibility. Next, to make certain that her house would be a peaceful home, she created rules for her sons and each one had a purpose. Nancy's criteria for her sons' behaviors included:

- never go to bed angry;
- always say good night before going to bed (whether you feel like it or not);
- never leave the house in anger (because you never know if you'll come back);
- no fighting is allowed (at least not in front of her or when she was home);
- be home by {specific time, based on the child}.

Though her guidelines made sense, she believed her sons considered them "warden rules." Nancy says they didn't understand why they had to be home while the other kids were still outside playing. No matter, the regulations Nancy insisted on were either value-driven, or provided a protective structure that would keep them out of trouble.

In addition, her rules created the peaceful environment that she set out to give herself and her sons. When Nancy tired of the daily struggles concernng work and family, she recalls, "The peace of mind in the evenings at home kept me going. Even though we had very few possessions, we had a *home* together."

Enlarging the sphere of influence to outside her home, she made church and religious involvement the third component of her purpose-driven life. Nancy actively served her congregation through Bible classes and committees. Through her commitment, Nancy found help, solace, and a supportive community. Nancy expected her boys to attend Sunday school and they did. Because she was at church much of the day, so were her boys. They got involved in church-related programs through which they developed a large portion of their social life. The church community was one way for Nancy to keep her sons away from and out of the kind of trouble that could easily find an adolescent boy.

In addition, the religious group offered a variety of social activities for Nancy and the family, and the programs provided additional structure. The church community opened their homes and hearts to them, as well as to other members of her faith. Nancy never had to wonder where she and the boys would be spending a holiday, or if there would be food for a celebration. They were always invited to someone's house where they would join with lots of others to enjoy fellowship. Nancy's church gave her and her sons a strong extended family.

Education filled the fourth slot of Nancy's system. Placing a high value on education, Nancy insisted that her children study and do well. Her boys knew from an early age that their mother would not consider their schooling complete until each received a college degree.

Firmly committed to their education, Nancy did whatever it took to make that happen. Whether helping a son who had difficulty learning to read, fighting a school counselor to ensure her sons received the necessary instruction, or applying for financial aid for college, Nancy focused incredible amounts of energy on her children's schooling.

The glue that kept all the parts of Nancy's system in place was expectation. The powerful mechanism worked for Nancy both in and outside her home. She rarely used physical punishment with her sons. Instead, she combined the powerfully strong but psychologically positive "intimidation of high expectations" with a firm "look" (that kind of determined look that only a mother can give to her children!). It worked. Nancy maintained control of her growing boys. As a result, if her children got into trouble at school or elsewhere, they were usually more concerned about how much their actions would hurt their mother than whatever punishment they would otherwise receive for their actions.

Not only did she hold high standards for herself and her sons, but Nancy articulated her principles to her neighbors and punctuated her words with respectful behaviors. She demonstrated her seriousness by not allowing her children to hang out with a child she felt was a bad influence. As a result, Nancy earned the respect of others in the neighborhood, even the street kids.

Interestingly, when the other neighbors recognized Nancy's serious intentions, they aided her in keeping an eye on the actions of her children. They would let her know what happened when she was at work or otherwise not around. And with that information, Nancy could secure control of potentially precarious situations before they got out of hand.

While Nancy struggled to maintain an upstanding lifestyle, many men sought the company of the attractive, single mother. She said they engaged in romantic sweet talk in an effort to persuade Nancy to give them some of her time. She says the men would try to flatter her by saying she was a "nice lady, and not like a lot of the women in the neighborhood." They often offered to help raise her boys.

At this point in her life, however, Nancy had given up being a bashful and compliant woman and was wise to men who merely wanted to "get over" on her, or who wanted to help her sons so that they could help themselves. Though she admits that being a working single parent had many lonely moments, Nancy did not think loneliness provided sufficient reason to lower herself and "succumb to seamy class living." She also made it clear to any man who was interested in her that she and her sons were a family. She refused to be involved with a man who was interested in her but not the children. Furthermore, Nancy only wanted to be involved with a man on her terms. She hadn't worked so hard to make a better life just to give it up for someone who did not share and honor her same values.

By the late 1960s, Nancy had been cleaning houses and supporting her family for nearly a decade. Around that time, while her sons were in high school and college, Nancy's church got a new pastor, the Reverend Pugh. Within a few years, the reverend had as great an impact on Nancy as had Sadie.

Reverend Pugh actively embraced the growing Civil Rights movement and participated in many programs that supported Civil Rights, including a Pittsburgh work-related, affirmative action-style program. Acting almost as a mentor, he saw more opportunity for Nancy than she could see for herself and encouraged Nancy to apply for a job at a local bank.

Used to cleaning houses, Nancy felt intimidated by the idea of working in an office. It took her quite some time and lots of encouragement from Reverend Pugh, but she eventually gathered enough courage to apply for a job and interview with the bank. Unfortunately, the bank only had an opening for a night position. Nancy wouldn't take the job because it meant leaving her youngest son, still in high school, alone each night in the projects without her supervision.

Fortunately, when Nancy explained her reasoning to the personnel manager, he found a day job for her. Nancy's first job at the bank merely required her to sort letters and checks. Though the low level position paid less than Nancy wanted, she recognized it as a new beginning and accepted the offer.

As always, Nancy started where she was and found ways to improve her circumstances. Banking offered her an actual career direction, and she made the most of it. During her nearly twenty years at the bank, she incrementally worked her way up from that humble first job and eventually retired from a supervisory position. In the weeks before her death, Nancy admitted that she was "still elated" that she reached that notable milestone.

By the mid-1970s, with her sons on their own, Nancy moved out of the projects and into a Pittsburgh suburb. Nearly ten years later, she met Charles Hill at church. A former church member, Charles had moved away from Pittsburgh several years earlier. As a widower, Charles returned to the church where he renewed his acquaintance with many congregants, including Nancy. Charles began courting Nancy, and soon the couple married. People who knew them, including her sons, claimed the two were "made for each other." The years with Charles, until his death from cancer in 1999, were the happiest days of her life.

A few years ago, Nancy moved away from Pittsburgh and closer to her dying mother. She moved into a suburban townhome, which she decorated beautifully—and kept impeccably clean. After her mother passed, Nancy stayed so that she could be near her sisters and extended family. She actively enjoyed the peaceful life she so treasured.

A few months before interviewing Nancy, she learned she had cancer. When diagnosed, Nancy immediately underwent surgery and began treatment. At first, her prognosis was good. Unfortunately, the good news did not last. The doctors informed her there was nothing more they could do locally, and suggested that she travel to another state and undergo an extreme cancer treatment; there were no guarantees, and little hope. Though she considered it briefly, she decided that radical and intense treatment wasn't what she wanted. She decided to look at her situation and make the best of it.

In her final days, Nancy was reflective as she affirmed, "Leaving McKeesport and the abuse and taking my boys with me was the best decision I ever made." Calling them *My Three Sons*, a reference to an old television show, Nancy expressed pride in how well they have all done for themselves. They all received at least an undergraduate degree and went on to achieve their own substantial successes. One son is a journalist. He was the one who couldn't read as a child. He now publishes a respected city news-paper. Another son, a teacher, heads the sociology department of a major university. Nancy's third son, also a teacher, managed the corporate training and development function for a large real estate company until his untimely death only six months after his mother's passing.

During her life, Nancy always focused on making her house a peaceful and loving home. She expressed concern that too many women "want things the quick way," and go about getting them any way they can. When asked if she had any advice for other women in similar situations, Nancy was firm and clear. "Do not compromise your life for nothing and nobody just to have a few quick things." Acknowledge where you are and ask yourself, "How can I better my life?"

If Nancy Hill could talk to you, she would tell you that once you choose to make your life better and devise a plan for doing so, **stay focused**. If distractions come along, tell yourself, "That's not what I want to do," and then get busy with some worthwhile endeavor or goal-focused activity.

After a life victoriously lived, Nancy spent her last days sur-rounded by children, siblings, and other loved ones. Prepared for her spiritual transition, Nancy waited to go to her new home—her most peaceful home. Just two days after the completion of this chapter, Nancy Hill died peacefully on June 25, 2003.

STEPPING STONES TO VICTORY

Nancy Hill had a three-part system for creating victory: **desire, expectation, and action**. She yearned for something better, including self-respect, a peaceful home, and an education for her children. Her expectation was that she could satisfy her desire in a proper and respectful way, no matter what her finances were at any time because she said, "I was a first-class lady." Her actions were well thought out, planned, and grounded in her value system. Her plans were always about what *she* could do to make her situation better.

Following Nancy Hill's three-part system, create your own process for victory. Record your answers in your Victory Journal.

1. If you could have something better than you have right now (and you can!), what would be your greatest, deepest *desire*? Think about this for a while. Would it be about money and power, or like Nancy, about self-respect and peace?

2. What are your personal expectations for yourself? For example, do you think you aren't worth more than you already have? Do you think that your life or your past has destroyed the goodness in you? Or do you think that no matter what you have now, you can expect more of yourself and do better?

   a. Let's presume you could have your heart's desire. In fact, pretend your life is on a number line and you can see where you are now and where your desired goal is.

      ☞ Where on the number line are you at this point in your life? Near the beginning, at the middle, toward the end?

    ❉ Where on the number line are you at the time you achieve your desired goal?

b. Once you have noticed as much as you can about your number line, open your eyes and write down all you remember, in as much detail as you can.

c. Once you have decided those two places, imagine that you are floating out to the place on your number line that is just past the point where you reached your goal. Step onto the number line and into the feeling of your goal. Now, turn around and look back.

Now ask yourself:

    ❉ What were the steps I took to get here? Notice them, one by one.

    ❉ How did I think about myself while I was on my way? Notice what you said to yourself, e.g., "How did I keep myself on track, and what kinds of positive things did I say to myself?" Also, "What were the feelings I had about myself as I watched myself making progress toward my goal?"

    ❉ How did others treat me? Notice how good it felt to be treated well.

    ❉ What negative or toxic behaviors did I change so that I could reach my goals?

    ❉ What did I learn to do differently so that I could be where I am today? Notice self-talk, positive behaviors, activities, friends and acquaintances, spirituality, education, etc.

    ❉ Using the responses, begin to set a new goal for yourself, and create a plan for its achievement.

3. Take *action*. Do something right now to make your goal more real. It could be a phone call to a college—or to your pastor. It could be deciding to end a destructive relationship. Whatever

it is, take one action right now. Take another action tomorrow...and the next day...and the next...

a. Review your progress.

b. Put your daily action step on your calendar the night before.

c. Do it.

7

Phoenix Rising

Jean Otte

"**W**ITHOUT ADVERSITY," JEAN OTTE BELIEVES, "AND without really, really tough things to deal with, you don't gain coping skills." According to Jean, coping skills enable a person to, on her own and with confidence, handle the twists, turns, and tragedies that are a natural part of life. Jean insists that preparing yourself to manage adversity is one of the foundations for successes in life. It is her method for creating her many victories. In addition to being the first woman executive for National Car Rental Systems Inc., the successful businesswoman is also the founder of the highly acclaimed Women Unlimited, a professional leadership development and mentoring program for women, and author of *Changing the Corporate Landscape*.

With her upbeat personality, sharp wit, and positive attitude, you wouldn't readily suspect just how well Jean Otte knows adversity. "Graduating" from one of life's survival schools at a very early age, her advanced degrees in "thriving" came one rigorous life step at a time. This Victorious Woman lived a lifetime modeling resolve rather than retreat, and triumph over tragedy.

Born in London, England, at the beginning of World War II in Europe, Jean knew little besides fear in her earliest years. Her father left to fight the war leaving her mother and her sisters on their own. They survived terrifying blitzkriegs at night only to find wreckage and ruin by day. It became commonplace for Jean to find buildings reduced to ruin, or see half a church left standing, or a neighbor's house suddenly missing a bedroom. Blackouts, bomb shelters, air raid sirens, and food rationing became Jean's way of life.

Jean's mother, along with many other women, worked outside the home throughout the war years. With no one at home during the day, even the smallest children attended school. At the tender age of four, Jean can still recall the sudden terror she felt when teachers hustled her out of the classroom and into a shelter, quickly pushing a gas mask onto her head and over her face. The war wreaked havoc in Jean's life; for years, the youngster knew little more than death and destruction.

Surrounded by grief and loss, Jean felt fortunate just to be living. She quickly learned that "if you got up and you were alive, everything else was a miracle." That simple but profound perspective instilled an attitude of gratitude and became part of her philosophy of life.

During the following recovery and rebuilding years, as Jean walked through the bombed-out rubble of London streets and played among the ruins, she made up her mind that simple survival would never be enough. She wanted more from life, though she had no idea how that would happen. Still, her youthful promise became the beginnings of the victory path that the adult Jean would later look back on with pride.

While the young girl felt grateful to be alive, the ravages of war left Jean "an incredibly introverted, scared child." She might have stayed that way if not for Mrs. Noonan. Not only did the kind teacher give Jean her first pat on the back, she found ways to help Jean through her fears.

Seeing that the bright young girl often hesitated to perform tasks, the wise Mrs. Noonan regularly suggested positive alternatives that helped her overcome her fears. When Jean felt too nervous to read out loud in class, Mrs. Noonan gave Jean the option to speak only to her, *and the class could simply listen.* After only a few one-on-one readings, Jean could perform the studious task regularly without trepidation.

Before long, a sense of trust and safety developed between the young girl and her teacher. When Mrs. Noonan suggested Jean take small risks, she did. When Jean shied away from a challenge, Mrs. Noonan often asked her, "Why do you think you can't do that, what's stopping you?" By naming her fears, Jean usually realized her disruptive concerns had no real substance.

With Mrs. Noonan's encouragement, Jean learned to see good and positive things about herself. Jean remembers, "She was a person who cared enough to tell me things that got in my way, things that were holding me back, as well as how things were being perceived by others."

Mrs. Noonan became Jean's first mentor and provided Jean with a powerful, life-affirming experience. Under her tutelage, Jean learned to recognize both her strengths and limitations. Through the encouragement of her trusted advisor, Jean began to feel safe enough to spread her wings. She joined the literary guild, theater group, school competitions, and similar extracurricular activities. As she put herself forward, she learned new skills and grew more confident. The success of her earlier accomplishments supported Jean's development as she grew into her teen years.

Her sixteenth year proved to be a key one for Jean. First, her father died. Next, as she grieved her loss, she watched sadly while her mother quickly became a "professional widow." Rather than taking charge of the family, her mother instead displayed a "dreadful negative attitude, expecting others to take care of her."

Sorrow and disappointment mixed with youthful impatience

and anger. One day, after an exasperating interaction with her mother, Jean had what she calls a "Scarlet O'Hara burnt-earth" moment. Tired of the friction in her home, Jean made a life-changing choice. On that otherwise ordinary day, Jean decided— *no matter what*—she would be happy in this life, *and* help others do the same. The pivotal moment changed her life forever.

After that, instead of feeling sorry for herself, armed with the confidence of her school time successes, Jean focused on being happy. To support her enthusiastic approach, she created a new standard for herself. From that day forward, if life dealt her "a crummy hand," she would neither fight against it nor give in to it. Because she already believed life was a gift, she made a point of actively embracing and enjoying it. Rather than settle for simple survival, Jean asked "What can I do to make this situation better?" Though still challenged by her mother, family matters, finances, and normal teenage angst, with "embrace and enjoy" added to her personal philosophy, Jean learned that nothing was insurmountable.

Also, while she didn't really think of herself as a risk-taker, Jean developed a thought process that enabled her to start taking more venturesome risks. Mixing her wartime learnings with Mrs. Noonan's "what's stopping you?" kind of question, Jean developed a winning methodology for her life. When confronted with a challenge, she looked at the situation, examined the pros and cons, and asked herself, "What's the downside—will I be dead? No? Okay then, I can go on!" It worked for Jean. Her life began to take shape.

By the time Jean entered her twenties, she had worked with British Telephone Company and British Airways in London. At twenty-one, the airlines offered her a job option to work abroad for a year on a labor exchange program between the United States and the United Kingdom; Jean considered the idea. On the positive side, it certainly fit the "embrace and enjoy" part of her philosophy. When she considered the cons, she reasoned that if there were a downside to this exciting journey, she could just go back to England. Deciding the experience would be an adventure, she accepted the offer.

A new country, new customs, and new thrills awaited the young woman. Her job enabled her to learn in a stressful but stable environment. One day, as she helped customers with flights and arrangements, a woman and her children came to her booth. In desperate straits, the small family had problems with their tickets. In the effort to straighten out their situation, Jean went the extra mile. Giving service with extreme care, she quickly expedited the woman's problem.

Jean later learned that she helped the family of Aaron Scheinfeld, a high-level executive who told Jean, "You are exactly the kind of person I'd love to have working for me." He told her that she had a job with his company if she ever wanted one. Jean did not think much of it at the time, but she kept his name and number...*just in case.*

Some months later, the exchange program completed, the airlines made plans for Jean to return to England. Jean had other ideas. Rather than return home, she decided she wanted to continue working in the United States.

In order to stay in the States, Jean would have to leave British Airlines and find a job with a U.S. company. She remembered Aaron Scheinfeld's offer, and though it took a while to get up the nerve to call him, she pushed past her apprehension. When she reached the executive, he made good on his offer. Recalling the moment, Jean straightens her shoulders and raises her chin, stating, "It was one of the first times I saw *and* seized an opportunity." Jean left the airlines and remained in the United States.

By her mid-twenties, Jean met a man, married, and had two sons. She also realized her mate suffered from alcoholism. She decided she would not live with the drinking. After ten years of marriage, when her boys were just three and six years-old, she made another life-changing and difficult choice and decided to get a divorce.

Though the prospect of being a single parent and raising two sons alone felt overwhelming, Jean faced her situation squarely. Anxious but determined, she fortified herself then with the same attitude that she currently advises other women to adopt. "These things are tragic and tough," she readily admits, "but none of these things is insurmountable."

As the head of her small household, Jean knew she'd have to support herself and her two sons. More importantly, she wanted to demonstrate two important life lessons. First, she wanted her boys to know they could be strong and succeed no matter what happened to them. She'd teach this by example. Second, determined not to fall into the same trap that her mother did, she decided that if she never again had a partner, she could take care of herself and would not be dependent on anyone. Jean considered it her responsibility to think of present and future ways of being self-sufficient. She faced the adversity of divorce and life as a single parent, then embraced the change and started over.

When she looked for work, Jean saw no difference between her responsibility to support her children and those of the men within a company. Yet as she went for one job interview after another, she felt disappointed that the world saw her situation differently. In the days before the women's movement began, she faced a frustrating but culturally acceptable corporate gender-bias. Not only did jobs for women revolve primarily around administrative support for male managers, but interview questions presumed a lack of serious and long-term viability. An interviewer once even asked Jean if she used birth control!

At the time, in spite of being smart, proficient, and driven, she could only find secretarial work with modest incomes. Not only did the available jobs not pay enough to support a family, Jean often felt her skills surpassed the administrative duties. Yet she needed to work, so she took a job and hoped for advancement. In the beginning, despite not feeling mentally stimulated or personally satisfied with work, her steadfast focus on supporting her family and raising her children helped temper the frustration.

As she did her job, Jean paid attention to the company's executive process. She began advancing her own agenda and using business-savvy skills that would take her up the executive ladder. While already a well-spoken woman, Jean improved her corporate communication skills. She developed a more assertive attitude and used it to influence the right people...and her career.

As she learned and grew, Jean got the attention of one of the executives, Jack Yurish. In a relationship similar to the one with Mrs. Noonan, Jack mentored Jean by both challenging her skills and championing her efforts. He told her tough truths about herself (the kind that no one really wants to hear) and simultaneously gave her suggestions for how to get ahead. At a time when only a handful of corporate women made it to the executive track, and even fewer received help getting there, Jack made the effort to be honest with Jean about her positive and negative qualities. He told her how her organizational and communication strengths could be utilized to benefit the company. He also let her know how she could improve some of her weaker areas, including how she could enhance the way she presented her ideas.

Though his words were often not easy to hear and his suggestions sometimes difficult and inconvenient to implement, Jean wanted to succeed. She trusted Jack enough to listen, learn, and develop her skills and competencies. The lesson she learned is one that she shares with women to this day. Difficult though it may be, Jean insists that honest performance evaluation is invaluable *if* it is given respectfully and in a constructive spirit. Moreover, "You have to be okay with accepting criticism. However, if nobody ever offers you feedback, how do you get better, how do you get promoted?" She also admits, "Sometimes it is *very inconvenient* to get to know ourselves better."

As Jean began working her way into management and through corporate glass ceilings, her career flourished. During that same time, she began socializing. Eventually she met Ron Otte, an executive with Trane, a company that specializes in heating and air conditioning systems. The two seemed to work well together and wanted the same things out of life. His steady manner impressed her. He became the love of Jean's life. They married, and looking back on their life together, Jean shares, "Ron was my rock."

With Ron and her two boys, Jean enjoyed the best that life could offer. Ron, an avid hockey fan, got involved with her sons and coached hockey teams as a hobby. The four of them spent many days rushing home from work, having dinner, and heading to one game or another. Family, work, and hockey meshed with everyday ups and downs to fill Jean's life as her sons grew into and through their teens.

Tragedy struck the Otte household when Ron was diagnosed with cancer. He followed standard treatments and together they fought the disease for two years. Unfortunately, Ron lost the battle and his death devastated Jean. The forty-nine-year-old widow felt lost.

For the next year or so, Jean suffered loss after loss. Just six weeks after Ron's death, Jean's mother died from Alzheimer's related complications. Then one son left home to join the Marines. The Desert Storm war broke out and he went overseas to fight. A while later, her second son graduated college, got married, and started a new life of his own. Next, Jean's sister died.

One after another, the events stacked up leaving a trail of incredible sorrow over a short amount of time. Jean prevailed and refused to give in to her pain. She worked persistently to keep her chin up, depending stubbornly on radical self-care. Though she had to make every effort to keep going, she believes that when someone, particularly a spouse or life partner dies, "You do a true disservice if you die with them; they aren't here to enjoy life—you are." Jean insisted that she would not dishonor Ron by giving up. In addition, she affirms, that "when the forest burns down and it's terrible, the forest burning down can give life to something that wouldn't have grown." Living with that perception, she woke up everyday and went about the business of living, believing that as one door closed, another would open.

As she handled the turmoil of her personal life, professional challenges arose. Another company purchased the one for which Jean worked. The takeover meant more change and the beginning of a most stressful period for Jean and her co-workers. They experienced a tremendous amount of downsizing and many people, including Jean, found the corporate transition overwhelming. Many of her co-workers gave into anger, depression, and resentment instigated by the corporate buyout.

As Jean strove daily to keep herself in good form, she remembered something that Ron would often say when coaching a hockey game. When describing a situation that could not be changed, he would pragmatically proclaim, "The puck is in the net." That meant that the only thing left to do was figure out how to have a different outcome the next time you have a shot at the goal, and make the necessary changes. Using Ron's hockey model as a metaphor for her situation, Jean realized *the puck was in the net*. As she surveyed the corporate landscape, she strategized, creating a positive outcome for herself.

Looking back, Jean believes her refusal to become bitter and angry became one of her greatest strengths. It kept her strong through the years of major life and work upheavals. Rather than resisting change, she chose to embrace it and see where it took her. At the time, Jean could barely see the good in her situation. Today, she is certain that tragedy gave her the push into something better.

At the same time, mentor Jack Yurish continued to champion and challenge Jean. Seeing her differently than she saw herself, she recalls, "He cared enough to tell me things that got in my way, that were holding me back." Through his guidance and coaching, Jean developed a better sense of how to advance her career goals. She learned how to master her influence, who best to align herself with, and how to get noticed without being perceived as obnoxious. As a result, she rose steadily up the corporate ranks and developed greater personal confidence.

Jean courageously moved ahead and broke through the ranks to become the most senior-level woman at her company—the first woman to do so. Her professional victories continued, and she eventually became a company officer and the corporate vice-president of quality management. She was charged with overseeing ongoing management development and employee education programs. In addition, Jean managed the quality improvement function as well as the process for measuring employee and customer satisfaction. In much the same fashion as her inspirational heroes, through every adversity and with each challenge, Jean became stronger. Rather than being a victim of circumstance, Jean Otte became victorious.

As Jean grew in professional stature and personal wholeness, she watched other women who did not—or could not—maximize their potential. As she did, she realized she wanted to work on a larger scale to help women better manage their lives. She believed that when a woman became more effective at coping with life's challenges, she would find more positive approaches to work and life and generate greater personal and professional success. Jean asked, "What, as a single individual, can I do?"

Her answer came with an idea to create an organization that would provide mentoring, networking, and ongoing educational opportunities for emerging executive women. She called the new venture Women Unlimited, honoring women's enormous, never-ending potential.

With a clear picture of what she wanted, she began to make plans, strategizing how she would tackle such a daunting task. She again sought the counsel of her mentor, who continued to encourage her to challenge her internal boundaries in order to push past the barriers to her goals. When she felt tired or stressed and wanted to give up, he'd ask, "What do you mean you cannot do this? What's stopping you?" Her answers always made the obstacles seem less daunting, and she persevered.

As plans progressed, years of networking and positively connecting with people convinced Jean that she knew many spirited and powerful people who would help make the Women Unlimited dream a reality. Depending on her alliances for assistance,

Jean got the help and support she needed to forward her ideas and get the new company started. She organized her wealth of experiences, and those of other successful women, into a format for developing women's management and leadership skills. Her diligent effort and hard work paid off when Women Unlimited became a reality.

Opening the doors in 1994, Jean Otte utilizes a combination of personal experiences, a valuable accumulation of life learning, and her own many passages through adversity to show other women how to succeed. With more than seventy-five corporate partners and a dedicated staff, Jean's Women Unlimited helps women "in the achievement of parity in the workplace through education, networking, and mentoring." Many corporations, including hundreds of Fortune 1000 companies have discovered the benefits of the Women Unlimited programs for their female executives.

As they learned and developed new skills and greater professional competence, thousands of Women Unlimited participants have created greater success in their lives. At Women Unlimited, women learn how not to sabotage their efforts and instead to make the most of their skills and assets through hard work, networking, and leadership development. Most Women Unlimited graduates excel in their workplaces. Many have been promoted to management and executive positions. Others have moved on and started their own businesses. In harmony with Jean's vision, the alumnae create lives that are more personally fulfilling and more professionally satisfying.

Women Unlimited has provided Jean with success and honor. *Business Week*, CNN, CNBC, *Fortune Magazine,* and many others have recognized her accomplishments with featured articles. She has received honors from Lifetime television, the Committee for 200, and the YWCA.

Throughout her successful career, Jean has shared her wisdom with staff, mentees, and participants. Her advice is rooted in her own experiences, both past and present. She tells women about the importance of integrity, a trait she holds in high personal regard. Jean also values a good laugh, chiding other women that "We don't put enough humor into our lives." Her staff calls her nuggets of advice "Otteisms." Her sage gems come from who she is, what she believes, and in the successes she has created from, and in spite of, her personal and professional challenges. Jean's words of advice are believable because they are filled with good common sense and the essence of Jean Otte herself. Having integrated her whole being into the organization, it comes as no surprise that her favorite compliment is, "You're so real."

Interestingly, Jean says that her life goes in ten-year cycles. Her current cycle, she says, has been very busy. However, as this set rounds the bend toward its ending, she is already asking herself what she wants to be and do next. Whatever she chooses, Jean has already decided she'll walk toward it with anticipation. On her journey, Jean won't be walking alone; energetically, Jean will have an army of women cheering her on to her next success!

"OTTEISMS" FOR WOMEN

Becoming victorious:
"Every woman has the capability of being victorious. Being victorious is living your life in a positive way that affects another human in a positive way. *That's victorious.*"

Change and challenge:
Jean has a lot to say to women about challenges and change. To begin with, Jean proposes that when you are faced with a difficult situation, "take a good hard look" and ask yourself:

  a. Is the puck in the net?

  b. Is it really as bad as I think?

  c. What can I do?

Then, start looking for solutions. If one solution doesn't fit, look for other approaches. Jean advises to keep searching for solutions and you will eventually find your answer.

Also, when facing a challenge that isn't working out the way you'd like, don't give up or turn back. Instead, Jean proposes that you review your situation and examine what has worked and what hasn't work. Ask yourself:

a. What have I learned?

b. What have I done differently?

c. How can I apply my new learnings?

d. What was the result?

Once this is done, Jean recommends looking at your answers and using what you discover to craft another approach or to generate a more appropriate solution to your challenge.

Finally, Jean contends that women worry so much about what people will say about them if they fail, that often they do not wholly pursue what they want. "We spend so much time worrying about what 'they' think about us—and...*they don't*," Jean insists, warning, "You can live your life with fear and uncertainty, but that's a terrible way to live." One of her remedies is to give up worrying about people's opinions of us. Instead, find a solution, make your plan, and take action; work with confidence, and believe in your ability to succeed.

❧ Emptiness:

Look at your life and ask what you can do to have meaning in it. Find something and *do it*. Even if you start with something small, do it. One small thing after another can lead you to a place of meaning.

Jean knows how much a sense of purpose has made a difference in her life. She has watched purpose and determination make a difference in the lives of others. It can make a difference for you—and even change your life for the better!

✎ Negativity:

Jean says that, like anyone else, she experiences days when her mood is negative. If in a bad mood and aware of how she's feeling, she asks herself, "Where is this coming from?" Recognizing what a waste of time being negative is, she gets up, moves, and does **one positive thing**. Jean usually chooses to call someone she loves and enjoy a positive conversation with him or her. However, something as simple as straightening a junk drawer, a file, or your desktop can move you out of the valley and into positive territory.

Also, Jean believes in using positive affirmations. She says them daily, usually to begin her day on a positive note. One of her favorites is, "We cannot direct the wind, but we can adjust the sails."

✎ Balance:

First, women need to get past the "mom can do everything" syndrome. Jean thinks that one of the most important lessons you can learn, both in and out of work, is to ask for what you need and want. Use phrases such as "It would mean the world to me if you..." or, "It would be great if you could make the arrangements...I don't feel like superwoman today."

"Don't be afraid to say 'no'." Jean knows first-hand that this is a difficult task; she is a recovering "I want to be liked by everyone" addict. Jean suggests you practice saying "no" in small ways so you can build yourself up to saying "no" to bigger requests and "then carry it into the workplace."

Jean said she was honest with herself when she was overwhelmed. She would admit to herself, "I got myself into this; I didn't have the courage to say 'no'." Over time, Jean has become better with balance. She noticed in her own life that when she began to say 'no' and set boundaries with clarity and expectation, her stresses were less and her life got better.

❧ **Succeeding in business:**

Women are often the keepers of information, have technical or interpersonal expertise, or possess some other skill that could help them move ahead in their company. Their knowledge may be just what they need to give them an executive edge, but they keep it to themselves or don't think it's anything important. Then an opportunity arises and someone who may be less qualified, but whose corporate savvy put him or her with the right person at the right time, often snatches it up. Failing to promote yourself to the right people is a major mistake that women in business make. "It's not who you know, but *who knows* you know," Jean advises.

To get attention and recognition, Jean suggests that you do something to show what you are able to accomplish. When complimented, rather than responding with a simple 'thank you,' she advises women to say something like, "I'm so appreciative that you noticed and took the time to say something because it was a lot of work. Would you mind mentioning it to my boss? Also, I'd welcome any opportunity to do it again."

Jean also says that when it comes to getting ahead, most women don't ask for what they want with clear, specific language. She tells women to approach their work with a plan and get help. Talk to those who have the ability to help you move ahead at work and say, "Here are my [clear, specific] goals; here's what I'd like you to help me with."

Another support women often don't take advantage of is mentoring. Jean advises that you find a mentor, someone you can trust to speak the truth. Your mentor needs to be open and willing to give you feedback—honest feedback—and you need to be open to hearing it. Jean admits that critical feedback is not easy to hear, but she also says that "very often you already know it." In addition, she insists, that without it, "You're probably going to stay stuck. If you don't hear the kind of feedback the right person can give you, you're going to be in the same spot—or worse, you'll start slipping back."

Aging:

A woman needs to understand that life is a process of reinventing oneself. Jean uses herself as an example, "I see myself as one who understands that I have to reinvent myself. I cannot be at sixty-three how I was at thirty-three."

"It's never too late to start a new journey; it doesn't have to be a big journey, it can be a little one. Just start it." That is Jean's directive. If you make a plan, take action. If you are hesitant about moving forward, your pep talk can be like one of Jean's: "Okay, I'm going to give this a shot. If it doesn't work, I'll try something else." You'll never know what works for you and what doesn't if you don't *try something*.

STEPPING STONES
TO VICTORY

1. Whatever challenges came her way, Jean faced them by making a choice to be victorious. Take a look at your life and your choices. Take out your Victory Journal and start writing your life story. It doesn't have to be book-length, but it needs to be complete.

2. When you're finished writing your life story, read it and highlight the moments where you made choices. For example, when Jean was faced with personal tragedy, she decided to honor her late spouse's memory by continuing to live her fullest life.

   a. Which of your decisions made a positive difference in your life. Which ones did not?

   b. Considering your choices, go back in your mind and remember what was going on inside you (what were you saying to yourself and how were you feeling?). Notice if there was a pattern to your thoughts and actions when you were making poor choices. Do the same with your powerful choices.

   c. Compare the two. What can you learn about your past decisions *now* that will help you make better decisions *in the future*? Write them down in your Victory Journal.

3. Many women live with the "what ifs" and use them as reasons not to take positive action. Mrs. Noonan asked Jean, "What do you think you can't do?" For the next month, keep a log of daily opportunities that require you to make a choice. When something you would like to do comes your way and you hesitate, ask yourself, "What's stopping me?"

If your answer includes a "what if," then let that be a signal to **halt your thought**. This is your opportunity to ask yourself if you are acting and reacting out of fear, or if you are making choices and decisions out of joy, love, and excitement for life. Is the "what if" coming from good logic or from fear? If the answer is logic, then use it as a guide. However, if the answer is fear, then challenge it by asking how realistic the fear is. As Jean suggests, ask yourself, "What's the down side—will I be dead? No? Okay then, I can go on!" If the fear is more about your discomfort than your reality, either get over it or move through it.

Remember, even when you feel as though you could die of fearful feelings, you can keep going. One method is to divide a task into the smallest steps, steps that are easier or less overwhelming. For example, getting a better job begins with clearly defining what a new job is. You can do that. Next, make a list of people you know. You can do *that*. Then, call one of those people and talk to them about your plans to get a new job; ask if they know anyone in your desired field. You can do *that*. You may have to call another person and ask the same thing. You *can* do that.

If you take the smallest of steps, you can develop confidence. As you cultivate confidence, you will feel less fear, and you will take bigger steps. Confidence comes with time, effort, and experience. Start small and build skills, one step at a time.

4. Mentoring became key to Jean's success. Having someone she trusted, Mrs. Noonan and Jack Yurish, to give her good feedback and encourage her made all the difference. Her company, Women Unlimited, stresses the mentoring relationship. Jean makes a distinction between the person who gives constructive criticism versus the person whose words simply cut you down. Do you know someone who can give you balanced feedback?

If you do not already have a person like this in your life, a trusted mentor, this may be a good time to investigate and find one. If you don't know a person, consider hiring a coach/ mentor. Whether you find someone or hire someone, Jean offers a few suggestions for choosing the right person. Your mentor should be a person you:

- respect;
- see as more accomplished or successful than you;
- feel you can trust.

In addition, consider that there are different mentors for different situations. If you're working and need more balance, find someone who has achieved a balanced work and family life. If you desire to be a manager in your company, identify someone who has done the same thing within the company. When you find the person who meets the criteria, the first thing you have to do is *ask* the person if s/he would be willing to mentor you. Be ready with an explanation of what that would mean to you: how much time it would take; how often you'd want to meet; how you'd like to be mentored; and how you'd help the mentor in exchange for the time and effort.

5. Jean got through the tragic year of deaths and losses by being persistent and stubborn in her self-care. In addition, Jean advises that "happiness is a skill—you need to practice it." Develop this skill by doing the following:

   a. For the next thirty days, **practice uncompromising self-care**. Write down two ways that you can do this during this period. For example, yours may be to spend time alone for thirty minutes a day and do something you love like reading a book, taking a walk, or chatting with a girlfriend without interruption. Include how you will fit the activities into your regular schedule.

   b. For the next thirty days, **practice radical happiness**. Write down two ways that you can do this during the next month. For example, list the ten best days or moments of your life. When you catch yourself worrying, being resentful, or thinking negatively, **consciously stop this thought process** and **shift your thoughts** to one of those special moments. Allow two to five minutes to dwell on your happy event.

c. Keep track of your results. Make this visual by using a notation in your daily planner or even create a chart to monitor your progress.

    ⚘ **Sample practice:**
    Each day this week I'll practice leaving my work at the office. To do this, I'll need to shift mental/emotional gears on my way home from work. I'll do this by [choose an action, such as listening to an audiotape in the car, stopping to buy flowers, taking a fifteen minute walk in the park] before I go home.

    ⚘ **Sample results:**
    I felt less stressed when I arrived home. Instead of mindlessly watching television just to decompress my day, each night I read a chapter of a book.

8

If I Were Brave
Patricia Painter

CANCER DISTINGUISHES ITSELF FROM ANY OTHER challenge in a very special way. Not only are people with the menacing disease fighting for their lives, there are a myriad of possible malignancies, and recurrences are common. Also, it is possible for someone, Patricia Painter for example, to be diagnosed with more than one form of cancer at the same time. Treatment for one cancerous entity may not cure the other; removal or remission of one does not prevent the other from causing death.

The fighting strategy for the ominous illness challenges even the most strong-willed individuals. From her vantage point as a cancer survivor, Pattie Painter believes that beating cancer often brings a unique victory to those who survive it.

Until diagnosed, Pattie considered herself a smart, upbeat, and very healthy woman. In addition to maintaining a fairly healthy diet with some exercise, she dutifully scheduled her "regulars," those annual appointments such as physicals, routine gynecological exams, etc. Her mother died from colon cancer and Pattie frequently had abnormal pap smears, so she felt strongly about the importance of early detection.

During her 2001 gynecological exam, a pap smear came back showing a problem. Since it was not the first time, Pattie knew what to expect. She would have the same standard surgical procedure as she'd had in the past. Six weeks later she would have a check-up and another pap smear.

Since she knew the drill, she barely thought about it when she scheduled the surgery. Afterward, the doctor didn't call, as usual. Presuming no news was good news, Pattie went about her active life as usual.

One Thursday night, the telephone rang. Pattie stood in the doorway of her modest country kitchen as she answered it. She heard her gynecologist's voice on the other end. He sounded oddly disturbed when he asked, "May I speak with Pattie?" Identifying herself, she waited for the doctor's response. Mindlessly moving toward the table, already set for dinner, she wondered what happened. His office hours ended earlier in the day. *What could he want?*

In a strained, clinical voice, he briskly told Pattie that she had cervical cancer. He was releasing her to an oncologist right away. He instructed Pattie to call his office on Friday and get the specialist's name and phone number. *Click.*

Pattie stared for a minute before she hung up the receiver. Stunned by the news, Pattie felt nothing except a dreadful numbness as she attempted to process the information. Just moments earlier, she might have thought of herself as a woman in peak condition, the kind of healthy that could easily be taken for granted.

Now, one terse phone call changed everything. *Cancer.* Her mother died from cancer...it had been a slow, painful death. Cancer. The word reverberated in her head, over and over again.

Pattie didn't know what to do first. She had questions. Why did the doctor end the conversation before she had time to think and ask those questions? What happened? How could this happen?

As soon as she could find her voice again, she called to her spouse. Hearing the alarm in her voice, Tom rushed from their living room into the kitchen. Pattie told him what the doctor said. He cried. She cried. Life had changed in an instant, and the fear-filled night became the first of many tearful ones the couple would share over the next year.

The stunning news put Pattie smack dab in the middle of a fight for her life. Wondering how she would manage, she began thinking of an earlier time and another overwhelming challenge. She remembered another night, almost twenty years earlier, when the man in her life walked out of their fourteen-year marriage. Until the cancer diagnosis, that black period stood as her greatest life challenge. All of a sudden, Pattie saw the first devastating experience with a fresh perspective. "You don't die from desertion, even though you think sometimes you might *want* to die. When you have a diagnosis of cancer, you *definitely know* that there is the possibility that you could die...it was certainly the greater threat."

Yet, at the same time, Pattie saw the similarity: sudden life-changing news, scrambling to make sense of what happened, fear of the future, and wondering what to do next. In retrospect, she also saw how the first challenge laid the foundation for a special kind of confidence and stamina, the same thing she needed to battle cancer. Desertion forced her life to shift to a new direction. Though she did not choose it, she did handle it. She successfully moved out of her comfort zone and onto her victory path. Retracing her steps and remembering how she created victory then would help transport her to a life-saving level in this situation now.

In her previous marriage, Pattie lived an average, middle class, suburban life with her spouse and two children. Rick worked in the office of a large manufacturing plant. Pattie worked as an administrative assistant with a pharmaceutical company. Because she came from a family of nine, most of Pattie's social life revolved around her children and her siblings and their children. Family get-togethers happened often, and she enjoyed them. Her hobbies included craft projects and singing, both of which she did for family.

If she considered the big picture, Pattie felt good about herself, their children, and her life. Though she and Rick had their ups and downs, she chalked them up to typical everyday stresses and thought their marriage was a good one. Little did she know...

About a year before their breakup, Rick became sullen and distant. Whenever she asked him if something was wrong—even asking him if there was another woman—Rick brushed her off. He insisted that his depressed behavior resulted from all the shop talk about rumored layoffs. It made him nervous, and he worried about losing his job. Pattie believed him. Even the newspapers often reported news about the downward spiral of the plant, and if it continued, Rick's job *could* conceivably end. So month after month, Pattie accepted his explanation.

One day, Rick abruptly told Pattie he needed some time away from her and the children. With clothes already packed, he quickly moved out of the house and moved in with his mother. Hurt and confused, Pattie tried to make sense of Rick's actions. She wanted to believe that, unable to handle the work-related pressure, he entered into a mid-life crisis of sorts. She accepted her rationalization as true and used it to explain Rick's leaving to their children. In the weeks that followed, it calmed her to think that Rick would overcome whatever he felt, they would work out problems as they surfaced, and then they'd get back together.

From the time he moved out, Rick sent Pattie money for the house and children. One month, his check bounced. She phoned her mother-in-law so she could speak to Rick. He was not there. Rick's mother told Pattie the shocking truth: Rick left town. She was sorry to be the one to tell Pattie, but Rick drove to Florida... to be with his girlfriend. *Girlfriend?*

In that brusque moment, the stunned Pattie realized how much she had deluded herself. Her marriage was over—*it was for real!* Girlfriend.

Learning the harsh truth felt exactly like unexpectedly being dunked into a tank of ice water. It got worse. In the weeks that followed, Pattie learned the astonishing details about Rick's other life. The "other woman" was not someone Rick met after their separation. Quite the contrary, *the other woman had been around through most of the fourteen years they were married!*

Pattie walked around her house in a daze. Going from room to room, she asked herself the same questions: What happened? How could it happen? How did she not know? Why did she believe his explanations? Could she have done something better, or different? Would it have made a difference? What should she tell the kids?

As her life imploded, Pattie knew two emotions: hurt and fear. She tried to deal with her pain, make sense of the betrayal, and figure out her future. At the same time, she still had to get the kids off to school and herself to work. Shopping still had to be done, meals made, doctor and dentist appointments kept, school functions attended, and so on. Though she wanted to crawl into a hole and hibernate until a better day, she could not. She still was obligated to do the mundane, everyday tasks for herself and her children who needed her.

The once happily married woman with a reasonably stable life slowly adjusted to being the newly divorced, single mom caring for her adolescent children—two *angry* young teenagers. With their father no longer around, at first they both blamed Pattie for the split. While she struggled with her own emotions, she also tried to understand how they felt. In less than a year, their life changed dramatically too. If she couldn't grasp what happened, how could they?

While Pattie and her children did what they could to structure their lives, Rick quickly married "the other woman." With that new reality, Pattie realized that, ready or not, *she alone had* to make decisions regarding homelife, school, house repairs, the mortgage, taxes, the car...and the future. In fact, she had to figure out, by herself, virtually everything for herself and her kids.

In rapid succession, Rick and his new spouse had three children. Though her teenagers talked to Rick whenever they wanted, Rick lived five states away and stayed busy with his new family. They only visited Rick for two weeks each year, leaving Pattie as the primary caregiver.

Day by day, Pattie faced the maze that became her life. She had one aim that overrode her confusion and pain. No matter what, she determined she would have a good life. First and foremost, that meant creating a stable environment for herself and her children. With that end in mind, Pattie says, "I worked even harder to be both a mom and a dad to them." The demoralizing desertion challenged every part of her.

In the past, Pattie often found comfort in prayer. So, she prayed. She also found strength in being positive. She often told herself and others that there was good in every situation, a silver lining in every cloud. Now it was time "to prove that I believed in my self-talk. Since I always said 'only good can come to me'...I had to believe, even though I didn't know how...that good could come out of this." Only good...*but how?*

Before long, Pattie realized she needed to make more money. Her company offered opportunities, but Pattie knew that a decent promotion with better pay required more education and skills. She had to go back to school. Her current job included a corporate education benefit. When she was married, she had little interest in using it because she wanted to spend her nonworking time with her family. Now, with a need-motivated goal, she grabbed the corporate perk. Pattie enrolled herself in college courses. On Saturday mornings, while her teenagers slept until noon, Pattie headed for classes targeting work-related subjects.

Over the next few years, education coupled with hard work paid off for Pattie. As she earned an associate degree, Pattie advanced her position and her income. She progressed from the entry-level secretarial and administrative jobs she previously held into supervisory and management positions. Pattie stayed true to her goal. With her professional successes, and with child support from Rick, Pattie and her children got the life she wanted them to have.

In addition, with each accomplishment Pattie saw new value in herself. Each challenge and victory, great and small, helped Pattie reshape her self-image into something that continued to improve. Upon reflection, Pattie acknowledged, "I always knew I was a valuable person, but the break-up gave me the determination to prove it even more. Each accomplishment, whether of my children or a promotion for myself, reinforced that fact." In time, Pattie succeeded in turning her difficult and painful experience into a personal and professional victory.

That was then.

Fast-forward to 1999 and the fifty-something Pattie: a happy, healthy, energetic, and enthusiastic woman. Through her victory over desertion, she developed a comfort level with her more independent self. A stronger Pattie learned to make better choices in life. She made them more easily and with more confidence.

Along the way, Pattie met Tom, a kind man with children about the same age as Pattie's. Their meeting, encouraged by an acquaintance of both of them, resulted in a serious relationship. The more they dated, the more Pattie could envision a lifetime partnership with Tom, kids and all! At the time of their marriage, the blended family included five teenagers. They sold both their houses and, with four of their five children still living with them, moved into a new home. Within a few years, all the teenagers became adults, married, and started families of their own.

On the workfront, a corporate merger presented Pattie the opportunity for an early retirement. She left her employer of twenty-five years and took a consulting job with a company that specialized in the pharmaceutical industry.

At that moment in time, if you had asked, Pattie Painter would have told you her life was a nearly perfect manifestation of her spiritual belief in good, along with her hard work, persistence, positive attitude, and love. As one century ended and a new one began, Pattie felt great about her family, relationships, and, in fact, her whole life. She felt excited as the clock struck twelve and ushered in a new millennium. As she reflected on her good fortune, she had no idea how much she would count on her past victory to pave the way for her greatest challenge yet to come.

During those first bewildering weeks after the cancer diagnosis, Pattie tried to understand what had happened. She seldom had health problems. She took care of herself. She didn't smoke, ate a healthy diet, exercised, and had regular checkups. When she had the occasional worrisome gynecological exam, she addressed it immediately and resolved it quickly. She could be the poster child for perfect health maintenance. *Except now she had cancer.* How could it be? She did everything right, so this had to be wrong.

Pattie's doctor wanted another pap smear. She expected some pain afterward, but her pain didn't stop. Upset and confounded, she called the oncologist and her general practitioner. Her regular doctor sent her for both an MRI and a colonoscopy. The results were bad. The MRI showed possible problems with both her liver and kidney; the colonoscopy clearly showed colon cancer, and the most recent pap smear confirmed the diagnosis of cervical cancer. She could not believe it. Cervical cancer, colon cancer, and based on unclear test results, maybe another cancer. It was that old "dunked in ice water" feeling all over again. How could all this be happening to her, she wondered?

Before she knew it, she was seeing dual oncologists. Her doctor referred to one oncologist as "the Michael Jordan of colons." The other oncologist specialized in cervical cancer. Pattie remembers joking that if one was the Michael Jordan of colons, she "hoped the other one was the Shaquil O'Neill of cervices!"

Pattie Painter quickly went from thinking she was a healthy woman with a loving future to questioning if she would be dead before the next Christmas. Even more frightening to Pattie, she wondered if she would die in the same slow, painful way her mother had. As memories of that agonizing experience flooded her mind, Pattie admits that at first all she thought about was death and dying.

During the next eight months, Pattie went from one surgery to another, undergoing a total of six. The procedures were complicated. Her doctors became a team, each one having to coordinate surgeries and treatments with the other. They dealt first with the colon cancer, then the cervical cancer. The final surgery was a complete abdominal hysterectomy.

Throughout the whole ordeal, good fortune smiled on Pattie. In the drama that became her daily life, whenever the doctors gave her a "best case/worst case" scenario for an operation, her condition always came out the best way it possibly could. Still, battling the disease month after month, the struggle with her health problems wore her down. Pattie began to wonder, "Who's beating me up?" Her usual optimism seemed rationed, coming to her only in the tiniest waves, for the briefest moments. She wondered how long she could continue to meet the challenges of cancer...*and if she could face her own mortality.*

Even after the final surgery, there were questions about the liver and kidney. Weeks went by before the doctors could check the organs again. Weeks of wonder and worry. Fortunately, once tested, the liver and kidney cancer scares were just that—scares.

During this time, her large family wanted to know her condition. They called for information, and to extend their good wishes. Though happy to know that people cared enough to call, she quickly tired of discussing her "latest procedure" with everyone. She remembers telling Tom, "I just can't take another phone call." It wasn't that Pattie didn't appreciate the concerns of her loved ones; she did. Pattie's disturbed feelings came from telling the latest news, speaking the same frightening words over and over again. She felt that the almost daily dredging debilitated her energy. While talking about various scenarios and possible outcomes, Pattie found it difficult to conjure up positive, life-giving power. With each recounting of her story, she felt as though she reinforced the negativity of her condition. In retrospect, Pattie realizes the distress was not about talking to others. On the contrary, her grief came because she did not want to hear, or more accurately *couldn't face*, the "crack in her voice."

Though facing her personal demons, at the same time Pattie did not want to isolate, or ignore, her large circle of family and friends. The loving people in her life wanted to know what was happening. She needed to find a way to keep in touch with others without losing touch with her inner self.

Pattie found her answer in the technology of e-mail. Pattie could write her message once, but communicate it to everyone. It became her saving grace. With e-mail, Pattie preserved important relationships, maintained important contacts, and received messages of support—messages she could save and, if she wanted, read again and again. Through this channel, she stayed connected; and at the same time, she protected her inner space.

In the process of sending e-mail, Pattie discovered something of even greater value than the communication with others. E-mail forced her to translate her thoughts and feelings into words. Throughout life, Pattie was a woman who always liked to appear strong and show her "happy face to the world." Writing helped her to express her angst, accept her vulnerability, and yet keep the deepest, most personal grief to herself. She wrote what she felt, and then censored what she sent. It enabled Pattie to face and handle her illness and her own mortality.

Through e-mail, she could accept the loving responses of family and friends. Pattie learned she could open herself up to the kindness of others in a way that she had not previously known, or even been comfortable with doing. Like good therapy, writing e-mail freed Pattie's mind and soul; it became an important instrument in the process of her healing.

Another part of her recovery process included prayer groups. Pattie and Tom attended church regularly. Tom served on several committees within the congregation. When Tom added Pattie to her own church's prayer list she felt happy, but not surprised. What amazed her were the other prayer chains that included her name, even those not of her own religion. Whether on a formal list or simply though an individual, Pattie felt as though everyone had her in their prayerful thoughts. She heard from former coworkers, colleagues in Tom's master gardener group, and people who didn't know Pattie but who knew her siblings and children.

Pattie felt blessed as it seemed everyone was praying for her. "There were so many people praying for me," she beamed, "even though I hadn't asked them to [pray]." The variety of denominations did not diminish her gratitude. Believing that "God is not a religion" and that all prayer is good, Pattie gratefully acknowledged all the prayer work done on her behalf. She is still in awe when she tells, "At one time...I was on prayer lists of seven different religions."

In addition, Pattie received an abundance of cards from family, friends, and former coworkers. Then, as people heard of her ordeal, she began receiving cards from cancer survivors. She did not know the individuals, but it didn't matter. "They were support cards," Pattie recalls, "not even necessarily get well, but just 'thinking about you.'" She seems still mystified by the encouraging effect it had on her. "I've always known that my family cared about me," Pattie acknowledges. Yet she admits, "The fact that strangers, people that I never met and possibly never will meet, can be that supportive is such an opening of the heart. You sort of expect your spouse and family to support you...but for a stranger to support you means that they had to go out of their way. I always felt the support of my family, but then I felt supported by strangers. Makes you feel wonderful."

So wonderful, in fact, that Pattie says eventually she "got to the point where I said to myself...I know I'm going to make it because I have so many people praying for me that I don't even need to worry about myself anymore. When I felt the positive energy vibrating from strangers, I really felt like I didn't have to pray for myself."

One day Pattie received a heartfelt letter from a woman who was a survivor of colon cancer. Though she didn't know her, the letter had a powerful impact on her. As she read the letter, the handwritten words touched her heart and spirit. Pattie experienced a turning point moment. She felt something inside her shift and though she can't explain why, "All of a sudden, *I knew* I was going to be fine."

As a matter of fact, as time would confirm, Pattie *was* fine. She still went through months of hospital visits, tedious tests, and short procedures. Because the doctors took aggressive steps while the cancers were still in the early stages, she did not need chemotherapy. As a result, her body gained strength after the surgeries. Her energy and enthusiasm returned and she began to feel like her old self again. Follow-up tests indicated the doctors got all the cancer, and gave her an excellent prognosis for long-term survival. In the end, Pattie emerged cancer-free.

Though Pattie counts surviving cancer her greatest victory, it is not the last one. Still traveling on her victory path, and now with time on her side, Pattie decided that there was more to accomplish in her life. Her ordeal with cancer brought with it the courage to ask herself two questions: "What do I like to do that is fun?" and "If nothing mattered, what would I do with the rest of my life?" As she thought about making a better life, she did so with a new and different viewpoint. She took a personal inventory and looked for fun in her life.

Pattie sat down, asking herself what those "fun" things were. Going back to her hobbies of crafts and singing, she realized she could develop those talents more fully. As she explored, Pattie says she knew she "was blessed with a very nice voice" and she loved to sing, but never seriously. She put singing at the top of her list, with an intention to raise her voice in song for others.

In the past, Pattie would not have considered singing professionally. But "having been through all of this," she decided she would go for it. What's more, she decided she could fuse her love of singing to a new, compelling desire to tell others about the importance of getting regular medical check-ups. Early detection saved her life; she wanted it to save others as well. As the new idea unfolded, Pattie recognized how she could have fun and, at the same time, serve a greater purpose by spreading some of the kindness she received during her illness.

While her decision was made, Pattie did not know her next step. Trepidation attached itself to uncertainty. One day, Pattie heard the song that changed the way she viewed her challenge. The song was "If I Were Brave" by writer/singer Jana Stanfield. She listened carefully to the words: "If I refuse to listen to the voice of fear, would the voice of courage whisper in my ear?" The words of the song haunted and challenged her to ask herself, *"What step would I take today, if I were brave?"*

It took a bit of soul-searching, but Pattie found both her direction and the courage. She moved one step at a time and got involved with a variety of groups. At first, she volunteered her singing and speaking services; then she began getting paid. Now she goes to meetings and conferences, speaking to women about the importance of doing "their regulars" (health/physical check-ups) and she sings at garden parties, weddings, and local events.

Today Pattie happily does more singing than she ever thought she would. To her great joy, she has performed at singing engagements that "even just five years ago I would have considered only as fantasies." She even sang at a long-standing Delaware landmark, the Hotel DuPont. Her performance, part of a cancer program, was one of the great thrills of her life.

Looking back over her two great challenges, especially through the eyes of her life-threatening illness, what does Pattie see differently? To begin with, Pattie says she uncovered a need to prove she could be "superwoman" and that being "super" created a lot of stress in her life. Because stress is so connected to the immune system, she learned to be judicious about how she uses her time. Now she focuses on her true priorities. Today she believes that painting the house when it doesn't need it, or being especially fussy about household matters, isn't as important as being with her children and grandchildren. In addition, she used to think of herself as a "holiday overachiever." She now thinks it isn't too important. In fact, her gift giving has gone from making all the gifts by hand to buying them, and most recently to giving gift cards. The only holiday and year-round activities Pattie keeps are the ones that are as self-nurturing as they are giving. If the activity is not both, she lets it go.

Finally, while Pattie always liked people, her experience has expanded her view. Today, Pattie believes "people are wonderful" and she is "overwhelmed by the goodness of people."

STEPPING STONES
TO VICTORY

1. Cancer is an insidious disease. Early detection is key. As Pattie
   Painter insists, "Everybody tells you that you need to do your
   regulars. But I'm living proof that *you really need to* because
   you don't have to feel bad to have bad things happen to you."

   Do you do *your* regulars? Why not make an appointment
   for an annual check-up including a mammogram and a gynecological exam—and do it today, before you forget or put it on
   a "to-do list" or "back burner" and never get to it.

2. Does your own self-sufficiency cause you to block yourself off
   from the goodness of others? Are you so busy being a superwoman that you never have time or room to accept kindness
   from others? Are you too busy to take time for yourself and
   for some immune-boosting rest and relaxation?

   If that's true, what are you willing to give up so that you
   can make the time and the space? Before you claim there is
   nothing you can give up, think again. Be ruthless about carv-
   ing out time and space. Do you really need to do one extra
   thing at work, or would you better serve yourself by leaving on
   time and stopping to buy yourself some flowers to brighten
   your dining table or your bedroom? Write down your thoughts
   and answers in your Victory Journal.

3. Pattie says that she previously valued herself, but her divorce
   made her more determined to prove her self-worth. Set aside
   your spouse/significant other, children, job, hobby, etc., and
   get down to only you in your life. Now, on a scale of one to
   ten, based on the way you think and feel about yourself, rate
   your own value? Do you rate high or average or low? If you

aren't experiencing yourself as highly valuable, what can you do to increase your personal sense of worth? Would you expect greater respect, be more assertive, take more time for yourself each day, be better at doing your "regulars"—or...what?

4. One of Pattie's favorite songs was from singer and songwriter Jana Stanfield. "If I Were Brave" is the song that helped Pattie make more positive choices in her life. The words include, "How far would I go, what would I achieve, trusting the hero in me." What would you do...if *you* were brave? Make a list in your Victory Journal. Would you go back to school for a specific degree, master a new skill, reserve thirty minutes alone for yourself daily, or set and live by clearer and more effective boundaries? Write down one item that would raise your level of self-worth or give you greater satisfaction in life. Then:

   a. Make it a goal;

   b. Devise a plan to do it;

   c. Commit it to someone else;

   d. Get support;

   e. Do it;

   f. Share your success.

9

Do What You Love
Alisa Lippincott Morkides

ALISA LIPPINCOTT FELT AS THOUGH SHE WAS NEVER going to discover what she was good at, the one thing that would bring her the success and satisfaction she craved. Excited by lots of ideas along the way, each soon fizzled, leaving her frustrated and discouraged. Career and entrepreneurial books all instructed her to find what she loved. "Find your passion," the self-help gurus directed. Alisa wondered what that would mean for her.

During college she became fascinated with coffee shops, and they continued to attract her attention into adulthood. However, though she still enjoyed visiting cafés, it was not a job. Decorating also appealed to Alisa, especially when it resulted in environments that radiated ambiance. But how could she make *that* a paying career?

Whatever else she did, wherever she was, Alisa continued the search for her right place in life, for the kind of work that would fill her spirit *and* her bank account. The solution eluded her for a long time.

Born into a family filled with scientists and mathematicians, Alisa Lippincott's life revolved around loved ones who were devoted to the sciences. Her chemist father worked for the Dupont Company. Her mother, a math whiz, had three scholarly brothers—one a mathematics mastermind and two nuclear physicists who were, literally, rocket scientists.

In her home, Alisa lived in a very pragmatic world, a place where equations and compounds were honored. Early on, through serious conversations and simple dinner talk, Alisa developed a keen sense of the family's "elitist attitude" around the scientific disciplines.

Contrary to familial predisposition, young Alisa loved history, writing, and the arts. In junior high, she taught herself to play the classical guitar. The intricate skill proved difficult to learn, but Alisa relished the challenge. Once she mastered the basics, she liked it so much that she wanted to be really good at it. To accomplish her goal, she often practiced until her fingers bled.

As a result of her father's job, the small family of four transferred frequently. Each time the family moved, it usually took a while for Alisa and her brother to know their way around, meet new people and make new friends. Loneliness often marked her first months in a new location. She filled the space with a variety of artistic pursuits, including playing guitar.

During those years, wherever they moved, the kitchen seemed to provide a warm and inviting place. Alisa developed a love for kitchens, viewing them as the heart of any home. Part of that experience included good food, especially scrumptious after-school snacks made even tastier with an accompanying cup of hot chocolate. Alisa *loved* baking the cookies and muffins that contributed to the hearth-like experience that filled her up, body and soul. All the great smells, the yummy tastes, and the cheery warmth made the kitchen a welcoming room.

As she moved through high school, Alisa thought more about college and her future. In striking contrast to the staid scientific and corporate jobs with which she was most familiar, she had dreams of being an entrepreneur. Alisa remembers how it felt whenever she thought of starting her own business. "It seemed," she recollects, "like a really wonderful thing to be able to be in charge of your own thing, to be able to develop a plan for something, to be able to create something from nothing and see it through."

Always having that idea in the back of her mind, Alisa began scratching the freelance itch at an early age. Once, while her high school counterparts took minimum wage summer jobs, Alisa began a small home-based bakery. She made tasty treats, cut them into sample-size pieces, and took them to pastry cooks at local restaurants and hotels. The chefs, impressed by the quality, ordered desserts. Each night, in the family kitchen, she filled orders for the luscious treats. The following morning, she delivered the freshly baked goodies to her happy clients. Though it only lasted a summer, Alisa remembers both how hard she worked and how much fun she had playing entrepreneur.

Another year Alisa parlayed her classical guitar expertise into an after-school job. She remembers thinking that "it would be really cool to teach the guitar, to make the money and to have a source of income." She marketed her services through local music stores and developed a clientele. At sixteen, she used the money to pay for one of her dreams, a summer adventure in Europe. She was proud that she had achieved such a goal.

Watching her sprout creative wings, the practical elders of the family expressed concern. In spite of her adolescent successes, when Alisa considered pursuing a liberal arts degree, her parents asked Alisa to think seriously about the kind of job she could get with such a broad-based and unfocused education. Concerned for her future, they encouraged her to follow the scientific tradition of her family. No matter how they verbally acknowledged Alisa's considerable creativity, the message she heard was, "if you

didn't major in math or science, you just really weren't bright."
Though Alisa knew she *was* bright, and wanted to *prove it* to her
family, the sciences were not her passion.

Still, growing up in the seventies in Wilmington, Delaware,
the corporate home of key financial institutions, Alisa knew what
determined a woman's worth: a prestigious college degree, followed by a brief stint with a major company, then marriage and
finally, life as a stay-at-home mom.

Haunted by youthful insecurity and her desire to be a dutiful
daughter, Alisa yielded to external pressures and did the "right"
thing. She convinced herself that being an entrepreneur was too
risky. Fear eclipsed desire and the urge went dormant.

Alisa went to college where she majored in chemistry. Though
she displayed no real talent for it, she did well and graduated.
Yes! She could be a part of the elite family tradition that surrounded her. Upon reflection, Alisa now realizes that she used
her college career to prove to herself that she could do it.

Next, Alisa accepted a job with a pharmaceutical company and
moved to Kalamazoo, Michigan, to work as a bench chemist. The
job paid well, and gave just due to the sciences—but she hated it.

After a year, she began looking for something better. Still considering starting her own business, she quit her job, moved to
North Carolina, and earned an MBA in finance. While studying,
her sleeping entrepreneurial spirit awakened. She wanted to make
the most of her new degree by going into business for herself.
Though not yet knowing what business to choose, the prospect
of being self-employed excited her.

Upon graduation, however, Alisa had huge school loans that
needed to be paid off, and corporate recruiters were offering her
incredible salaries that were hard to pass up. Logic won out over
creativity and, once again, Alisa put her entrepreneurial urges a-
side. She accepted a job with the Rohm and Haas Corporation
and later took a job with The Franklin Mint.

While she made a good income and enjoyed what her money
could buy, she recalls feeling like a bird in a gilded cage. In her

heart, she wanted to break free. Though bored with the work, her rational mind regularly reminded her...*the money was so good*.

For several years, Alisa continued to wrestle with the appeal of security versus her desire for exciting work. At the same time, the thirty-year-old woman felt some pressure from her parents and grandparents. Though proud of her accomplishments, they wanted her to settle down and start a family.

Around that time, Alisa reconnected with Michael, an old acquaintance. Romance blossomed into a whirlwind courtship and the pair married within the year.

An engineer and self-proclaimed computer geek, Michael had his own computer software business. His work took him to different places and Alisa quit her job to travel with him. They lived in Dallas initially, and then Michael retained work in his hometown of Chicago. His parents were in poor health and seemed to get more fragile each month. So, while living in the famed windy city, Alisa helped care for her aging in-laws. Though she sometimes felt she lived a dutiful life, she also admits it was a pretty good one. Her entrepreneurial drive slipped into neutral, and Alisa enjoyed a temporary reprieve from the nagging, gotta-do-something urge.

In time, however, the old drive kicked into gear. Alisa wanted to grow something of her own, for her own success. She knew nothing else could take its place, and she would not be satisfied until she succeeded.

Filled with energy and enthusiasm, she again decided to start her own business. The problem was...*doing what?*

Alisa began searching. In her travels, she discovered Chicago's famous Thorne Rooms. She became fascinated with the painstakingly constructed dioramas that combine history and architecture. The miniature rooms are filled with furniture reproductions, all built to the same exacting scale of one inch to one foot. Each one depicts the architectural design and furnishings of a specific era both in Europe and America. The more Alisa learned about the rooms and their history, the more she wanted to make them herself. She felt challenged by the detail of the miniatures; they stimulated her creativity.

Alisa gave the project an energetic start. She researched and studied the models, and then taught herself. Her apartment soon filled with wood, drill presses, saws, and other equipment. A few months into the work, however, Alisa realized her creative limits. Becoming skilled enough to sell the miniature rooms successfully could take years and years. Though she loved the learning process, she understood that the time required to reach the necessary skill level ensured a slow payoff. Looking back, Alisa admits, "As an amateur, I wasn't bad; as an artist, I wasn't there... I wasn't going to make it in that world." She felt disappointed with herself.

A short time later, Michael's business brought them back to Delaware. They bought a house and settled into suburban living. They agreed that it made sense for Alisa to handle the family finances. She worked out a household budget and began building the couple's nest egg.

All the while, the yearning for a successful business of her own grew stronger...and so did Alisa's frustration. Taking into consideration her background, including her MBA, she scanned the professional landscape for entrepreneurial possibilities. Alisa decided to pursue a career as a financial planner. Rolling out a pragmatic new strategy, Alisa sought work with a financial company, through which she would take the required courses and gain experience. Once she had a handle on how to run a financial planning firm and had some successes under her belt, she would open her own small business supplying financial advice.

Though the idea did not stir her passion, Alisa felt purposeful and the plan gave her a straightforward track on which to run. She proceeded quickly. She found a job with the company that is now American Express, where she daily learned about her newly chosen profession. She enrolled in courses and earned the designation of Certified Financial Planner.

During the process, she continued looking for other potential opportunities. Alisa considered becoming a builder so she could construct houses. She even went as far as obtaining a contractor's license. She also developed an idea for creating an eBay-like Internet car dealership. Some of her proposed ventures came and went in a flash, others simply withered away, and a few evolved into business plans before being discarded.

Alisa had so many ideas that went nowhere that the people who knew her well teased her. One of Michael's associates often joked about her ideas, calling them "Alisa's idea du jour." While comedy at her expense sometimes hurt her feelings, she refused to let it dampen her spirits or sabotage her efforts. Even as she prepared to launch her new business in financial planning, her vexing quest for passion-motivated work continued.

"Do what you love," the career and self-help books kept saying. Alisa looked deeply inside, trying to sort out and understand what activities best fit that description. She thought about the pleasure she got from playing and teaching classical guitar, the satisfaction of making and selling baked goods, her excitement over the unique Thorne Rooms. *Hmmm.* She also loved the unusual and the creative, especially when it came to building things and creating environments.

In addition, Alisa never lost her penchant for coffee shops and cafés, the pastime she developed during her undergraduate days. She still haunted them, often going out of her way to find new ones, soaking in each experience. For no particular reason except curiosity, when she visited a store, she observed and evaluated it. She routinely critiqued the food, service, ambiance, and everything else, measuring them against her personal preferences. She would sit quietly with a shop's touted brew-of-the-day while she amused herself with ideas for improving the shop, wondering if adding a different food or offering a different kind of service would improve a store's overall profitability. Like a fun game, the practice both stimulated and relaxed her.

When she considered her most joyful activities, she frequently wondered how she could do something with them. Michael's business did well, and she felt confident in her ability to make financial planning a success. However, her heart seemed to open up when doing something, *anything*, with the arts. *Do what you love.* What could she do that would be both fulfilling and profitable? She asked and asked, but no satisfying ideas surfaced. Disheartened, Alisa moaned silently, "Am I ever going to find what I really want to do?"

Not one to sit around and be depressed about what she did not have, Alisa focused on the tangible tasks at hand and pressed forward with the quantifiable and lucrative financial business. If nothing else, at least she knew that venture would scratch her entrepreneurial itch.

Her plans progressed while she talked with many brokerages, chose a broker-dealer, and negotiated an all-important contract for services. After adding that ingredient to the mix of education, credentials, and experience, she finally had a solid foundation in place and was ready for the next step—writing her business plan.

On the day she began, Alisa sat down to write. Nothing happened. Her usually creative and prolific thought process seemed like a vast wasteland. In the days that followed, she tried to come up with ideas, but the ink in the pen might as well have run dry. As the pages of the calendar turned and the winter months made way for spring, Alisa felt cheered as she watched the world coming alive again after the long winter. As she listened to happily chirping birds, she wished their sounds would carry with them the needed ideas and strategies that eluded her thoughts. Yet as hard as she tried to summon innovative energy with which to craft a business plan, she found none.

What Alisa *did* find were other, unwanted thoughts and ideas noodling around in her brain. Day after tedious day she pushed them down, further and further, into her subconsciousness. The persistent, guttural messages told Alisa the idea already had the earmarks of a boring business. Afraid to pay attention, she wanted to ignore them. She had too much invested in her plan. She couldn't quit now...*could she?*

Days passed with relative unproductivity. Though feeling tired and stuck, Alisa convinced herself to keep going. She thought of the people who poked fun at her laundry list of ideas. She wondered if they were more in touch with her life than she was. For so long she wanted to have her own business, and now she had the opportunity. This business just *had* to work; Alisa couldn't face yet another idea dissolving into thin air. She remembers telling herself insistently, "I have to prove to myself, once and for all, that I *can* run a business!"

It was May 1993 when, in the midst of her turmoil, Alisa welcomed a break in her routine. The appreciated diversion came in the form of a long-planned trip to Italy with Michael and some friends. Alisa looked forward to the holiday and believed that a few relaxing weeks in the Tuscan sun would dislodge the mental block that plagued her. Anticipating a renewed energy, Alisa visualized herself returning from the trip and sitting down to write. She saw herself breezing though the business plan with the exciting and innovative ideas that, so far, eluded her. For the time being, Alisa could set aside the grueling mental work and prepare for her trip.

Once in Italy, the small group chose their activities, deciding to spend some time together and some time apart. Alisa loved Italy and wanted the most personal experience she could have. Sometimes, rather than joining the others and experiencing all the usual tourist excursions to museums and galleries, Alisa took another route. Indulging her fondness for coffee shops, Alisa made the rounds of the many local espresso bars. Some days it was if she'd died and gone to java paradise!

What happened to Alisa in those tiny taverns of Italy was life changing. As she viewed the world from café table to café table, she noticed how people *regularly took time* to enjoy an espresso. It wasn't just people stopping to get something to drink. What Alisa watched were people indulging in what she calls, "the lost art of actually having conversations with each other...changing even a small thing like drinking a cup of coffee into a quintessential experience." She reveled in her people-watching experiences at cafés.

One morning while drinking a cappuccino on the rose covered stone terrace of a charming pension in Fiesole, Alisa gazed upon the splendor of the hills before her. The early sun kissed the Tuscan earth and it shone with a golden glow. The lustful beauty of olive trees brushing against the sky merged with the ambiance of the café. It filled her up and she felt unbelievably good. "This is great," she thought to herself. "This is life, this *is living*." It was like being in heaven, she remembers, a moment in time that she never wanted to end.

So rich was the experience, she wanted to share it with others. Excited thoughts swirled in and around ebullient feelings. What bubbled up for Alisa was the idea of having a "bunch of kitchens" that provided the warmth of being someone's home, a place that encouraged great interactions and great experiences. The idea focused on "having really quality things, especially coffee...coffee was a great business idea to wrap the concept around." In retrospect, Alisa realizes, "an experience is really what I wanted to create...specialty coffee was the way, the vehicle to do it."

Alisa's life changed in one powerful instant. She felt as though everything she did before then made her ready for that one watershed moment. After years of unknowing preparation, she asserts, "Something *finally* spoke to *everything* that I was."

Immediately, she started thinking through the possibilities. Starbucks had recently gone public, so the concept was not totally foreign in the United States. However, she knew cafés were still a very new concept in her steeped-in-tradition town. Later that evening, when she caught up with her spouse and friends, Alisa wondered aloud about this being the perfect time for her upscale town to have its very own espresso café. The small group, long past getting excited over her brainstorms, gave her patronizing responses. Alisa didn't care. She loved both the concept and the challenge; this was something she could sink her teeth into and not let go.

For the rest of the trip, and all the way back to the United States, her mind raced. From the beginning she wanted to differentiate herself from any similar kind of place. *How would she do that?* Would she duplicate the Italian café mood, or something else? What would she call her new place? Would it work in Greenville, Delaware? While the questions came fast and furious, so did the answers.

In the confinement of the airplane's cabin, thousands of feet above the earth, her traveling companions listened to her excited chattering. Everyone wondered if this would be just another one of Alisa's madcap ideas, or if it would materialize into something more. No one, even Alisa, could have guessed how this latest inspiration would develop and what legs it would have.

When Alisa returned, she immediately discarded the financial planning idea. Though a nagging parental influence warned her not to let go of something so practical, she quieted the voice by telling herself, "I can always go back to that...what I want to do now is write this [espresso café] business plan and see if there's a spark here." She started right in on it...and never turned back.

First, Alisa chose a name for the new shop. Playing off the French word *brouhaha*, meaning, "to create a hubbub," Alisa called the new store Brew Ha Ha! It was a fun name and reminded her of the sound of coffee brewing. Her idea was to make Brew Ha Ha! a gathering place where neighbors could meet for conversation over great coffee and good but quick food. She wanted to create a throwback to an earlier time, "a part of our past," she reminisces, "lost with the onslaught of the sanitized, fast-food chains."

Next, she began to write. Almost immediately Alisa noticed a difference from all the previously written plans. With the other plans, she had to practically force herself to write them, laboring over words and ideas. With this plan, Alisa says, "I had an energy I'd never felt before." She took it as a sign that she was *meant* to do it.

When she put pen to paper, there was no strain or struggle;

the ideas in her head flowed into words on paper. The more she wrote, the more excited she became. Brew Ha Ha! spoke to her creativity, her fascination of building something from scratch, and her love of cafés. Her background in finance proved to be a definite asset. Even her chemist capability found a place as she experimented with ingredients and created great coffee concoctions. As she worked, she saw how the progression of her life and skills brought her to a perfect place in time and opportunity. Brew Ha Ha! was her great "ah ha."

Alisa completed the business plan in record time. At the end of two weeks, she finished the first Brew-Ha-Ha! plan. By June 1993, Alisa was on her way!

Though her ideas filled Alisa with passion, not everyone shared her enthusiasm. In fact, the people close to her became some of her greatest critics. From the start, Alisa knew she might not convince them of her seriousness, but she would try.

She began with Michael, the path of least resistance. When Alisa explained why the Brew Ha Ha! idea had merit, Michael reminded her that she said the same about her last "great idea" and questioned how long her excitement would last. He knew their savings provided the couple with a small financial cushion, but not enough for a business start-up. Though he earned a good income, the money fluctuated, and Michael expressed concerns of financial balance and stability. Just the same, Michael trusted Alisa with the finances despite his nervousness. He went along with Alisa's plan to use their savings and even agreed to tap into their credit line if necessary. Considering her business idea history, Alisa believes he supported her the best he possibly could. He was the only one who did.

When Alisa told her parents, they were confused. Her father wanted to know how her new idea made good use of her education. He also wanted to know why Alisa had such an aversion to having a normal job with a normal company and a stable income that included benefits. Her mother felt the same and asked Alisa why she needed to take such a risk when instead she could either stay at home or find herself a safe, secure position.

The feedback from friends and business colleagues covered everything from outright negativity to subtle disparagement. Some questioned her actions and asked why she would take the kind of risk that created enormous debt. Others asked her if she had the "stick-to-itive-ness" to see it through.

Though disappointed by the responses, she could hardly blame anyone for being overly cautious and skeptical. Her prior track record for follow-through on ideas wasn't great. She understood to them it seemed almost schizophrenic—financial planner one minute, barista the next. Worse yet, her new business idea was a flamboyant one, and about as far away from financial planning as a person could get. And that name, Brew Ha Ha! Where did *that* come from, people wondered, telling Alisa the public would never accept such a name.

As her circle of family and friends heard about Alisa's latest idea, everyone took a "wait and see" attitude. Obviously, they were not likely investors, but she did wish for some emotional support. However, based on their responses, Alisa knew she was on her own.

Over the next few months, Alisa visited local commercial rentals sites and eventually secured a location in a small shopping area. Next she focused on décor, supplies, vendors, staff, and dozens of other business requisites. The list seemed endless, and the tasks more daunting than she imagined. She knew virtually nothing about the restaurant business; now she had to learn everything she could, and quickly.

Alisa began with more traditional information sources like the Small Business Administration. However, 1993 information on cafés and coffee shops followed old and out-of-date models. So Alisa scoured the library for books that met her needs. Next, she bought a current copy of the annual "best of" edition of *Philadelphia Magazine*. She combed its pages looking for specially selected muffins, scones, and desserts. When she found ones she liked, she looked for the manufacturer of the award-winning goodies.

She called the company, told the owner or salesperson about her plans, and asked if s/he wanted to supply her store. She faced mixed responses. Some people thought she was a "fly-by-night" dreamer and told her so. But others took her seriously and worked with her.

When it came to actually getting the desserts as well as other supplies, only the paper company would deliver directly to the store. Frustrated but undaunted, Alisa decided if they wouldn't come to her, she would go to them. She contracted with vendors and agreed to pick up her merchandise at their warehouses.

In addition to suppliers, Alisa needed to know what to do inside the store. She started talking with people in the food business. Alisa asked around and got help from coffee vendors as well as people who were already in the peripheral businesses such as bakeries and suppliers of cafés. The vendors gave her samples of everything from deli meats and sweets to cream and cocoa powder. She asked their advice on everything from "How do you make espresso?" and "Show me how to work this machine" to "What do you think of this location?" and "How many cups of coffee do you think I'll sell a day?" In addition, during their conversations, vendors would ask her if she had purchased certain items. From their questions, Alisa figured out what else she needed. Day after day, one step and one task at a time, she moved forward.

Alisa's challenges did not end with locating supplies and researching courses of action. Money quickly became a major issue. Initially the budget matched her savings and Alisa thought that if her projections were off a little, if she needed to, she felt confident she could stretch the dollars to match the needs.

Alisa soon discovered that the company's projected expenses, based on figures supplied by someone who she thought knew the right answers, turned out to be substantially higher than expected. When projection met reality, Alisa found that everything from construction to supplies cost more than she anticipated. Alisa exceeded her budget within a few weeks, and she quickly used all their savings and then maxed-out their credit cards just getting the store opened. Problems with working capital forced Alisa to liquidate her Individual Retirement Account, costing her a whopping forty percent penalty!

Afterward, not only did she not feel emotionally supported by anyone in her close circle, but also the financial risk caused those same people to express serious concern. The pressure to succeed was intense. During moments when Alisa wondered if she could really pull it off, if nothing else, the stress of indebtedness kept her going.

As she moved ahead, Alisa bought equipment, obtained necessary licenses, and oversaw construction. As she daily set about creating the environment that matched her vision, Alisa gained more confidence. While the tiny store took shape, she interviewed prospective staff and hired one person. They'd work at the counter side-by-side. Together they counted down the days as they prepared the store for customers.

Alisa rode an emotional roller coaster during those final weeks before opening the first Brew Ha Ha! Exuberance one minute, doubt the next, tired all the time. What if the townspeople did not like the café? Alisa had plenty of people telling her how the quaint, posh, and *very* traditional town was not ready for her kind of shop. *What if she failed?*

Finally, seven months after Italy, on a cold December morning in Greenville, Delaware, the first Brew Ha Ha! opened its doors. From that first day, people noticed. Whether rushing to work or shopping for the approaching holiday, people took time to come in and check out the place. Situated near several offices, specialty stores, a restaurant, and a bookstore, people wanted to see what this new, oddly-named store was. Once inside, patrons found a warmly painted and eclectically decorated shop. Though barely large enough for the counter and a half-dozen or so tables, it felt like a cozy place to be—like the warm, comfortable feel of the kitchens Alisa so loved.

In the beginning, while she established herself and her business, she did everything. As a hands-on owner, not only did Alisa work behind the counter, she also picked up deliveries from vendors and cleaned up before closing each day. In addition, she kept the books and did payroll. The hour-long drive from Wilmington to Philadelphia to purchase bread, muffins, and other supplies became a weekly ritual. During the ice and snow-filled winter months, she faced poorly plowed and badly salted roads to visit her five different vendors and buy the necessary provisions. She worked hard and it paid off.

Though Alisa did some advertising, her greatest publicity came from her customers. As the word spread around town, her clientele grew. She began seeing the same faces coming in the store each day.

Alisa felt the first rush of success, but challenges quickly replaced the thrills. The small space, though cozy for customers, presented storage problems. With no on-site place for supplies at the café, Alisa kept most items at her house. Each day she brought with her the day's deli provisions, along with fifty-pound tubs of brownie and muffin mixes that would soon become the freshly baked goods found on the counter. She also brought in the rich, enticing specialty cakes made of chocolate, coconut, nuts, and other delicious ingredients. If she ran out of something during store hours, she either had to go home to get it or do without.

Then, Mother Nature decided to throw Alisa a curve ball in the form of snow and ice. During Brew Ha Ha!'s first winter, fourteen storms pummeled the area. People made their tedious way to work on ice-covered roads often in bumper-to-bumper traffic. They found little time for an extra stop. Many events in town were cancelled. Fewer customers ventured out for errands, choosing instead to put them off until driving conditions improved. Delawarians seemed to be in hibernation, and the café struggled through many winter days when weather-related problems slowed business. It seemed as though only people with four-wheel drives could get to the store—and Alisa thanked God for them. While all the local businesses felt the pinch, the fledgling Brew Ha Ha! struggled for survival.

Through those dreary first months of 1994, Alisa wondered if the store would make it. From the upbeat reaction of patrons during those first few weeks, Alisa knew she created a winning place—but it only counted if she could tough it out during those awful winter months.

When the last ice storm melted and spring arrived, Brew Ha Ha! was still in business. Before long, the store became a place where regulars came for their morning coffee and the locals liked to meet. A couple of businessmen from nearby offices spent so much time in the café that they tried talking Alisa into installing a payphone so they could take calls there. Helped along by some excellent press coverage in the area's major newspaper and magazine, Brew Ha Ha! quickly became a place where the "movers and shakers" met to make decisions and deals over coffee.

Alisa conquered the start-up, and she survived the long winter. She knew she had a victorious venture in the works. She felt good about her success.

The crazy and stressful process taught Alisa two valuable business lessons that she used in all future corporate development. First of all, she found out that, "You don't have to figure it all out the first day. Start with a goal and a plan. Do a lot of research and talk to a lot of people." Alisa began with a goal to have a store opened in six months, and created a plan for making that goal happen. While she admits, "Every plan has a lot of flexibility around it," at the same time she also insists that there must be a basic structure at the start. Alisa's business plan helped her understand the basic needs, such as financing, a suitable location, furniture, equipment, construction, a menu, and supplies. The rest of it, the lessons for running a successful operation, came one day at a time.

Secondly, in the process of overcoming her reticence about asking for help, Alisa gained an understanding so valuable that it soon became a permanent part of her personal repertoire, and something that she regularly passes along to others. "People are willing to help," Alisa insists. "Yes, there are people who *will* say 'no' or who won't take you seriously. So you move on to the next person...*you keep going.*"

How do you find people who are willing to help? Alisa insists that help is always available, but it is a matter of unreservedly asking for it. She says she often hears women say they do not know what to do or how to get started. They complain that everybody closes the door on them. Based on her own experiences, she refuses to give credence to that kind of negative talk, emphatically maintaining, "There's no excuse for that, especially in today's world, with the Internet [you can do] all kinds of basic research... you can learn so much through the Internet."

As the first store took hold, Alisa saw the bigger picture come into focus and prepared to move ahead. The only idea that motivated her as much as opening her second store was her eagerness to extricate herself from the details of everyday management. She didn't like dealing with scheduling, and could easily be talked into giving one employee or another a break. Though her kindness helped the workers, it often hurt the business.

Thinking that administration might not be her strength, Alisa decided to hire a store manager. Her first employee, an energetic and hard-working woman, seemed to have an instinct for the business. Alisa promoted this woman to manager, paying her salary out of what would have been the first year's profits. Alisa considered it a worthwhile expenditure because it freed her from the more tedious parts of ownership. Alisa then set about opening the second Brew Ha Ha!

As Alisa enjoyed the benefits of success in her professional world, life on the homefront began changing. Like Alisa, Michael loved his Italian experience. Wanting more of it, he aggressively looked for business there. Though in the past Alisa usually traveled with Michael, her new business made it impossible for her to join him. When he found work in Italy, planning to be there for at least a year, Alisa already had plans for the second store in motion. Michael moved overseas, leaving Alisa and Brew Ha Ha! temporarily on their own.

Though Alisa was comfortable with this new arrangement, the change had a direct impact on her in the form of added obligations. Though it was the opportunity of a lifetime for Michael, his work abroad left Alisa solely responsible for caring for their home in addition to building her new business. At times it felt overwhelming, but the busy Alisa took it in stride.

Within a few months, Alisa found space for a second location in a nearby town. Happily, this time she didn't have to use her personal savings. The success of the initial store enabled her to secure a bank loan for store number two. Cutting her entrepreneurial teeth in Greenville, Alisa thought she knew what she was doing. With one store under her belt, she presumed the second opening would go smoothly.

Instead, it gave Alisa nightmares. One construction problem followed another. Her first contractor fell behind in his work. Before she knew it, he left town. Working one day and gone the next, the man left Alisa only sawdust and half-built shelves. Staring at the mess in disbelief, Alisa wondered how she could salvage the disaster.

Alisa searched her resources for help. Luckily, she found other tradesmen fairly fast and became the project manager. With long hours and substantial effort, the new subcontractors completed the work in a timely fashion. Relieved, Alisa opened the second Brew Ha Ha! on schedule.

Unfortunately, her calm was short-lived. Shortly after the new store opened, Alisa learned that she neglected to obtain a mandatory legal document. Frustrated and annoyed, she took down the welcoming "Now Open" sign and applied for a certificate of occupancy. Every day became a financial loss until she worked her way through government red tape and acquired the permit she needed.

Next, the contractor who had come to her rescue began having money problems. When he failed to pay his subcontractors their wages, they called Alisa. The stresses made her head spin.

Looking back, Alisa is still amazed that the store finally got underway. However, once truly open for business, the store did well. It actually broke even in its first week—a level that usually takes the average business several years to achieve. The store's rapid success amazed even Alisa.

More importantly, Alisa learned lessons that would have an effect on every other Brew Ha Ha! As a result of her construction disaster, the company designed all future stores in-house and also acted as the general contractor for all sites. By doing so, Alisa and her growing team gained greater control over the building process, including costs and timing. Though each successive store had its own unique challenges, the process worked much better.

As Alisa's knowledge and experience grew, so did the company. By 1997, Brew Ha Ha! had expanded to eight stores strong. In 1998, *INC Magazine* named Brew Ha Ha! one of the fastest growing companies in the country. The *INC* 500 award thrilled Alisa and motivated her to seek greater achievements.

Alisa had fun growing the business but the daily practicalities still annoyed her. As she did with her first store, she continued delegating the dreaded daily detail work to staff, most of whom were young and inexperienced college students. To keep the business on track, Alisa hired an operations manager to oversee the daily happenings. Though he had the experience she wanted, he only lasted six weeks, not even long enough to make a dent in the work.

At that time, she turned to a consultant she retained for other business matters. He began handling operations for Alisa on an ad hoc basis. Craig* was a smart man with business experience. This strong-willed man displayed considerable confidence. She liked that about him, and admired his decisive manner.

Before long, in addition to a salary, Alisa offered him a small partnership in the company. Craig accepted. Glad to have someone with a vested interest in the company overseeing those critical details, Alisa trusted him to be strong in the corporate areas where she was weak. While Craig handled the accounting, Alisa did what she did best—open new stores.

In 1999, Brew Ha Ha! grew by four more stores. Each store had different obstacles, and Alisa met each challenge with persistence, determination, and a stunning new confidence acquired over the past few years. Each new location turned a profit within a short time of its opening. Alisa believed she had a winning strategy.

While the glow of success grew brighter at work, it darkened at home. As Alisa became more adept at confronting problems in business, she felt ready to tackle marital issues that she had previously pushed aside. When she discussed her concerns with Michael, she realized they would not be resolved. In the millennium year, Alisa and Michael separated. The next year, the couple filed for divorce.

Though they parted amicably, the end of her marriage had a profound emotional impact on Alisa. Her work energy dissipated, along with her desire and drive. During the year-long separation, Alisa feels as though she "lost her way...lost the passion." She mentally "checked out" of her thriving company. Life seemed like something of a blur.

While talking to divorce lawyers about a settlement, Alisa paid little attention to growing the business. She paid even less attention to accounting details and personnel matters. If she noticed disturbing indications like decreased profits and increased payroll, she questioned Craig. He typically told her everything was fine and he had the matter under control. She willingly accepted his answers. Since she seldom looked at supporting data with real interest, Alisa trusted that whatever Craig said was accurate. The less she had to think about the business, the better she was.

Looking back, she admits that even when she thought things were bad, Craig "seemed so sure, and I wanted to believe him." And, she confesses, "In the past I gave my power over [to men] because I did not think I was as strong as that, *as they are*." So Alisa ignored the many warning signs of a deteriorating business. In the midst of her personal turmoil, denial served as a powerful stress-reliever.

As the divorce became final, Brew Ha Ha! faced a crossroads. The company grew out of its line of credit. It expanded so quickly that the profits had not yet caught up. The company had two choices: Alisa could either stop growing it, or she would have to seek venture capital.

For Alisa, given everything that happened, she decided to stop opening stores for a while and take some time to regroup and renew. While she did, Alisa trusted that Craig would pick up the slack. She would later regret her blind faith in him.

In the spring and summer of 2001, Alisa had an unsettled feeling. Though she knew intuitively that something in Brew-Ha-Ha!'s operations did not seem right, she "hoped against hope" that it would all be fine. Though she often told others that studying the numbers bored her, in reality, she felt overwhelmed when it came to the company's bookkeeping. Almost as a backlash to her pragmatic upbringing, she seldom read the reports with any real focus. Alisa ignored the inner warning.

Shortly after the events of 9/11, when those sad autumn days brought unexpected financial losses for so many companies, she decided to take a look at the company's income statements. She found something that disturbed her. She already suspected that the company's spending exceeded its income. When she talked to Craig about it, he told her not to worry. He assured her that they would make up for increasing costs with greater sales. They never did. As she stared at the numbers, Alisa felt a shock wave of disbelief go through her body as the totals confirmed her fears. She searched the papers again and again, each time hoping she would find something she missed the previous time. She did not.

In the days that followed, she viewed all the new reports, waiting to see an improvement. Yet no matter what way she looked at the numbers, she came to the same troubling conclusion.

Alisa's instincts told her that "this is not working...I need to step in and do something." But still healing from their divorce, Alisa questioned her own capabilities. She rationalized and told herself that she didn't need the extra stress and responsibility of running the business. Rather than take action, she closed her business eyes and hoped the small chain of stores would soon turn around.

Her lethargy became the company's worst enemy. Alisa soon saw the company free-falling into failure.

Again, she questioned Craig. He responded with patronizing answers. No longer satisfied with his snappy replies, Alisa pressed him for better answers. He surprised Alisa with defensive, even angry responses. His sharp retorts gave Alisa a sudden and unwelcome jolt of reality. The bright businesswoman calls it another "watershed moment" and one she *really* didn't want.

Over the next few days, Alisa came out of her divorce-induced daze and forced herself to take an in-depth look around the company. She saw rampant disorganization and employees with little interest. With bad numbers and bad morale, Alisa felt like an observer watching her business headed quickly toward a brick wall. Suddenly, like the water from a boiling teakettle, Alisa saw all her work and effort evaporating before her eyes. What had happened?

Backtracking in her mind, Alisa realized that she made a mistake by turning the reins entirely over to someone else. She so wanted to grow the café company that she willingly let go of the administrative side of the business. The same strength that got Brew Ha Ha! to a place of success became a limitation. She erroneously thought she could get away with turning mundane matters over to Craig and not bothering with them.

Looking in the mirror of her life, Alisa faced reality. Though her marriage ended, Brew Ha Ha! lived. True, it was gasping for air, but still breathing. "I can do better than this," she told herself. She made another critical decision.

The next day, Alisa went to work and immediately fired Craig as the business manager (and eventually bought out his small share in the business). Now what? Frightened but resolute, she encouraged herself by declaring, "Maybe I don't have a clue what I'm going to do...but I can't do worse than this." With that determination, on the brink of bankruptcy, Alisa started over.

With renewed energy, she sat at her desk. From the drawer she took out a clean, white sheet of paper and started writing. Feeling as though she had a business professor on her shoulder, she mapped out a plan. "I wrote what I knew I had to do, right then and there," Alisa recounts. "I wrote a one-page job expectation for each direct report." Using a simple "so we're clear, here's what I'm looking for from you" format, Alisa listed the responsibilities for each position. She developed a quick, incentive-based performance system revolving around an end-goal, and took the time to make sure everyone understood clearly what she wanted as an outcome, "so that we could all work on the same goal." She embarked on a no-nonsense, no-compromise course; Alisa had no other choice.

Her new mandate forced Alisa to advance her skills to another level. In the past, she seldom fired or laid-off anyone. In fact, until now Alisa usually avoided staff confrontations. She told herself she preferred a "democratic" work environment. While the thought of firing people made Alisa uncomfortable, the possibility of losing her business felt worse. Now in survival mode, Alisa accepted nothing less than guerrilla determination from herself and her staff. She started enforcing policy, and refused to make exceptions for anyone.

During the days when she had focused on growing the business, Alisa had lost touch with things like the costs of supplies. She quickly learned that expenses had skyrocketed. Alisa needed to cut thousands of hours and a few hundred thousand dollars from the payroll. Not only did that mean discharging nearly half the office staff, it also required renegotiating prices wherever and on whatever she could—with every vendor and employee, and for as much as she could.

Alisa worked hard at keeping the business afloat. It took nearly eighteen months before Alisa saw light at the end of the tunnel. By this time, however, she had accepted a hard truth: she had a weak management style. Often too pliable with staff, she avoided conflict and let too many interpersonal issues go by the wayside. That behavior *had* to change. In order for that to happen, *she* had to change. Demonstrating both willingness and resilience, Alisa gradually developed new work skills.

With newly acquired wisdom, Alisa changed her involvement with business operations, particularly with regards to delegating. Alisa learned that in business, "One has to look closely at motive when delegating." She realized that, in the past, she simply gave away the work that bothered her rather than assigning appropriate tasks. And instead of expecting accountability, she delegated control. In doing so, she weakened the business and diminished her own abilities, allowing herself to feel inept. She fell into an unconstructive pattern of listening to negativity. She warns other women, "You get into a cycle of 'I just can't do it'...the inner voices, the outer voices...you just don't know [if you can do it]. I never tried."

With her mind fully back into business mode, Alisa tackled the emotionally challenging task of developing a tough-minded attitude regarding daily business details. She changed the way she handled everything from budget expenditures to employee days off.

In retrospect, she holds only herself accountable for the near failure. Taking back her company was "more of a learning experience and probably better" than anything else. While Craig's actions were a catalyst, he was only "one prototype" of a person to whom Alisa regularly relinquished her authority. Alisa needed to develop stronger business skills, and sooner or later, she had to learn that lesson. In addition, Alisa concedes, "What I found is that I needed to trust myself and believe in myself, instead of giving my power to someone else."

Facing the business with even greater confidence, Brew Ha Ha! entered a new era. With renewed clarity about what she wanted and how she wanted to grow, Alisa had a new lease on life. In the past, she knew she could build something from nothing. Not until now did Alisa really believe she could maintain and sustain it as well. She always chose to hand off that responsibility in the past to someone else. Before, she wanted to depend on someone else, allowing herself to believe someone else was stronger and better at the tough stuff than she was. Bringing back the nearly failed venture convinced Alisa that she could function as well, if not better, than someone whose interests didn't match her own.

In less than ten years, Alisa found a passion, nurtured it into a successful business, let it sink to near-death, and then saved it from ruin. With her better business skills, she vowed to strengthen the business even more by making each store better than ever. She made it a game, trying out new products, varying the menus, and tweaking the environments to create greater ambiance. She had fun seeing what worked and what did not. For the first time, Alisa could honestly say, "This is really *my* business."

Today, in addition to being home of the famed Wyeth family, the internationally renowned Longwood Gardens, the beautiful and often painted Brandywine River, a host of historical sites and museums, and a plethora of credit card and other financial institutions, the Brandywine Valley area also boasts twelve Brew Ha Ha! locations. Each one is a place where the local folk go to meet each other. In addition, tourists from all over the world find respite from a day of sightseeing. For nine years running, Brew Ha Ha! has been named "Best of Delaware" by *Delaware Today* magazine. Cable television's Food Network featured Brew Ha Ha!, calling it one of the best cafés in the country for its eclectic character and warm ambiance.

Alisa continues to embody what she learned. While she plans for the future of Brew Ha Ha!, Alisa still oversees the daily operations of the company. Instead of adding stores, she focuses on enhancing things in each store and improving market share. She added espresso and catering services for local groups and businesses, and offers classes for customers wishing to develop their personal barista skills.

By this stage of her career, Alisa knows that even the most creative people must take control of the everyday essentials of their dream. While delegating is often necessary, relinquishing accountability for the non-creative details is only an invitation for failure. Like the mother who has a child, the process of giving birth is only the beginning of a long journey filled with work, responsibility, and love.

On the personal side, Alisa enjoys a new life with new spouse, Chris Morkides. Dating the never-married, forty-something man of proud Greek heritage proved she still had an appetite for risk-taking and challenges. Their courtship culminated in her own personal "big, fat Greek wedding" in 2002.

Today, Alisa is learning to balance married life and professional success. Marriage to Chris brought with it a greater focus on all the good in her life. She places greater emphasis on family and personal happiness. Alisa practices living in the present moment, which enables her to enjoy life more.

Her business challenges taught Alisa to be a better manager and handle conflict more effectively. Alisa passes on an important lesson about emotions in business. She warns women that petty jealousies and trivial rivalries waste valuable time and precious energy. When a woman finds herself feeling envious, resentful, or judgmental, or being the target of someone else's negative feelings, she suggests rising above those feelings by asking, "How does this relate to my goals? Does it propel me forward?" If the answer is "no" and there's nothing to learn from it, *let it go*. Focus instead on only those activities that support your goals and propel you forward.

While she still faces daily challenges common to any business, rather than allow the pressures to overwhelm her, Alisa looks at the tasks before her and asks herself, "What can I do in a day?" She does what she can, one day at a time.

Her new attitude works for her...and works very well.

As for the future, Alisa admits she will continue to look for challenges. Borrowing from one of her favorite movies, *Shawshank Redemption*, Alisa quotes, "You've got to get busy living or get busy dying." She chooses living life to the fullest.

Whatever the outcome, Alisa will always know how victorious

her journey has been. Though she made mistakes and nearly lost it all, Alisa is proud that she chose to take risks. While she still sometimes gets overwhelmed, she pushes through and keeps going. Greater strength and more confidence are her rewards—the hard-won trophies Alisa earned as she made her way to the top. Living her life fully and with sparkle and zest, she is happy to be fully engaged, instead of standing on the sidelines watching others, as many people do. Today, confident that she can handle the challenges life tosses her way, Alisa exudes the spirit and energy of a truly Victorious Woman.

STEPPING STONES
TO VICTORY

Alisa kept looking for her passion. Once she found it, she took action and created her victories, both in creating Brew-Ha-Ha! and by later turning the company around.

Being passionate about something is essential to being happy. What are you passionate about? If you don't already know your passion, the following exercises may help you figure it out.

1. In your Victory Journal, write at the top of a page "Activities That Get Me Jazzed and/or Bring Me Joy." Head another page with "I Feel Creative When I..."

   a. For the next week, spend some time considering those things that make you feel excited, joyful, and creative. Some suggestions to spark your thought process:

      ❧ Think about what you liked doing as a child and teenager. Was there something you enjoyed but gave up because people said it wasn't practical?

      ❧ If you could go to college *today*, what would your major be...and why? If you already have a degree, how would you use it differently today than when you graduated?

      ❧ Think about conversations with friends. Do your conversations have any recurring theme, such as love for animals, eating out, reading, entertainment, telling jokes, or helping others with problems? You may decide to be a veterinarian; book, restaurant, or entertainment reviewer for a newspaper or magazine; stand-up comedian; or psychologist.

b. Record what comes into your mind. If nothing surfaces right away, don't be concerned. Sometimes the ideas are stimulated by focused thought, but don't immediately come into your conscious mind. Instead, your thinking may produce the ideas at odd or unexpected times, such as when you first wake up or while you're doing something mindless.

c. Keep a tiny notebook with you at all times, as well as next to your bed while you sleep. Jot ideas down as they come to you. Transfer them to your Victory Journal so you can keep track of them and reflect on them in the context of other things you are writing.

2. Once you get an idea, test it. Begin by doing research to determine if it's something that really interests you. You can begin on the Internet, but also check out your regional career center, the community college, and your local library. Your reference librarian can be a great asset during your investigation. Also, local night schools offer a variety of courses. Check to see if there's a class you can take to learn more.

Next, contact people who already work within the particular field that interests you. If you want to start your own business, call local business owners and talk to them. If medical research is your passion, call a research lab or pharmaceutical company and ask to speak to the head developer. Ask for just ten (or fifteen or twenty) minutes of their time.

If you feel nervous or intimidated, keep this in mind: Alisa deduced that when a woman approaches a potential resource person with only a vague notion of what she wants, people are not likely to take her seriously. While the golden key turns with a woman's willingness to ask for help, the door opens only if she is able to communicate what she wants directly and effectively. Alisa discovered the importance of getting to the point quickly, and *clearly* conveying her vision and strategy to others. She learned that without honing the art of competently presenting her ideas, she'd spin wheels and get nowhere.

With that in mind, be clear and concise when you talk to someone. Tell them why you are calling and what you want in three or four sentences. You may want to write it out first and practice aloud until you are comfortable with your words. If someone agrees to meet with you (by phone or in person), make an appointment to meet with them and:

a. Arrive at their office or home early enough to compose yourself. Have an agenda and bring questions with you, marking the top three you want answered.

b. Stick to your agenda, ask the questions, and stay only as long as you agreed. Before you leave, ask if s/he knows anyone else you should talk to for more information.

c. Send a thank you note **within two days**—do not put off conveying your appreciation.

Keep this in mind: when Alisa asked, people gave her answers; then, she asked more questions. They asked questions, too, and their questions stimulated her thinking. Little by little, the picture got clearer and the steps became logical. The clearer you are, the more likely you will achieve your goal—and that is your objective.

3. Alisa wants women to know that information gathering may boil down to a numbers game...and the business facts of life. "There *are* people who won't help you," she acknowledges, but emphasizes that "you just move on to the person who will. I know it's easier said than done if you're shy...but one of the ways you can know if you can make it, or overcome an obstacle, or make it in business is that you *don't get discouraged if someone says 'no'*. And you're going to have a lot of people who are going to say 'no.'" If you conquer the fear of asking for help, *then you can overcome pretty much anything.*

As you search for assistance and move toward your goals, you're likely to be rejected many times. So that you don't give up, plan in advance what you will do when that happens? Do you have a mentor, supportive friend, coach, or someone who will champion your efforts even when you feel like quitting? Make an appointment to talk with them regularly, specifically about your progress. Specify that you only want constructive feedback and no criticism. Write down the positive things they tell you in your Victory Journal so that you can refer to them whenever you need to remember to keep going in spite of rejection or disappointment.

4. If you're still excited, take action. Set a goal, create a strategy (a list of steps to achieve your goal), and get moving! Keep track of your progress in your Victory Journal and refer to it frequently to remind you of how well you're doing.

5. By turning her head away from less pleasant parts, like personnel management and financial record keeping, Alisa gave control to someone else and almost lost her business.

   Knowing your strengths and weaknesses can be crucial to any venture. It often makes good sense to find someone to work with who's strong in the areas where you're weak. However, this can work against you by keeping you in the dark.

   Valid strategies for your success should include a process through which you can garner knowledge without maintaining daily control or micromanaging. For example, if a partner or significant other has the responsibility of the household finances, make a point to look at the monthly bank statements and credit balances; ask when you don't understand something.

   What are your weak areas and blind spots? How will you deal with them so you know what's going on without getting overly involved. In your Victory Journal, make a list of three areas of vulnerability and how you will compensate for them.

EXAMPLE:

<u>Problem Area</u>	<u>Solution</u>
I dislike micromanaging my staff, and they hate me doing it. But more than once I've gotten "called on the carpet" because one of my staff did not perform their job as required or expected.	I'll have a fifteen-minute meeting each week with every person who is heading a project. I'll ask them to prepare a summary of their activities, tell me what their challenges are and how they plan to move forward, and if they need any help from me.

10

Reaching New Heights
Mary Thecla Lomnicki

WHEN YOU LOOK IN THE MIRROR, DO YOU FEEL good about what you see? How important do you think your body image is to your happiness, success, and well-being?

If you're like most women, you probably look in the mirror and want to change something about your looks. In a culture obsessed with thin, young, hard bodies, the message seems to be that a woman's worth is established by her dress size while sexual prowess can determine her power level.

When we don't measure up to the unrealistic images touted by the movies, television, and magazines, many of us feel discouraged and unwanted. We try harder to be "just right." We diet and exercise so much that we support an eighty-five million dollar a year industry that caters to our preoccupation. Cosmetic surgery is commonplace. Plastic surgeons can change noses and chins, augment or lift breasts, smooth out wrinkles, and make us look ten years younger. What we cannot improve, we try to conceal with clothes that hide, elongate, and minimize our supposed flaws.

With so much emphasis placed on appearance, what happens to the woman who cannot hide her physical dissimilarities? When, no matter what she does, she will never match the airbrushed or softened photo images that determine today's beauty standards?

Some women make themselves miserable. They allow the perceived flaws of their external facade to control their lives. Their thoughts, actions, and behaviors reflect low self-esteem and lack of confidence.

Other women, like Tekki Lomnicki, ultimately create a victory.

Born with diastrophic dwarfism, Tekki cannot hide her nonconforming physique from the world. There is no way to conceal the fact that she stands only three-foot-four-inches tall and walks only with supports. If you're an average-sized woman and wanted to talk with Tekki eye-to-eye, you would have to kneel to do so, and might even have to tilt back on your heels. While you might feel uncomfortable with the way she looks, she would not.

As a little person, Tekki navigates her way through the world of average-sized people. Whether she is getting into a car, trying to reach a public restroom's sink and soap dispenser to wash her hands, or just wants to see what the salad bar offers, Tekki faces challenges most of us cannot even imagine. In addition to her logistical concerns, she tolerates the curious stares and uncomfortable smirks of average-sized adults and teens every place she goes. Little children stand in front of her and try to figure out how she is the same size but looks so much older. Tekki often chats with them until embarrassed parents apologetically hurry them away.

In spite of how differently she looks from the idealized media images, Tekki is confident of her worth and finds her power. She acknowledges, however, that she didn't always feel that way. Her path to victory has been a long, difficult, and circuitous route.

Born into a Polish-Catholic family during the late 1950s, her challenges began while still in the womb. As a breech baby, Tekki struggled to be born as her mother endured hours of labor. When she finally arrived, she was blue. The doctor couldn't get her to breathe. Expecting Tekki to die, he handed her over to the attending nurse, Sister Mary Thecla, for baptism.

In order to perform the ritual, Sister Thecla needed a name for the baby. She quickly thought of her own spiritual patron, Saint Thecla, a second century Christian, who survived being tortured for her faith and lived to be ninety-eight years old. She later became known as the patron saint of a happy death. That day was her feast day, a special day set aside to pay homage to the saint and her life. On that day of honor, the good sister would name the infant Mary Thecla.

In the cold, antiseptic white delivery room of Resurrection Catholic Hospital, Sister Mary Thecla administered the sacrament. While doing so, the clergywoman sought guidance from Saint Thecla. In prayer, as she poured the baptismal water over the infant's head, she tearfully petitioned for the baby's peaceful passing.

Suddenly, instead of going quietly to her death, the tiny infant began to breathe. Within seconds everyone within earshot could hear newborn Mary Thecla screaming her way into life.

Her mother, lying close by, felt elated. Though physically and emotionally exhausted from the precarious events of her daughter's birth, she jubilantly believed she had witnessed a miracle.

In the hospital room, shock gave way to joy, and then turned to action. The medical team scrambled as their focus changed from waiting for death to preserving a life.

Examining the baby, they saw her clubfeet and legs so twisted they resembled a pretzel. Only moments later, the doctor and nurse began applying plaster casts to the baby's legs to encourage her poorly developed and very pliable bones to grow straight. The procedure signaled the beginning of years of painful medical treatments for Mary Thecla, soon nicknamed Tekki.

The 1960s presented little advancement in the treatment of dwarfism-related conditions. Tekki had a variety of problems. She developed scoliosis, and her hip did not fit well in its socket. Hip and knee replacements had yet to be developed. As a result, her rigid body only moved on its own with the help of crutches.

When forced to walk on her toes due to a too-short achilles tendon, the doctors followed the common medical wisdom of the day and surgically stretched the tendon. After four surgeries, with ankles fused into a motionless position, she had no flexibility and very little rotating movement between her legs, ankles, and feet. With so much pain and physical trauma, the young girl had little choice but to confront life's harsh realities.

Yet from the beginning, Tekki's parents made the decision not to treat her as disabled or different. In fact, they barely addressed her dwarfism. Tekki did not actually realize she was a dwarf until high school, when she met another little person. Until then, she blamed frequent surgeries for stunting her growth.

During those early years, Tekki's parents focused on helping her to walk. Her father decided early on that he would do anything in his power to make that happen, while her mother prayed for Tekki's healing.

By the time she started school, Tekki's average-sized family had grown to include two younger brothers. Treating their children equally, her parents looked for comparable mental and social developments from each of them. They expected each child to do household chores, develop social skills, bring home good grades, and be involved in school activities.

Not only did Tekki do well in school, but around the house she also engaged her brothers in sporting activities. She enjoyed baseball and developed her pitching arm, as well as demonstrating considerable skill batting a ball into the outfield. The three siblings made up special rules for running, so Tekki could compete equally with her brothers. She could wrestle with both of them and when the boys started playing soccer, Tekki did too. In fact, because she could run with her crutches and kick the ball, she became pretty good at the challenging sport.

As they grew up, Tekki's brothers became super protective of their older sister. If anyone teased her about her size, they would fight the person who taunted her.

During adolescence, the young woman slowly absorbed a little of each parent's personality and passions. Her mother, Dolores, demonstrated a great faith and at her insistence, the family circle revolved around Catholic dogmas and traditions. Tekki learned about God, the saints, and the power of prayer from her mother. The religious mother of three had particular devotion to Saint Bernadette and frequently prayed for Tekki and her physical challenges.

Tekki's father, Eddie, provided an earthier education. The businessman, a tailor by trade and owner of a garment factory, made most of his daughter's clothes. Something of a daredevil, he often took Tekki and her brothers for spectacular rides on his motorcycle. They often tooled around town, laughing hysterically as the wind wildly tousled their hair.

During Tekki's many hospital stays, after working long hours at the factory, Eddie visited his daughter. Though frequently getting to the hospital after regular visiting hours, the brash, unyielding, and outspoken man would "swear his way in" so that he could see Tekki. Once at her bedside, Tekki recalls how the stark hospital room would brighten with her father's presence. The pale green walls and fluorescent lights seemed less cold when Eddie sat next to her on the bleached white sheets.

During his visits, Eddie delighted Tekki with outrageous tales about the characters he knew from his factory. His anecdotes gave the tiny patient a happy lift and fueled her imagination, paving the way for a future passion for storytelling.

Her father's risk-taking and outrageous behaviors balanced her mother's more pious personality. Tekki appreciated the contrast. Each parent satisfied a different aspect of her nature. She enjoyed the variety.

Aside from surgeries and recovery periods, when Tekki had to be carried everywhere, both her parents expected their daughter to get along normally. Eddie pushed Tekki to take risks and she got his message: "You can do anything you set your mind to do." She saw her father as invincible, and she believed she had the same indomitable genes.

Throughout her childhood, if she felt down or depressed, her parents would tell her, "Stop feeling sorry for yourself, you're no different from anyone else." Looking back, Tekki remembers that their attitude made her feel good and strengthened, as though she *could* be like average-sized children. She worked harder and fought more to be a "regular kid," in spite of her disabilities. As a result, she expected more from herself and accomplished more than she otherwise might have.

Though she recognizes the positive influence of that attitude, Tekki also acknowledges that it prevented her from fully feeling the emotional impact of her physical dissimilarity. In fact, Tekki recalls, her parents made so much effort to focus their attention on issues that did not relate to her size and disability that she "didn't even feel that it was okay to go there." She never realized how profoundly she grieved for her unusual body and did not truly "deal with the sadness around being different." Consequently, she harbored deep feelings about "not being good enough," subconsciously believing she could never measure up to her average-sized peers.

As a result, Tekki developed an extraordinary ability to disconnect from emotions relating to her size, disabilities, and her body image. Although she now thinks her attitude became a protective barrier during her youth, those sad feelings mushroomed in her soul and became the deep, dark secret she kept from everyone—especially herself.

Her parents' encouragement and a healthy relationship with her brothers enabled her to easily make friends with the neighborhood boys. During the early years, Tekki had more boy than girl friends. Her parents, especially her father, goaded Tekki into seeing herself on an equal footing with the boys. It served her so well in the workplace that later in her life a therapist told Tekki to "go home and thank your parents."

By junior high school, the contrasts between Tekki and the other children became more distinct. Classmates started growing taller. Boys looked at girls with new interest and the girls responded. Though Tekki could share some of the new excitement with her friends, like hair and make-up tips, other rites of passage eluded her.

When the girls began wearing stockings every day and showing off their legs, Tekki did not. In those days before pantyhose, stockings provided nothing but pain and trouble for her as she struggled to pull a garter belt over her legs and hips. Sometimes she felt like a referee in a match between her nylons and her unbending feet, straining to get everything straight and attached. Except for special occasions, Tekki resigned herself to wearing "extremely nerdy" short white socks. The boys noticed by *not* noticing.

Unable to compete socially with the other girls, Tekki began her teen years with feelings of ambition combined with loneliness. Those feelings lessened one summer when one of her classmates underwent treatment for scoliosis. Like Tekki, Cassie wore a full back brace. At the end of the school year, finding common ground between them, they developed a friendship. They enjoyed a wonderful summer of swapping stories and sharing girlish giggles. When they returned to school in September, though they saw less of each other, they remained friendly.

In late October, the school presented its annual Halloween talent show. Cassie's brace came off just in time for her to participate in it. On the day of the performance, Tekki sat in the audience as Cassie danced onto the stage wearing a leotard and tutu. Appearing for the first time in front of a large group without her back brace, Cassie treated the show as a sort of coming-out party—like a butterfly emerging from her cocoon. When the audience saw her, they rose to their feet and applauded her triumph.

Through the darkness of the theater, Tekki peered over the seats in front of her and at the brightly lit stage. An angst-ridden knowing crept into her mind and permeated her body. Comparing herself to Cassie, Tekki realized *she* would *never* be cured of her condition. She remembers thinking, "There was no 'fix' for me...no matter how long I wore my back brace, I would never be miraculously cured [of being a little person]...I would always be different." The full force of that reality hit Tekki for the first time in her life, and it devastated her.

Though the new and difficult awareness registered in Tekki's mind, she did her best to deny her pain. She pressed onward. Unlike Cassie during her spectacular stage show, no one applauded Tekki's daily victories. In fact, almost no one even knew the challenges she faced, how completing even the smallest of tasks often demanded an incredible strength of will. While the rest of the world thought nothing of dressing themselves, tying their shoes, or climbing a steep set of stairs, the same acts demonstrated mammoth achievements for the young girl.

By the time she entered high school, Tekki felt "swallowed up" by the eight hundred-member class. Like most teenagers, her appearance became a huge part of her life. Physical differences became even more apparent, and her self-talk reflected it. "I will never be as attractive as an average-sized girl," she would tell herself and feel sad by what she believed that meant. Much like the overweight girl, the one who is too tall, and the girl with striking, prominent features, Tekki believed she would never be good enough or pretty enough to attract a boyfriend.

Convinced that "I don't deserve to be treated well because I'm weird looking," when it came to dating, Tekki tolerated unacceptable behaviors from boys. If she went out with one and the boy looked longingly at an average-sized girl, she blamed herself. "I'm a fat pig," she berated, "so it doesn't surprise me that he would look at other women. It's natural." And her self-talk continuously affirmed her negative body image. Decidedly telling herself, "If I were thin, or if I were tall, he wouldn't look at other girls," she allowed boys to put her down. Always, she believed she had the problem. Seldom, *if ever*, did she consider that the boys she dated had their own insecurities or were just plain jerks.

Fortunately, in the spring of her freshman year, Tekki looked for an extra-curricular activity and found the theater—and Les Zunkel. The young teacher inspired Tekki and believed that anyone could make it in the theater. Encouraged by Mr. Zunkel, Tekki says she became absorbed into the make-believe world. She felt as though she fit in and, as a result, she thrived. In addition to making sets, acting, singing, and directing, she played many substantial parts. By playing different roles, she could be whomever and whatever she wanted. Through Tekki's theater experience, her heart opened up and she felt free.

Much to her surprise, as a result of her theatrical exploits, she gained some prominence in school circles. She enjoyed the positive attention and had a lot of fun. Her senior class voted her homecoming queen, though she is quick to point out the contest stressed popularity rather than beauty. Still, when she graduated in June 1974, she approached college in an upbeat mood. She felt good about herself and her future.

That fall, Tekki entered Rosary College, initially planning to earn dual degrees in French and English. She quickly shifted her focus to English alone, thinking it would better match her career interests, especially the theatrical ones.

Though she had a healthy respect for her studies, like most college students Tekki also enjoyed an active social life. Since she knew no other dwarfs (Tekki did not become a member of the Little People of America until age twenty-five), she dated average-sized men. She found the greatest mutual attractions with guys who stood out in a crowd, ones who either looked different from the norm or who displayed rebellious behaviors.

In contrast to her high school crushes, college dating took on a different and more serious tone. She wanted to find love and romance. Unfortunately, like many young women her age, Tekki lacked a strong, positive sense of herself. Though she had much to offer, like her high energy, kind spirit, and quick wit, she still didn't think a man would be attracted to her for all her good qualities. Without a positive internal experience, and wanting to be appealing to men, Tekki concluded that sex offered a logical doorway into a relationship. Also, the physical connection provided two additional benefits. Physical attachments enabled her to be in touch with her own body in a pain-free way and, at the same time, they provided a way for Tekki to compete with average-sized women.

Once with a man, Tekki usually idealized a dating connection, often putting high expectations on the relationship. Losing herself in the daydreams of love, she remembers needing constant reassurance of a boyfriend's affections, even if it meant that they talked down to her or treated her badly. She painfully recalls, "I had no worth if that person didn't love me. I would fantasize the relationship to such a degree—sort of the 'knight in shining armor' thing—that when the men were just real people, I couldn't take it and thought I was worthless."

When a liaison did not work out the way she wanted, Tekki would feel seriously let down. Sometimes the boyfriend could be blamed, but often her own belittling self-talk contributed to the weakening of the couple's bond. After time, to avoid disappointment and affirm her worth, she began to sabotage her relationships by anticipating endings, conceding, "I got out before they could break up with me."

During those days, her love life followed a prickly pattern: meet a boy, go out, become intimate, break up. Though she seldom got involved with more than one boy at a time, she maintained a steady succession of boyfriends or "serial dating" as she now refers to it. Though her behaviors stemmed from a fear of disappointment and rejection, the love 'em and leave 'em attitude enabled Tekki to feel in control and push aside her feelings of being "not good enough." Tekki would later discover how those debilitating emotions played a recurring theme in her relationships, one that insidiously entered most all her interactions with both men and women through much of her early adult life.

By her junior year in college, she felt ready for new academic challenges. Encouraged by her challenge-loving father, Tekki took advantage of a college-sponsored program to spend a semester in London. Soaking up the historical and theatrical culture, she enjoyed the country's unfamiliar customs and newfound friends.

During Thanksgiving, Tekki's mother visited her daughter in England. Her mother had not been to Europe, but often said that if she ever had the opportunity, she wanted to travel to Lourdes, France, and visit the shrine of Saint Bernadette. According to religious legend, The Blessed Mother appeared to Bernadette, then a lowly peasant girl, and spoke to her. In the days and weeks that followed the apparition, many healings took place at the spot, and it became a world-renowned shrine.

Wanting to do something nice for her mother while she visited, Tekki arranged for the two to make the trip from London to Lourdes. Tekki had only a mild interest in going, but liked her mother's excitement. At the time she had no idea how the excursion would become one of the most significant emotional experiences of her life.

They arrived at the world-famous grotto during the off season. Without the usual throngs of tourists and religious groups, the two women could enjoy the experience almost without interruption. They walked up to the shrine. There, on top of a steep hill and nestled in a stonewall alcove, they saw a statue of the Blessed Mother reportedly in the exact spot she had appeared to Bernadette.

Though Tekki admits that she seldom followed the rituals of her faith during that time in her life, she could not ignore being touched by the awesome experience. When she sat on the benches that dotted the holy space, she couldn't help but feel its sacredness. Her soul soaked in the powerful energy of the holy place as she heard the tinkling sound of water trickling through the grey-black stone that encircled the statue. The heart connection she felt compared to nothing in her experience, and she recalls it as one of the most profound moments of her life.

As the pair departed the holy shrine, both felt moved. Shortly afterward, however, on the way back to their hotel, a vague but disturbing feeling overtook Tekki. She remembered how, as a young girl, she often heard her mother telling people that a visit to this holy place would result in Tekki's healing. The long forgotten childhood memories flooded into her conscious mind and agitated the peacefulness of her soul. As the bus rattled down the road and back into town, Tekki began thinking how her mother must have felt because, still disabled, Tekki obviously failed to be granted "the cure."

The more she thought about it, the angrier Tekki became. By the time they returned to the hotel, she could barely wait until they entered the small hotel room. Once inside the sparsely furnished room, Tekki blew up at her mother. Feeling the old "not good enough" and "Why can't you accept me for who I am?" feelings, she sarcastically apologized to her mother for not being granted a miraculous healing.

To Tekki's surprise, her mother looked stunned by the accusation and the defensive apology. Calmly and quietly, the older woman sat on a hard, wooden chair. She looked at her daughter with tears in her eyes and spoke quietly. "I didn't come here looking for a miracle," she whispered. "I came to thank God for all that you are."

Her mother's expression touched Tekki's heart, and humbled her. She remembered the Cassie experience and how hard she took the realization that she would always have a disability. She spent a lifetime wanting to be "regular" and "cured." Until that moment, she never really understood that she had unique qualities—having nothing to do with her size—that made her stand out from others in a positive way. The moment changed her life. "Wow," she thought as the words sunk in, "I'd better live up to [her gratitude to God]."

After her mother returned home, Tekki thought about the trip to Lourdes. For the first time, Tekki no longer presumed that her mother thought she had the kind of problems only divine intervention could resolve. She began to understand that for many years, like many daughters, she must have projected *her own feelings of insecurity* into every conversation she had with her mother. Instead of hearing whatever positive things her mother might actually have been saying, she filtered the words through her own lack of confidence. Under the impression made by the faulty interpretation, she reacted negatively toward her mother, and toward herself.

At the end of that semester, Tekki returned to Chicago. It astounded her to think that, for years, her mother actually felt proud that she never gave in or gave up...and Tekki had never realized it. Tekki felt proud to know that her mother admired her strength and resilience. In the years that followed, the mother-daughter relationship grew even dearer to both women.

The experience started a new pattern in Tekki's mind. Amazed that she could have misinterpreted her mother's conversations for so long, Tekki began questioning other feelings, especially the ones that focused on her impressions of other people's perceptions of her. She wondered if "not good enough" could be coming from her and *not* from others, as she always presumed. The thought process eventually led to a personal epiphany—but not for a while, and not until she faced the private demons that lurked deep inside.

After graduating from college, while still dabbling in theater, Tekki used her English degree to secure a job in advertising. She worked her way up to copy chief, a manager of copywriters. A few years later, deciding she wanted more time and flexibility to develop her stage interests, she left the regular working world to freelance.

Around the same time, her father suffered congestive heart failure. He had a history of heart disease and had recovered from two heart attacks, one at thirty-five and the other at forty-five. At age sixty-three, Eddie's heart gave out and he did not recover.

Unbelieving and dazed, she kept asking, "How could he die?" It seemed impossible to her that the invincible, risk-taking, and motorcycle-riding businessman could be dead.

Feeling numb and dumbstruck by the loss, Tekki grieved her father's death deeply. To medicate her feelings of grief and sorrow, she used men and relationships much the way another person might use food or alcohol. However, the affairs didn't make her feel good. Instead, she still felt sad and empty.

Tired of the dating merry-go-round, Tekki began rethinking her relationships. Curiious if being with average-sized men created too many insecurity issues for her, she stopped dating them. For the first time, Tekki focused her interests on men who were also little people. She thought, "I wouldn't have the same problems. I wouldn't be competing with average-sized women... I would feel total acceptance."

Unfortunately, instead of feeling better and more comfortable, nothing changed. "What I didn't know is that I didn't accept myself," Tekki explains. She had yet to learn that without self-acceptance and self-love, nothing else worked. Neither of those positive feelings can come from anyone outside. Both are gifts each woman must give to herself.

Though other dwarfs could better understand Tekki's physical challenges, when she dated them she didn't feel more secure or cherished. Tekki discovered that, while they shared similar physical experiences, many of them also experienced the same negative feelings about being different. Those feelings often surfaced in a relationship. As a result, Tekki still felt the need to use the same "dump him before he dumps me" sabotaging behavior. The serial dating she thought would dissipate when she dated other dwarfs did not stop.

After a while, Tekki began thinking that if the same behaviors happened with both average-sized men and dwarfs, maybe it was not about them. She realized that if the pattern played out with all men, then "something was going on with me for putting up with them." In addition, she started thinking that the intimacy she craved had more to do with some unknown need than true desire.

The more she considered it, Tekki began seeing how easily she could lose herself in a man and his life. As she recalled her relationships, she noticed that when a boyfriend did not constantly reassure her by professing his love, she became anxious. She realized she needed a man's approval and acceptance more than she wanted or thought could be healthy. Confused, she began questioning herself and her motivations.

Then she met Craig at a Little People of America meeting. Afflicted with brittle bone disease, he used a wheelchair. Though very small and odd-looking, Craig had an exceptionally funny, Woody Allen-like sense of humor. And in spite of his disability, he lived something of a thrill-seeking life. He taunted fate by engaging in risky activities like horseback riding and skydiving; over the years, he had broken over a hundred bones performing his daring escapades.

Tekki and Craig dated a few times and had a lot of fun together. He made Tekki laugh and she fell in love with his "devil-may-care, every-day-is-a-party attitude." Though they had a few kissing sessions in the car, it didn't go further. One night Craig came back to Tekki's apartment. After kissing for a while, Craig began advancing the activity. While he did, he told Tekki, "Well, you're not the girl from Ipanema, but I love you." His words stunned her. "I couldn't believe my ears," Tekki remembers painfully. "I realized that even with a little person I wasn't good enough. I did not say anything at the time, because I felt terrible about myself." Still, an icy chill came over Tekki and she ended the evening.

The next weekend, Tekki and Craig double-dated with two of Tekki's friends. She noticed him shooting lascivious looks at every average-sized woman who walked past them. While it bothered her, she said nothing. Other, similar incidents occurred, but she tolerated them out of a fear of being alone. "If I were without a boyfriend," she admits, "then there was something wrong with me. I wasn't desirable."

One night, as Tekki and Craig shared an intimate moment, he began singing to her. "You are so beautiful," he crooned...and then emphasized "to *me*." Tekki understood the implication of his intonation. She lost it. Scraping together whatever dignity and self-love she could muster, she screamed, "I am beautiful to a lot of people." In that moment, Tekki understood that she no longer wanted to feel less than other women. She no longer desired to feel that she must have a man in her life. She wanted to be finished with men who looked suggestively at other women, frequented strip clubs, or demonstrated behaviors that felt disrespectful to her.

After long hours of soul-searching, along with helpful support from friends, Tekki faced the fact that she had a problem. As any addict who desired sobriety would do, she sought therapy and a twelve-step program for recovery. She found the first of several therapists and joined Sex and Love Addicts Anonymous (SLAA).

Through months of therapy and support group meetings, Tekki began to understand how she used sex to assuage a deep loathing for her own body. With the encouragement of both the recovery program and her therapist, she decided to abstain from sex and relationships. Instead of using her body to mask or medicate her feelings, she forced herself to get in touch with the profound grief she felt about her body and its differences.

At first, being honest about her feelings proved to be challenging. Though she successfully dealt with her disability daily, Tekki had a lifetime pattern of denial about her body image. She had no real sense of her inner self or what made her special and unique, except for her size. Now it seemed that her recovery focused on nothing else. The singular concentration annoyed her, mostly because she'd spent a lifetime ignoring or denying those all-important feelings.

Simultaneously, Tekki got in touch with previously unconscious hidden jealousies and a surprising but powerful anger she felt toward average-sized women. Once aware of it and though it took considerable time and energy, Tekki began addressing the newly discovered feelings with therapy and new, self-affirming inner dialogue.

Tekki stuck with it, and became more willing to get through to her true self. Rather than use any of the unproductive patterns that enabled her to feel better, equal, or in control, she focused instead on every sensation, "being with the feelings," and letting them come out.

Throughout her first year in SLAA and in keeping with the program, Tekki dared herself to find ways of expressing her feelings that did not include a romantic encounter. Instead of peeling off her clothes for a man, instead she shed unwanted emotions. She realized that, whether with her parents, boyfriends, or others, she consistently had made up negative stories about what they thought or how they felt about her. Sitting in her apartment, looking at the pictures and knick-knacks that chronicled the thirty-odd years of her life, Tekki cried for hours on end...for her dwarfism, her fused clubfeet, her twisted back, her poor body image, and for every good trait—like her sensitivity and wit—that she neglected to celebrate while searching for love. She grieved for how often she incorrectly mind-read a boyfriend's intentions and sabotaged her own success in a relationship.

In spite of her fears, and trusting that she could weather the storm of painful revelations, she started conversations and opened dialogs. In doing so, she spoke honestly from her head and heart rather than from a fear of rejection. Instead of presuming she knew what others thought or expected, she asked, "This is what I think you expect of me, what is the reality?" As a result, she began to establish some great relationships with family, friends, co-workers, and even former lovers.

Breaking through the emotional numbness that guarded her during childhood, Tekki allowed herself to feel vulnerable. She patiently practiced the twelve steps, beginning with "I admit that I am powerless over sex and romance and my life has become unmanageable." As she worked her way from first to last, she wrote about her experiences in a journal. Slowly, the adult woman, silenced for so long, began to emerge.

As healing gradually replaced hurt, Tekki began to understand something new about herself. "I had never brought out the real me in a relationship," Tekki concluded. She began to see that she denied her true self in every relationship, with men *and* women. Appreciating herself in a new way, she discovered, "What made me different was not my body; what made me different was my gift of being able to be with people, to really listen and have compassion."

Then she wondered that if she could no longer use sex, love, or fantasy to survive, *what would she do instead?*

Her days at Resurrection Hospital came back to her. She endured those awful weeks with storytelling. Sister Mary Thecla's anecdotes from her Polish upbringing, and her father's chronicles from the garment district made her laugh, cry, and dream. Mr. Zunkel's acting and directing lessons transformed her high school days into a great experience. She always had a passion for the theater, enough so that she gave up a steady, paying job for greater flexibility and time to pursue acting. Yet after all that, she felt as though she still just dabbled in the theater.

Slowly it dawned on Tekki how much her body image affected her ability to fully embrace the acting profession. Throughout her life she resisted parts that had a "Mini-Me" feel to them, as well as those that made gratuitous use of dwarfs. When she did well in a significant role, Tekki doubted the praise she received. Through her narrow self-deprecating prism, she couldn't see how a compliment reflected the depth she brought to a character. She invariably questioned if the good wishes came because she played the part well or because she did well...*for her size.* As a result, she never thought she could be "good enough" and talked herself into self-fulfilling mediocrity.

When she stopped using men to distract her, she began developing a greater love for herself and her many talents. She came to understand that if she wanted to act, she would have to work harder and take her true passion more seriously. She would have to find her niche by creating it, something she wouldn't be able to do by just dipping her toes into the theatrical waters. If Tekki wanted to be everything she could be, she had to plunge fearlessly into the thespian ocean. She challenged herself to "forge a career in theater and find a heart connection with audiences who could relate...because of the differences inside of them." Remembering her father's message to "go for it," Tekki decided she would put all her energies into acting and become fully engaged in pursuits of the stage.

With that goal in mind, she started writing more, took classes, and joined a playwriting group. Rather than giving the acting profession virtual lip service, she devoted herself to the true work of an actor, including asking for constructive critique, something she had previously avoided.

The greater her effort, the better she got. Happily, her "creativity finally blossomed." The more seriously she took her work, the less seriously she took herself. Feeling more relaxed about herself and her body, she bared her soul and entered into a fuller experience of life.

She soon heard about The Blue Rider, a small experimental theater in Chicago's artsy Pilsen neighborhood. Its director, Donna Blue Lachman, created improvisational theater based on personal experiences. When Donna Blue offered a performance and composition workshop, Tekki signed up. The class gave Tekki the opportunity to expand the parameters of her talent, and confront obstacles to accomplishment.

As part of a discussion, she wondered aloud how she could be an effective actor if she could not move around the stage the way other actors could. Lachman heard the pain in Tekki's voice. She shared with her a story about one of her own mentors, Devora Bartonov, a former ballerina. Being of advanced age, the ballerina could no longer move around the stage the way her counterparts did. Yet she refused to allow her lack of movement to be a concern. Describing the body as a vehicle, the dancer explained that it is the spirit that moves a performer. Slowly but gracefully raising her aged arm and pointing upward, she affirmed, "Your *soul* points the way though space."

As Tekki heard the story, something good exploded in her head and she instantly understood. She had a seismic shift in her thoughts about ability versus disability. All this time, the continual negative focus on body image prevented her big heart and jovial soul from finding their best expression through her full-bodied, powerful voice. From that moment on, Tekki decided she would *let her soul point the way*, allowing the power of her words to carry the story to her audiences—even if her body could not.

As though fulfilling the old adage, "When the student is ready, the teacher appears," the Blue Rider workshop generated a new level of openness within her. Suddenly freed from the sabotaging thoughts that stole her passion, she turned a corner and walked in a new direction.

Not long afterward, an old friend from her advertising days invited her to visit him at his new home at Harbin Hot Springs in California. Tom knew about SLAA, Tekki's therapy, and her dreams for the future. He seemed convinced that Tekki would find the spa experience healing. She reluctantly agreed to go.

Harbin Hot Springs reminded her of a hippie place, one that time forgot. People had traveled to this spa for over a hundred years to soak in the healing pools of water. Nestled deep in the woods, the health resort generally attracted a comfortable, almost disheveled-looking crowd of people sporting ripped jeans, beads, and crystals.

After passing through the vestibule of the lodge, Tekki nervously entered the "clothing-optional" area. Wearing a robe, she walked toward the springs. She didn't know what she'd do when she got to the water. She wondered what people might think of seeing a dwarf walking around naked.

On that soft summer night, she looked at people with no clothing, and also no awkwardness. To her amazement, as she laid her robe on a nearby chair, she felt no discomfort or self-consciousness. In the dim light of sunset's afterglow, she saw a sea of bodies. Some were tall and lean while others were short, fat, thin, smooth, or wrinkled. Tekki saw people with short hair and men and women with hair growing to their waist. She also saw people whose bodies showed the effects of life, some showed the ravages of past illness, while others revealed surgical scars or missing parts.

Instead of the embarrassment she expected, it suddenly struck Tekki that the spa allowed people's truest humanity to shine gloriously. The real life images that surrounded her stood in stark contrast to the airbrushed and make-up laden facades that are often passed off as reality, the veneer-only pictures that tend to diminish the average person.

As she approached one of the pools, she noticed the wide, peaceful silence. Step by step, Tekki began her descent into the warm waters. Little by little, she let go...of anything and everything. As the water enveloped her body, it became a powerful force for healing. After a while, floating atop the warm water, she watched the moon rise gloriously into the sky. She delighted in the spectacle of the twinkling stars. She felt comforted by the silhouette of the evergreen trees against the night sky.

While she embraced the experience, an amazing scene unfolded before her eyes. A mother and her two adult daughters entered the water. Tekki noticed the older woman had only one breast. While adjusting to seeing a mastectomy for the first time, she sensed a beauty about this particular woman, a serene, almost saint-like quality. It captivated Tekki.

As the younger women guided their mother down the small steps and into the water, they held her close, and Tekki could hear them telling her, "We love you. You are still beautiful."

As she watched the three women and their sacred experience, a new awareness washed over Tekki. Her heart conveyed a new thought to her mind, helping her to realize, "My body was just a container of sorts, that my soul was what counted." She also began feeling, "how precious my body is since it is the one I was given." The internal revelation became another turning point. For the first time, she respected her body, and in that moment, Tekki says, "I began to love my body."

Afterward, she threw herself into theater work, and "everything started happening." She and two friends, Michael Blackwell and Nancy Neven Shelton, wrote their first play. As they prepared to present *When Heck Was a Puppy: The Living Testimonies of Folk Artist Edna Mae Brice* at The Blue Rider, Michael met the mayor's spouse at a local cultural event. He invited Maggie Daley to the production. Though she could not attend, she sent her staff. They loved it.

As Tekki's good fortune would have it, Maggie Daley and her staff already had an idea to provide a program involving disabled children and the arts. As they began putting a plan together, the team sought teachers and performers for the project. After her team saw *When Heck Was a Puppy*, Mrs. Daley recruited Tekki, asking her to be one of a team of artists who would develop and present a workshop for children.

Until then, Tekki never considered doing any work with kids. Yet once presented to her, the idea "felt like home." In constructing the workshop, called The Magic City Camp, Tekki created a space where disabled children could test their talents, work with each other, and have fun. She taught them how to write a play together, and showed them how to act in it. Her young playwright performers included children with cerebral palsy, brain damage, and other physical disabilities.

As Tekki worked with the children, she saw herself through their experience. She recognized that a child's uniqueness came from personality, not disability. Not only did that help her integrate that knowledge into her own being, but she also "began to feel like a warrior for equality for children with disabilities."

The initial workshop effort proved so successful that Maggie Daley brought Tekki back for another year. At the end of the second year, Mrs. Daley decided to bring The Magic City Camp into Chicago's award-winning Gallery 37. It became part of The Connections Program.

Shortly thereafter, the same creative trio formed Tellin' Tales Theatre, where the performers "gather the stories of groups and individuals" and use them to facilitate heart healing. Tekki loves her work with Tellin' Tales. It attracts other actors and writers who tell their own stories through performance.

In 1998, inspired by The Connections Program, Tekki created a project she called *Six Stories Up* for her Tellin' Tales Theatre. Its mission is to bring together diverse groups, including children with disabilities, and "create theatrically innovative performances using mentoring and collaboration." The objective is to help both performers and audiences "recognize their commonalities and build a sense of community."

Partially funded by a city arts grant, the annual project pairs six well-known storytellers with six Chicago middle school children who work together with a diverse stage crew. The mentoring program culminates in a full theater production.

For the first few years, with money from fundraisers and generous donors, Tellin' Tales rented space for *Six Stories Up* from The Blue Rider Theater. When the theater closed its doors, Tekki searched for other places to stage the production. Because the show's theme centered on hospital stories of patients, they sought the patronage of Dr. David McLone, a noted pediatric neurologist. With his assistance, Children's Memorial Hospital agreed to partner with Tellin' Tales to produce *Six Stories Up in Pediatrics*, a show promising patrons "hilarious healing, contagious laughter, and infectious fun."

Of all her accomplishments, Tekki is most proud of her work with *Six Stories Up*, including her ability to keep it running year after year. Through the program, Tekki passes along to children with disabilities the same messages of hope and encouragement that she received from her father, Mr. Zunkel, and others who supported her progress along the way. Her victory path is wide enough for Tekki *and* the young people, as she helps them take steps toward creating their personal victories. She has high praise for the children, professing, "More and more kids participate and gain self-esteem...[they] learn that they can do anything they set their minds to."

At the same time, the children teach Tekki. Their unique talents become an illustration of their multi-faceted gifts and vulnerability, as well as her own. Their candor forces her to be always honest about the scope of her physical capabilities. They help her remember that she does not have to hide her disability when she can't do something because of it. Also, they remind her to keep on loving herself just the way she is, dwarfed body and all.

Her work with children is beginning to come full circle. Tekki recently brought back several graduates from her first project. Seven years after their first *Six Stories Up* adventure, the disabled youths returned as mentors for adults who never before participated in theater. With guidance from the teenagers, they wrote, produced, and acted in a full-length play. They called the turnabout *Six Stories Upside Down*.

When she reflects on her achievements, including the small victories of daily living, she surprises herself. A retrospective picture does not reflect the daily struggles. "Sometimes I don't know how I had the strength to jump into the unknown," she laughs. But experience taught her simply to look at the next action and say, "I'll do it." Step by step, the days add up and make a life — and create a victory.

When she feels like giving up, which Tekki admits happens "just about everyday," she remembers that life goes on, and there is always new growth taking place both in the world and within her. "When the sun comes up, it's a new day," she waxes philosophically. When she wakes up to it, Tekki sees an untouched canvas and finds a renewed strength. She keeps going and gets stronger.

Also, through a spiritual alliance called The Institute for Self-Actualization (ISA), Tekki has learned that "at the point of quitting...we as humans are at the edge of something really successful and exciting—and if we go for it and don't quit—we get to the next level...I know that if I don't quit...I get more and more support." As a result, Tekki learned that even when the strides are short, the progress is sure and her victory assured.

Though Tekki will always have to deal with dwarfism and disabilities, she has reached a point of acceptance and peace about her life and her body. Tekki now understands that her problems of the past occurred not so much because her body held her back, but instead because *she* held back her body. Now she embraces *all* of whom she is, including the beauty of her stature.

STEPPING STONES
TO VICTORY

Having overcome many challenges that stemmed from her disabilities and a poor body image, Tekki cautions women not to let physical attributes dictate quality of life. "Stay true to yourself," she advises. Focus less importance on your physical imperfections and more on your unique and special qualities. Tekki promises, "If you are able to show your heart, your beauty can't help but come out...from there, **your soul will shine**." Start now.

1. Choose five positive, non-physical characteristics or behaviors that make you special. Write these in your Victory Journal. Think about qualities like integrity, determination, positive attitude, and behaviors such as being assertive, a skilled problem solver, a good mentor, or an excellent listener.

    a. Write three examples or short stories of how those personality traits helped you make a difference for yourself, a family member or friend, or at work.

    b. When you're finished, read your stories. How do they make you feel about yourself? Record those feelings in your Victory Journal.

2. Get a bigger picture of yourself. Ask three family members, friends, and co-workers (three each!) to tell you *one characteristic* about yourself that makes you *positively different*. Ask them if they can tell you a story that demonstrates that characteristic. Record their responses in your Victory Journal.

3. Because she didn't want to be alone, Tekki found herself tolerating men's demeaning behaviors. The relationships failed

to fill her up, and instead they drained her energy and distracted her from fulfilling her purpose in life. Have you had a similar experience? Have you ever allowed a partnership, one that was supposed to be loving and supportive, to become all-consuming and invisible to yourself?

    a. Write the story of the relationship(s) in your journal.

    b. After writing it, read your story and think about how it happened. Usually, a woman accepts bad behaviors when she has a mental or emotional need that she believes cannot or will not be filled. What need were you trying to meet in this relationship? Was it acceptance, love, attention, the need to be needed, or something else?

    c. What are other, more positive ways that you can get that need met? If you can't think of any yourself, talk to others. Generate at least three other ways of having that need satisfied.

4. When your needs are met, you are not in a constant state of wanting. As a result, you feel better about yourself and are more likely to grow into your potential. In your journal, make a list of twenty-five needs. Here's a sample list of needs:

    ❧ to be accepted, approved of, praised, loved, heard, validated, listened to, cared about, in control, self-reliant, in balance, mentally strong, emotionally strong, physically strong, secure, responsible, irresponsible, quiet, passionate, remembered, and valued.

    a. Of your twenty-five needs, what are the top three needs that are important to you daily? Circle those three.

    b. To get those needs met, you must help people in your life know what to do for you. For example, if you need balance in your daily life but are extremely busy, ask someone (spouse, parent, friend) to help you. Maybe they can stay with your kids for an hour each week to allow you some alone time (and ask three people, so you get three one-hour breaks). If you need to be heard, especially by your partner, ask him/her to agree to give you a block of time each day or a few times each week during which s/he will give you undivided attention. If you want to be praised, tell the people in your life how important it is and ask them to tell you when you do something praiseworthy.

5. To build greater self-esteem, think about someone who makes you feel less than who you are. What does s/he do that makes you feel that way? How can you stop it from happening?

   Write down five situations and their accompanying, affirmative responses.

EXAMPLES:

Situation	Response
Jeff never requests my help, but tries to guilt me into doing something. He drops hints to make me feel bad until I give in and he gets what he wants. I don't like the manipulation.	From now on I'll tell him, "Guilt doesn't work anymore. If you'd like my help, you'll have to ask for it." And then I'll stick to it.
Martin never lets me finish a sentence. I feel that this is disrespectful and as if what I have to say doesn't matter to him.	When he interrupts me, I'll tell him, "You cannot interrupt me while I'm speaking." I'll repeat it until he understands...or refuse to continue our conversation.
My sister always criticizes my words, actions, and opinions.	I'll say, "I don't accept criticism, only feedback. Be constructive, or I don't want to hear it."

6. Tekki found support through her theater friends, SLAA, and ISA. Having a person or group that supports you in the process of change is critically important to your success. As you practice getting a bigger picture of yourself, getting needs met, and stopping unsupportive behaviors, a mentor can be a great help.

   a. Who can you find to mentor you in developing those traits? Create a list that includes professional personnel, such as psychologists and life coaches, as well as a trusted family member or friend, a teacher, or guidance counselor.

   b. Contact two of these people from the list. If they are paid professionals, set up appointments and get started. If they are "volunteers," set up a regular time and place to meet. The easiest place may be a local bookstore or coffee shop...*and you buy the coffee!*

11

Shaping Life's Challenges into Personal Victories

WHEN CONFRONTED WITH A DIFFICULT CIRCUM-
stance, how does the Victorious Woman motivate herself to take the first steps toward victory? Does she depend on
inner drive alone or do particular external conditions push her
forward? Staying the course, especially when the odds are against
her or the path gets rough, is often a greater challenge. How does
a woman do it? These are some of the questions I sought answers
for in my quest to define the Victorious Woman.

Through interviews and group discussions, I listened to countless individual stories. These accounts validated some of my pre-
conceived theories, and debunked others.

I presumed, for example, that victory always began with a

deliberate, thought-out choice. In fact, it occurs most often as a courageous response to an unwanted turn of events, such as illness, abuse, or abandonment. When Maureen Ingelsby returned home one night, she saw John's packed suitcases. Her puzzlement turned to shock only moments later when John told Maureen he was leaving her and their five children. She had no plan and no thoughts, just confusion. Victory resulted from a resolve to keep her family together. When Alisa Morkides opened up an espresso café and it became a success, she defied the odds. However, bringing the business back from near bankruptcy challenged her internal resources in a wholly different way. What she learned from this experience bestowed a victory with a richer and more satisfying texture than success alone could ever have provided.

After analyzing the life stories of these victorious women, a specific pattern became apparent. I noticed that certain thoughts and behaviors were followed by palpable actions that enabled a woman to shape a victory out of personal difficulties. The Victorious Woman Model emerged. While the archetype itself confirmed many of my presuppositions, other aspects of the Victorious Woman did not.

I assumed that when she finds the right direction, a woman gets on track and keeps going. In reality, however, at the outset of the journey, few women step onto their victory path with ease and confidence. All agreed that their experience felt more like climbing the uphill side of a mountain. Also, on the way to their victory, most experienced considerable anxiety while developing assertive and empowering responses to problems. Toni Kershaw simply wanted to be the best mother and agonized as she struggled to balance her own health requirements with those of her bulimic and anorexic daughter. Though Nancy Hill did not want to continue cleaning houses, she felt nervously ill-equipped for office work and almost didn't interview for the job. That small step alone became a victory in itself. In order to advance to victory, both women pushed through their discomfort and learned to overcome previously unproductive behaviors.

Time and again the centerpiece of many discussions became the very definition of victory in relationship to women. As dialogs developed, I discovered that, for the most part, women seldom thought about victory in ways that relate to a feminine model. The general understanding of victory seems to take place only within the framework of seemingly masculine constructs such as war, sports, contests, competitions, and politics.

As women, if we want victory to be a theme in the book of each of our lives, we need to define it in a way that is meaningful and relevant to us. A woman's victory must be something that is acknowledged and respected. We cannot allow it to be considered a trite event.

With both individuals and groups, first attempts at defining a feminine model of victory evoked murky characterizations. As conversations continued and women dug into their inner beings, they became clearer and more literal. They described the Victorious Woman as one who "knows who she is, comfortable in her own skin," "realizes her value," "makes choices," "believes in herself," "overcomes obstacles and they become strengths," "able to take risks," "lives her passion," and other positive characteristics.

When considering their own relationship to victory, a number of women experienced light bulb moments. One woman summarized the words of many when she admitted that, even though she used the word "victory" all her life, until our discussion she would never have thought about it in terms of anything *she* ever did. Afterward, she realized she would forever relate to victory in a whole new way.

After studying the Victorious Woman, I realized that not one victory transpired because a woman waited until some Good Samaritan rescued her. On the contrary, each victory resulted from proactive, practical, and focused thoughts and behaviors. Though she may have sought help and accepted assistance, the Victorious Woman set a process in motion and followed it through to the end. When Maureen Ingelsby's marriage suddenly ended and she became a single mother, she made a plan and took immediate action. Her first job did not pay well, but it allowed Maureen to bring her two pre-school children to work with her. At the same time, it bought her some time while she looked for another opportunity. When one came along, she took immediate, positive action and moved up to a better-paying position.

On the way to a victory, each Victorious Woman improved, grew, and thrived in spite of the trials and tribulations of her difficulty. For each woman, victory is *more than* successfully surviving a situation, overcoming obstacles, and achieving a particular desired outcome. For Pattie Painter it meant maintaining a positive attitude during her illness. Lilly Zook developed a greater sense of personal worth that enabled her not only to leave her abusive marriage, but also to learn new skills that contributed to her independence. Tekki Lomnicki moved from denial into personal power to become a stronger and more powerful individual.

Whatever the difficulty and however successful the outcome, the process of becoming victorious defined the woman. Victory means *making a statement about how you choose to live.* It clearly separates the kind of life that is chauffeured, powered, and operated by others from one in which destiny is the vehicle and the woman is the driver.

Throughout the interviews, I observed differences in the way a woman recounted the events that led to victory. A victorious narrative didn't downplay a woman's hard work; it clearly conveyed their effort, sacrifice, and energy invested in the process. Moreover, not one Victorious Woman spun the details of her personal story into a showcase of cheeky bravado. Through their authenticity, I determined victory is honest and not pretentious.

Indeed, victory had its own expression in each woman. Satisfaction and self-assurance emanated from deep in her soul, conveyed with a style all her own. Effervescent women such as Pattie Painter, Alisa Morkides, or Jean Otte became calmer and more direct. In contrast, soft-spoken women such as Toni Kershaw or the weakened, dying Nancy Hill almost startled me with their firm conviction. Whatever a Victorious Woman's personality or however different her pitch or inflection, each one claimed her victory and spoke about it with fervor and certainty.

Finally, few women ever perceived the difficult circumstances as thresholds to victory. On the contrary, each Victorious Woman found herself thrust into an undesirable situation and felt overwhelmed. Then something happened in her thoughts and feelings, and she took actions that shifted her into victory mode.

Through the remarkable interviews and intriguing stories, I discovered several interesting facets to a woman's victorious journey. Most notably, she travels the victory path:

- while managing multiple responsibilities such as family, work, and caregiving;
- in a series of steps rather than a single Wonder Woman-sized leap;
- in a non-linear manner where one segment or task does not necessarily follow the other as an automatic first-second-third directive. For example, support does not necessarily come at the beginning or end, but can show up in different places along the way.

As I continued to evaluate the process, four distinct categories emerged: *victim*, *surviving*, *advancing*, and *victorious*. These are not fixed phases but instead Stepping Stones toward victory, each characterized by specific patterns of behavior. When a woman stays both present and focused, the Stepping Stones become solid spaces in which a woman can get her footing while surveying the future and deciding what she needs to do next. Conversely, if a woman is uninspired or reactive, a Stepping Stone can lead to mental paralysis and inactivity, thus becoming the permanent pothole in which a woman gets stuck.

My hope for this book, and my wish for you, is that after reading these chapters you will be inspired to set out on your own journey to victory. The path begins with the Stepping Stones. As you read, think about which one you are on now, and how you can move to the next one.

STEPPING STONES
——————— and the ———————
VICTORIOUS WOMAN MODEL

THE "VICTIM" STEPPING STONE

If something tragic happens—a woman is raped, scammed, mugged, or devastated by a car accident or some other one-time event—she is victimized. What follows is a difficult and sometimes overwhelming period of time. Eventually, however, she finds a way to live with the tragedy and moves on with her life. Being victimized by an external event does not mean a woman has to become the Victim.

Some women, however, choose to stay victimized and adopt a victim mentality. The Victim does not readily distinguish herself from other women. She is not a certain height, weight, or ethnicity and can be found at every socio-economic level. She can be tough or sweet, dour or funny. You probably would not notice the Victim in a crowded room. That is, not until you talk with her. Her words and tone of voice convey an attitude and a belief system that characterizes her victim way of life. Her downward spiral may not have begun with a tragic, undeserved, or unfair event, but she can surely tell you of several in her life.

Usually thinking submissive and resigned thoughts, the Victim colors everything with a "poor me against the big world" attitude. Somehow this woman always seems to lose at the game of life, always ending up with the short end of the stick. Her overriding belief is that "they don't think I'm good enough," and it feeds into anger, frustration, and depression. Her conversation is dotted with phrases like "it's not fair" or "s/he is out to get me." She finds evidence that supports her dejected thinking in everything that happens. She tells others about her plight, and often garners their sympathy...at least for a while.

The Victim behaves in ways that enable her to be easily wronged, allowing her to be a ready participant in her own maltreatment. She seems unable or unwilling to make decisions in her favor, even when the choices appear black and white. This woman is often emotionally needy, uses poor judgment, and even when well advised to be on guard, gets into situations that can only end badly for her. Frequently, physically or emotionally dependent on the patient kindness of others for her care, she becomes hostile if she does not get it. She may not stay at a job for a long period of time, sometimes being fired for a bad attitude or work skills or quitting because she thinks her boss or co-workers are against her. She can also be the woman who is easily taken in by a fast-talking guy who sweeps her off her feet but who leaves her pregnant, broke, alone, and dependent on others.

When faced with an obstacle, this woman easily gives up the fight, convinced that she's under attack by some person or some system. When speaking with others, her words often reflect the poignant and distressing belief that no matter how hard she tries, somehow she *just can't win.* Using defeatist self-talk, she convinces herself and others that "no matter what I do, I never get ahead," and complains, "I tried but, like always, I got screwed."

When this woman is offered help by way of advice, she's likely to become defensive and even angry. She quickly snaps back with an angry retort like, "I don't need you to tell me what to do, I just need [a ride, some money, a job, etc.]." Somehow, she either cannot or will not make the connection between her irresponsible or problematic behaviors and her sorry predicaments.

Often the Victim tells her story to others. Her version of life touches people and draws them into her circle. The dramas are almost always wrapped in her cloak of powerlessness and helplessness. This woman conveniently avoids telling others of her complicity in creating the soap opera-like stories. She neglects to disclose how she is always late for work, tried to get away with something illegal and got caught, or consistently dates alcoholics and abusers.

In truth, she isn't always aware of how her thoughts, attitudes, and beliefs influence poor outcomes. She also evades opportunities to become more cognizant of her personal responsibility or contribution to sabotaging behaviors.

One such woman, Eleanor*, found herself deserted by her spouse and left alone to care for her four children. She didn't know how to proceed, so she did nothing except cry to her mother. She waited around until, through her mother's prompting, siblings intervened and moved the family to her mother's house.

Once settled, Eleanor found a good job. However, she drank heavily after work hours and expected others to watch over and care for her children. She disrupted her mother's household so much that she was asked to leave. Someone else took her in, but she repeated the pattern. Exasperated, her relatives found a rental home for the small family so they could live on their own.

After a while, she found a boyfriend and became even more irresponsible about childcare. Eleanor's children frequently got in trouble in the neighborhood. In time, her sisters convinced Eleanor to place the children in a subsidized boarding school in another part of the state.

Year in and year out, she cried to family and friends about how much she missed her children, and how hard it was to put them away. While that may have been true, Eleanor failed to tell anyone that she seldom visited or sent care packages to the children for whom she supposedly pined. When the children came home for vacations, she maintained her routine of working during the day and partying with her boyfriend at night, leaving the children alone day after day.

Like other women who make victimhood a way of life, Eleanor's hardships provided the backdrop for drama that consistently ended with, "What else could I do? I had no other choice." All the while, however, Eleanor enjoyed the pity and sympathy of many family members and thrived on the attention.

Tracy* is another woman who chose the victim lifestyle. She often found herself out of work and struggling to stay afloat.

When she joined a church group, Tracy quickly told everyone about her difficult state of affairs. She asked several people for help in the form of rides, resume writing, and informal counseling. Churchgoers did what they could, but soon discovered she had a somewhat demanding attitude and was barely appreciative of the help she received.

Through the efforts and help of one kind soul, she received some governmental assistance so she could acquire job-related computer skills. The funding agency sent the woman a check for tuition instead of paying the computer school directly. Shortly before the courses began, Tracy attended a Star Wars convention. At the event, seemingly without concern for the consequences, she spent the training dollars.

When the supportive church members questioned her use of the money, Tracy justified her behavior by crying about how depressed she felt and how spending the tuition money made her feel good. Some responded to her irresponsible behavior with sadness, others with annoyance or anger. When they expressed their feelings, Tracy became angry and defensive. She told them they had no right to tell her how she should spend *her* money.

Before long, most of her allies pulled away, feeling that they only wanted to help people who helped themselves. In response, the unapologetic woman quickly launched into her "people are always against me" rhetoric.

Within a few months, since Tracy no longer had the money to upgrade her job skills, she could only find low-level, unskilled work. She left the church, gave up her apartment, and moved in with her mother. The unhealthy move supplied Tracy with years of self-pity, as well as the attention and unearned compassion of others around her.

Every day we hear stories of women who make a behavioral pattern out of overshopping, drinking, lying, irresponsible sex, and other unproductive behaviors that satisfy their immediate emotional needs. In the meantime, they live in denial of their victim mentality, insulating their insecurity and delaying their emotional maturity. Challenges are overcome mostly through the efforts of others. When those who assist such women are absent, they seem lost and unable to cope.

The Victim feels helpless against life's challenges and *decides to stay that way*, even though she often does not realize it. She carries a lot of emotional baggage, and though it weighs her down, the Victim prefers to keep it with her at all times. Rather than find her own healthy, moral, or wholesome solutions to difficult situations, she stumbles unconsciously through life, letting it swallow her up—and then resigning into a hell of her own making.

Most likely you know at least one woman who falls into the victim category. For whatever reason, it seems that far too many women believe being a professional victim is an acceptable way of life.

However, when a woman becomes aware that she is stuck in a victim pattern, she *can choose something different*. When Jean Otte's spouse died of cancer and her company went through a buyout, she could have retreated into victimhood. Instead, she chose another route. Rather than resisting change, she chose to embrace it and see where it took her. Today, she is certain that tragedy and unexpected change gave her a push into something even better.

It took Lilly Zook a while to disconnect from a victim life. Though the dramas of her abusive marriage seemed like a never-ending, vicious cycle, Lilly eventually made better choices, proving that the pattern *could* be broken. As Lilly also demonstrated, the process can take some time; it also requires internal strength, planning, and forward movement. Yet if only one woman shows that it can be done, then she is proof that every woman can opt out of the Victim rut if she chooses to do so.

For a woman with a victim mentality, the method for moving forward begins with making **one small but positive choice**, such as expecting more from herself. Nancy Hill did it by routinely keeping her house neat and clean and taking to heart her friend Sadie's "you can make a home out of an old shack" adage.

With small but consistent steps, the Victim can inch her way steadily into surviving mode. One small attitude adjustment or one consistently practiced new behavior can change her fate and begin creating a better future. For example, a woman can refuse to be talked to with disrespect. If she tends to be late for work, she can choose to change and consistently be on time. She *can* walk away from being a victim, make progressively better choices, create success, and end up with her victory. It takes courage, time, and patience, but it is attainable.

THE "SURVIVING" STEPPING STONE

This does not reference a game that involves eating odd and gross food or getting voted off an island. It is also not about the woman who survives some kind of devastation like beating cancer, living through a plane crash, or jumping out of a burning building into safety. The woman who lives through a situational, one-time misfortune is a trauma survivor.

Instead, the Surviving Woman seems to have an indomitable spirit, but she habitually feels like she loses every conflict, dispute, or confrontation whether it is to a child, a spouse, or a boss. The Surviving Woman keeps fighting rather than giving up, but she often loses sight of exactly what she will win when the fight is over.

The Surviving Woman treads wearily through her life. Though she commonly works really hard, she usually doesn't feel she gets satisfaction from her efforts. Neither happy nor unhappy, she is also not quite content and frequently feels overwhelmed.

Unfortunately, the Surviving Woman is often her own worst enemy. Many carry the pain of some past hurt or are angry over an old incident like a broken promise, an opportunity lost, or a wrong done to her. She thinks of it often and somehow blames either the episode or the offending person as the reason why she can't go further. It becomes a self-fulfilling prophecy.

Day-by-day, year-after-year, she longs for more—a better job, a more loving relationship, or a better standard of living—but she has stopped seriously striving for a lifestyle upgrade. Some of the same "it's not fair" victim threads are woven together with a hopeful, "it'll get better soon" attitude. Together, they create the undergarments of a tough armor. The Surviving Woman wages a private war between herself and the world, one that seems to her as an ongoing struggle.

One of her greatest challenges is emotional honesty. The Surviving Woman does not vent her emotions in a healthy manner. Instead of learning how to campaign for what she wants and argue constructively if she doesn't get it, she stuffs her feelings deep inside. Anger, resentment, sadness, and more linger beneath the surface. Often the smallest incident can cause those pent up emotions to burst, spewing toxic emotion onto her children, her parents, store clerks, or anyone who is around in that moment. Then she feels even worse for allowing herself to get out of control and hurting others by her actions. She strives for control, but never finds it. Instead, she finds herself overcaring and even less resourceful in healthfully articulating her negative feelings.

The Surviving Woman often lives in a state of low-grade but chronic depression, though you would seldom know it. Year after year, she hides her feelings and her disappointments by feigning a positive attitude and putting on a happy face. Others may never realize her desperation unless or until something monumental happens and pushes her into a bona fide burnout.

Over time that young woman who may once have conveyed a light and energetic confidence shifts into wistful daydreams and moves to "someday, I'll..." Something clicks inside and she lets her real feelings go mentally or emotionally underground. Maybe she is overwhelmed by the feeling of powerlessness, fears the pain of failure, needs security...or something else. Whatever the underlying reason, the woman masks her true self and becomes the Surviving Woman.

Before Pattie Painter learned that the man she married had a girlfriend, she lived a surviving life. Though she suspected some kind of disconnection in her marriage, when she questioned her spouse, he had logical responses for his behaviors. She went along day by day and made her family both her priority and her pleasure. Pattie might have stayed that way until she learned of "the other woman." Though at that point she could have stepped into victim mode, instead she chose to take control. The event propelled her out of surviving and into advancing. She developed and grew as she advanced, laying the foundation for her later victory over cancer.

Whatever a woman's rationale, she takes on a surviving lifestyle by giving up her own self-validating dreams and goals—usually in favor of satisfying either a non-productive emotional need or the agendas of others. She often becomes an expert at accommodation and compliance, easily giving others what they want. Sadly, she seldom gets the same cooperation when *she* wants to do something. Though she sacrifices for others, she frequently doesn't ask, or even think to ask, that someone give up something for her. However, if she does ask, the people she indulges have lots of reasons why they can't meet her need but assure her they will help another time...yet that time never seems to come.

Eventually, this Surviving Woman feels drained and disillusioned. Rather than stray far from the accepted female archetype, **she settles** for the familiar. In the process, she gives up her personal sense of freedom. Eventually, she becomes someone so far from her authentic self that she feels she has few choices, and will do anything just to maintain the status quo.

An example of a Surviving Woman is Rebecca.* As a twenty-two-year old college graduate she had a bright future ahead of her. Her diploma brought with it considerable debt in the form of student loans and Rebecca felt angry about it. She blamed her parents for not paying her college tuition so she could start her working life debt-free. Rebecca felt she had to make job choices based on money rather than preference. She complained about how her supposedly forced-choice jobs led to wretched working conditions, bosses who were against her, and other hardships.

To balance her work hardships, Rebecca threw herself into other interests. She created an exciting social life. She traveled both at home and abroad. She enjoyed nice clothes and drove a cool-looking car. Eventually she met a man and the two married. After Rebecca had the first of her two children, she decided to be a stay-at-home mom. By the time her second child came along, feeling somewhat dissatisfied with her marriage, she threw herself into selfless motherhood. She expected her children to live up to her sometimes unrealistic expectations and became overly protective of them.

Though her spouse worked long hours at his job and seldom spent time with her or their children, Rebecca didn't consider herself unhappy. She occasionally made snide remarks that resonated resentment, and occasionally talked about returning to school for an advanced degree, but she did little to change her surviving pattern. If you asked her, Rebecca would tell you that she had a good life. Yet she seldom seemed truly happy.

Though Rebecca, like other Surviving Women, is light years more responsible than the Victim, she never accepts accountability for self-sabotaging behaviors. In fact, she seldom recognizes them or the damage they do. Instead, she argues that she's the long-suffering giver who never gets her fair share back either from people or situations. She daydreams about being powerful and sometimes longs to do to others what she perceives they do to her. She demeans other women who've created success, especially those who balance work and family successfully. She takes silent pleasure in creating scenarios about what would happen if she stopped being the overcaring spouse or mother, the ever-present caregiver, or the diligent employee. She insists that it would "serve them right," seldom understanding that her self-sacrificing ways may be doing unnecessary damage to both her and her relationships.

Without a doubt, the Surviving Woman usually wants to do

more and be more. Unfortunately, instead of using tragedy, anger, frustration, or dissatisfaction to push up and out of survival mode, she continues to plod along. She is frequently unrecognized, under appreciated, and under compensated. She knows it, but because she either keeps her feelings inside or denies them, they surface as resentment wrapped around passive-aggressive behaviors, hypochondriasis, or psychosomatic illnesses, and unfortunately, sometimes real, life-threatening physical illnesses.

Whether at work or in the neighborhood, this type of woman tends to indulge in some degree of rumor mongering, though it is seldom blatant. She tends to target other women who have already moved past surviving. Offended if someone calls her a gossip, she prefers to think of herself as an information gatherer who gets recognition for being "in the know." She enjoys other people's problems so she doesn't have to look at her own. She justifies her behaviors as a way of leveling the playing field—no doubt it also helps her to feel powerful.

Yet when the Surviving Woman wants to make a better life for herself and sets goals, she usually gives up before achieving them. Whether she desires to find a new job, lose weight, have more "me" time, or achieve some specific personal or professional goal, when she is coached and asked to think of solutions, she reverts to "yes, but..." mode. She has an endless list of reasons, a.k.a. excuses, for why she can't do it and the goal cannot be achieved. "Yes, but...it wouldn't be the holiday without the cookies and all the gifts," or "Yes, but...I *always* do that for [the kids, my parents, my spouse, my co-workers]; they'd be disappointed if I didn't." The Surviving Woman gets started, but gives up when the pressure from family gets too great. She finds herself too submerged into the lives of others, or her own insecurities get the better of her.

The most striking thing about the Surviving Woman is that, though she's often talented and accomplished, she still gives her power over to others (usually a spouse, children, or company) and sabotages her own dreams. That nearly happened to Alisa when she turned over the most critical portion of her business to someone else. After all the hard work of creating her initial success, she almost lost everything because she wasn't ready to accept the responsibility for the financial and personnel matters she didn't care to handle. When it came to those key issues, she slipped temporarily into surviving mode. The difference between Alisa and the true Surviving Woman is that when Alisa saw the damage, she took swift, take-no-prisoner actions to get back on track. The Surviving Woman may not have wanted to hurt her partner's feelings, and might have waited until it was too late.

Toni Kershaw modeled the Surviving Woman with an enabling pattern she created, developed, and allowed. Her family became so dependent on her to meet their needs that they became annoyed when she wanted to do something just for herself because it took time away from them. Rather than dealing with the resulting disturbance, and striving to keep peace, she complied with their wishes. She lived in that pattern for many years.

In order to make the slide into surviving, a woman allows herself to be distracted from her goals by others. At some point, she stops thinking that her life is ever going to be the way she really wants it. She decides instead to keep what she has and tries to make the best of it, presuming change is simply not possible, desirable, or convenient. She focuses on the agendas of others, whether it's a spouse, parent, child, boss, or volunteer organization. Her own agenda takes a back seat to all else, and she usually puts her needs and desires last—and then runs out of time.

Eventually, she transfers her dreams to her spouse or children. She overcares and overdoes in her efforts to help them succeed. Meanwhile, she tends to criticize them when they're not fulfilling her opinion of their potential. Her criticism takes on many faces. It may be direct and verbal, or it could be passive-aggressive and take the form of ignoring or guilt.

Sometimes, however, she finds a person outside the family, such as a friend, boss, minister, or colleague. She may become so invested in their drama that she neglects her own family. Either way, she lives her own potential vicariously through someone else.

Though constantly making choices and decisions that reflect self-abnegation, the Surviving Woman does not relate her own thoughts and behaviors directly to her dissatisfaction. Instead, she proudly professes that *somehow* she manages to survive each on-slaught of the world's wrath.

Reactive energy distinguishes her from both the Advancing Woman and the Victorious Woman. Like the Victim, she is not likely to take action until and unless something happens and forces her to do so. The Surviving Woman moves forward only when she's pushed or sometimes pulled along by someone else, often while she's kicking and screaming all the way.

Yet the Surviving Woman can shift her behaviors and cognitive patterns to become the Victorious Woman. Tekki Lomnicki found a non-productive lifestyle and used it to supply power and control. Her sexual escapades helped her to deny the issues she had with her own body and her personal insecurities. Tekki matured into taking greater personal responsibility for her life. Once she did, her life changed, and as a result, she embraced victory. Only after she stopped surviving and stepped into a better mental and emotional place did Tekki begin experiencing the successes that made her feel holistically good about her life.

Like the Victim, the Surviving Woman has the personal power to change her thoughts, modify her behaviors, and live a more substantive life. The ability to anticipate, choose, take control, and respond to situations proactively is *the major difference* between women who are victimized or surviving and those who are advancing toward victory.

THE "ADVANCING" STEPPING STONE

Though success and victory may be synonymous, one does not perfunctorily presume the other. I spoke with numbers of women who were extremely accomplished and highly successful yet not necessarily creating a victory, at least not yet.

Few women transcend from victimized or surviving to victorious in some magical instance. Whether the victory comes over a long period of time or happens more quickly, a woman must rely on the scaffolding of *advancing* to support her success and prevent a swift return to an undesired place in life.

The advancing Stepping Stone is like a garden for growing victories. It's a step a woman takes when she sets a goal and creates a strategy. In advancing mode, she assesses her own strengths and limitations, knows the characteristics she needs to develop, and strives for self improvement. Through the process of positive change, she adds skills to her behavioral toolbox, broadening and expanding her capabilities and gaining a sense of mastery.

As a woman advances her life, rather than wait for some big demonstration or development such as a new job or some physical change like a weight loss, new hair style/color, or plastic surgery, she gets busy on the inside. The Advancing Woman focuses on less visible but more powerful manifestations. Taking an active role in family finances, speaking up at a business meeting, or saying "no" to someone else's self-focused request may be one of the most difficult challenges of her life and demand the greatest internal courage.

Though no one can see what takes place within the woman who moves from victimized or surviving into advancing, it makes little difference to anyone else but herself. The steps may be small and not very noticeable to others, but that does not lessen the challenge or degree of difficulty. Yet, when taken consistently, the smallest steps add up and eventually become a victory path.

The first significant internal shift a woman makes in order to move from surviving to advancing is a change in her awareness. When she sees, for the first time, how her unassertive or accommodating behaviors get in her way, she can never again *not* see them. Though she may take some time to develop the courage to take action and make changes, awareness is the beginning.

Secondly, the Advancing Woman develops critical emotional

competencies. In contrast to the wonderful emotional gifts that most women are born with, such as intuition and sensitivity, other equally important proficiencies aren't traditionally stressed in a woman's development. Both the Surviving and Advancing Woman recognize their significance.

Yet knowing and doing are two very different things. One is passive; the other is active. What separates the Advancing Woman from the Victim and the Surviving Woman is her **active willingness** to develop these distinct capabilities and grow into them comfortably. Specifically, once she understands the importance of the skill, she learns how to incorporate it into her life, and then practices using it.

As a woman moves around the Stepping Stones from victim or surviving and into advancing, she begins adding new behavioral patterns to her existing repertoire. Six key characteristics for advancing include: *self-control, initiative, achievement drive, organizational awareness, leadership,* and *influence.*

1. **Self-control**. When women think of self-control, it's usually in regards to restraining emotions or maintaining a diet and exercise regimen. However, in this instance self-control means maintaining control of her life by establishing effective boundaries, having a working personal agenda, and recognizing that she and her priorities have equal importance with those of others in her life such as a spouse or significant other, children, parents, work, and friends. The Advancing Woman understands that acknowledging her own needs and acting on them enables her to maintain a high level of self-esteem. She sees giving and receiving as a two-way street, expecting the important people in her life whose needs she accommodates to oblige her when she needs them.

   The Advancing Woman sees self-control as a necessary proficiency for making sure she has private time, being able to indulge in a hobby, and having time to connect with other adults who are not in her family. It could also mean starting a business, having a home-based career, or going back to school for an advanced degree or upgrading job skills. Whatever the specifics, the critical element is that a woman is in charge of her life by advancing her personal goals.

Without self-control, a woman easily shifts into the detrimental lifestyle of overcare, a systematic progression of losing herself into the agendas of others for whom she cares. Others begin thinking a woman's time is theirs to use. It drains both the woman's strength of mind and will. She becomes a Surviving Woman and sets herself up for an unfulfilled, potentially unhappy life. At the same time, if she is a mother, she breeds dependent children who develop unhealthy expectations for women.

Instead of being an overprotective mother, the Advancing Woman benchmarks her mothering skills by her child's ability to be independent, interdependent, and self-sufficient. Children can still feel loved *and* take care of themselves. As they mature and develop greater confidence, the Advancing Woman is progressively freer to find time to focus on her own goals. It's an invaluable and never-ending gift for both mother and child.

The Advancing Woman learns that her partner, children, and others benefit when they see her placing equal priority on her own life as well as that of her family. Neither her sons nor her daughters grow up believing that a woman's job is to give up her identity for the sake of her family. Instead of martyring herself for her family, she maintains a sense of herself and her excitement for life. While she is taking care of her needs, she isn't making inordinate sacrifices that inhibit adult relationships and hamper the maturity of her children.

Pattie Painter gained greater self-control when she gave up overdoing everything, especially on the holidays. She replaces the stress brought on by making gifts, excessive baking, and micromanaging each event with gifts, cards, and only those homey touches that make her feel good. Whoever misses a particular food or decoration has the option to pitch in and do it themselves.

By maintaining self-control, the Advancing Woman can preserve the essence of who she is. She can be authentically happy, and that emotion flows from her, gracing everyone.

What are you doing to strengthen your self-control?

2. **Initiative.** Broadly speaking, this implies openness and action. More specifically, it means the ability to see an opportunity and be ready and willing to act on it. When working with others, it means having the credibility, confidence, and comfort level to present different ideas and approaches to problems.

I often notice how a woman spots an opportunity and then talks herself out of acting on it. She might keep innovative thoughts to herself because she believes her idea will get shot down or hesitates promoting herself because she is afraid others will perceive her as showy or aggressive. As a result, a woman too often communicates ideas with a feeble conviction that dampens her credibility.

At the same time, I also see women seizing opportunity in spite of the fear of rejection or failure. Alisa Morkides knew Brew-Ha-Ha! could surely have failed from the start, but she went ahead anyway. Nancy Hill took a low-level job in a bank at a time in our history when prejudice was legitimately institutionalized. Kathy Clark took risks in spite of the corporate "good old boys" who waited for her to fail.

When was the last time you risked taking the initiative on a project for your own self-development or personal satisfaction?

3. **Achievement drive.** A woman with active achievement drive enjoys the benefits of self-control by acknowledging her personal goals and aspirations, choosing a direction, and creating a working action plan. Without it, a woman too easily relinquishes her own dreams and allows her ambition and the urge to achieve to go underground. She may set goals and truly

mean to achieve them, but at the first sign of an obstacle she gives up. Frequently, she replaces her own ambitions with the mantle of caregiving.

On the contrary, the Advancing Woman keeps in touch with her inner desires and articulates them into clear intentions, goals, and objectives. While she may have dreams for loved ones, she also sets her sights on personal accomplishment, even knowing completion may take some time. When faced with obstacles, she does not make excuses and give up. Instead, she finds ways around or through the difficulties and keeps going. The Advancing Woman understands that she is at her best when she strives for personal performance improvement and success in the areas that make her feel happy, satisfied, and worthwhile.

While each Victorious Woman relied on achievement drive to get through their particular challenge, not all came by it easily. Nancy Hill and Lilly Zook didn't think they could do much of anything for a long time. Yet as they moved out of victim, through surviving, and into advancing, the tiny spark of victory fanned into a flame. Nancy progressed from cleaning houses to working in a bank. Her achievement drive gradually encouraged her to seek better jobs, eventually retiring as a bank manager. Lilly is steadily learning new skills, seeks higher education, and walks a victory path laden with hope.

How is your achievement drive? Does the idea of achievement frighten or excite you? Notice what happens inside your head and body when you think about it. You might feel a rush of excitement, suddenly overwhelmed, a sense of urgency, fear of failure, or a myriad of other thoughts or sensations. All of them are normal. What counts is what you do next.

What is one thing that, if you knew you could achieve it, you would do in a heartbeat? What's stopping you?

4. **Organizational awareness.** Rather than make solid connections with a variety of people, many women find one or two

buddies and form a comfortable clique. Whatever happens, whether it's on the job, at home, or in the community, she views events through the small prism of her tight circle. Her growth seems limited to her group's knowledge, opinion, and acceptance.

Conversely, as a woman advances, she maintains her close friendships, but also expands her sphere to include others. As she does, whether thinking specifically about a task or more generally, she grasps the bigger picture. When she does that, she's able to see how her skills and abilities fit and what talents different people bring to the experience. If she is working on a project, she can pinpoint a group need. She knows how to best contribute as well as who to contact to promote herself in the experience. She also knows what expertise others have to share.

Kathy Clark depended on organizational awareness to promote the programs she initiated. If Kathy recognized a need that could be filled, the Career Closet for example, she knew who had the expertise and authority to make it happen. When she approached those individuals, she'd established enough credibility within her field to be taken seriously. People took action and made the valuable outreach a reality that benefited many disadvantaged women. Tekki Lomnicki casts a wide net for her theater involvement with children. *Six Stories Up* depends heavily on Tekki's organizational awareness. Not only does she have to know what she can and can't do, she has to know scores of others who can best participate to make the experience great for the children.

The Advancing Woman nourishes a variety of strong relationships outside of her own groups or work areas. *What have you done recently to expand your organizational network?*

5. **Leadership**. Through leadership, you're able to promote your ideas in a fashion that persuades others to listen, and if required, take action. Spearheading a project with authority and

cooperation is one example of leading others. Among other important characteristics of good leaders are the ability to guide, mentor, and inspire others.

Many women are natural leaders. Some obviously demonstrate their ability all the time. For others, it lies dormant, either undeveloped or squashed at an early time. Still others received the social or religious messages that they should take a back seat to others, or they may not have the desire or ability to lead at this time.

Jean Otte developed greater leadership skills while climbing the corporate ladder, during a business buyout, and while she served her company as an officer and vice-president. One of the functions of her current company, Women Unlimited, is to assist women in developing their leadership skills as they grow their talent.

For the Advancing Woman, the study of leadership is vital both inside and outside of the home. She can learn the characteristics and develop them by reading, asking for help, and finding a mentor. For practice, she can begin in small venues, such as a local community group or with a professional organization.

How can you practice leadership in what you do every day?

6. **Influence**. Influence is the power to produce effects, especially indirectly. In other words, influence is your ability to establish your credibility, gain clout within your circle, and let others know who you are and what you know.

Exercising greater influence is something that nearly every Advancing Woman could do better. We could take a few lessons from men on this one! Watch how men promote themselves and their assets by tooting their own horn. When they do, they usually increase their credibility and acquire the status they need to convince others of their worth.

At the same time, take note of the women (like yourself) who demonstrate remarkable accomplishments yet impress no one, often because nearly no one knows how amazing they can be. When there's a need or opportunity to put forth an idea or champion a cause, these women commonly don't have the influence to sway anyone. Often no one will even listen because they never develop enough credibility or clout with the people in power to be heard. Remember Jean Otte's advice, "It's not who you know, but *who knows* you know," Throughout her executive career, Jean made sure the right people knew she could teach, train, manage, and organize.

One woman, Sue*, would have benefited by exercising her influence. She was a manager in an office of a mid-size company. Without her, a critical portion of the company could not function. Sue led her department masterfully, did her job seamlessly, worked hard, and strove for excellence. Not wanting to toot her own horn, few people ever knew how much she and her department contributed to the company. Sue believed others would notice and give her credit.

Yet when compliments came, she tended to downplay her efforts, often shifting recognition to her secretary or some other helpful person. While others deserved the kudos, they wouldn't have had the same opportunity without Sue's insight, intuition, or leadership ability. Sue's self-effacing attitude made it difficult for others to see her as a powerhouse. Few people, including the owner, recognized the importance of her work.

In another department, but at the same managerial level, Renee* did little and delegated everything to her subordinates. She had little knowledge of what it took to create her department's success. Yet Renee understood influence and had finely honed the skill. She heavily promoted each small success to the president, other department heads, and throughout the company.

When the owner prepared to sell the company, he kept a bare-bones management team. He saw Sue and her salary as another line item in their budget. Her position disappeared and she lost her job. Why? Sue never made an effort to promote herself or her impressive skills, always believing her good work would be evidence of her skill. After eliminating Sue's job, it didn't take long for the company president to recognize that key responsibilities were not being addressed.

In contrast, Renee so carefully nurtured her influence that she stayed, but her staff left. Though she did her best, without her supportive department Renee quickly became the weakest link in the skeleton management team. The president realized months later that he had made a critical mistake.

How often have you noticed that people who are less qualified are given preference over those with more competence? The difference is in the ability of one person to create greater influence than another. People don't know what you can do unless you tell them; telling the right people is influence. When Pattie Painter began a singing career, her influence led to paid gigs. Maureen Ingelsby's influence induced a magazine writer to feature her in an article about real estate agents.

How can you make creating influence a regular part of your daily life?

The woman who takes the time and solidifies the preceeding six traits in her life is more likely to experience success as well as feel better about her life. To advance in her life, she must actively grow her talent in these areas.

As you consider expanding your repertoire of positive emotional competencies, be patient. Consider the process of growth analogous to that of a lobster. As a lobster develops, it eventually outgrows its shell. It leaves the hard shell that has protected it for so long and faces the sea with a new, soft shell. At first, the lobster is vulnerable and the shell is easy to puncture. Over time, it becomes as hard and comfortable as the old one. The process of growing out of the shell continues and shedding occurs again.

For the Advancing Woman, the inner journey is probably the most difficult yet most exciting one a woman will ever take. She is likely to make mistakes and find plenty of obstacles on the path. Yet in the process, the Advancing Woman forges the internal steel needed to create satisfying successes in her life, whether she chooses personal or professional achievements, or both. As she integrates and aligns these behaviors into her personality, she boosts her self-esteem and raises herself to her proper place in the world.

From whatever Stepping Stone a woman begins, the advancing characteristics help a woman live her best life. In addition, when a woman establishes herself as an Advancing Woman, she is more likely to be ready to create a victory when the opportunity arises.

THE "VICTORIOUS" STEPPING STONE

Being a Victorious Woman is something of a double-edged tribute. The circumstance that led to victory is one that each woman would have preferred not to experience. Maureen Ingelsby didn't plan to be deserted by John. Jean Otte wanted Ron to be with her always. Toni Kershaw never expected a conflict between her own health and that of her daughter. Alisa Morkides would have loved to have someone else handle the less exciting parts of her business. No one would ever desire Pattie Painter's cancer diagnosis, and Tekki Lomnicki came into this world with a set of physical difficulties that few of us can fathom. Both Kathy Clark and Lilly Zook only wanted to live happily ever after with the men they married while Nancy Hill's abusive marriage pushed her into victory.

As life would have it, not one Victorious Woman had a crystal ball to predict her outcome. With no way of knowing what life had in store, she had no special motivation to prepare for her particular victory.

The stories in this book show that there really *is* no preparation for the challenge itself. However, each Victorious Woman stepped forward and took control of her life *in a way that made a victorious difference.*

While the Stepping Stones provide direction, the Victorious Woman Model is the game plan. The model's sections are interdependent, and it seems that growing one competency automatically leads to the development of another, almost as if by osmosis. Though presented in this chapter as a linear list, the reality is that the system is more octagonal. A woman usually begins with awareness, but moves around in a variety of ways. However, when you choose to use the Victorious Woman Model, you can trust the validity of its use in providing a framework for creating your own victories.

THE VICTORIOUS WOMAN MODEL

❧ Awareness:

When Lilly Zook got the first inkling that her abusive husband may not always be right and maybe she wasn't always wrong, she experienced something known as divine discontent. Divine discontent is something that springs from the highest part of your being and causes a woman to question her way of life or her choices. Whether she knows about different lifestyles, until she has a reason to challenge the status quo, she usually doesn't. When she decides she no longer wants whatever has gone before, and she's willing to have something better, her awareness shifts.

Many events can precipitate a shift. A woman may choose to either be a stay-at-home mom or one who works outside the home. One day she realizes that her choice created some heretofore unknown difficulty and she has a new awareness. She rearranges her priorities and makes new choices.

Similarly, after years of friendship with her grade school buddies, a young woman suddenly finds these relationships empty. While she is still single, they all are married and have children. One night, after a girls' night out, she realizes they have nothing in common anymore. Though the changes happened gradually, her awareness shifted almost instantly.

A change of awareness is often a first sign of an impending change. It almost always happens at the beginning of a victory, but can also happen during stages along the way.

Awareness.

☞ Courage:

What image enters your mind when you think of courage? Through each Victorious Woman, I learned that courage is about the strength to face challenges *in spite of* the fear. As Maureen Ingelsby said, she knew there were a hundred things that could've gone wrong and "it could have all gone sour." Yet she and the others step into their victory in spite of the odds. Courage is an essential element of this model.

When suddenly left alone to care for five children, Maureen summoned courage to face the next day. Pattie Painter faced the cancer diagnosis and multiple surgeries with courage. Neither one of them pretended the challenge was less then it was. Both recognized the enormity of their situation. But instead of letting it overwhelm them into being victims, they faced their challenges head-on.

Courage is the willingness to face the naked truth, recognize the challenge, and make the decision to overcome the obstacle. That could mean getting out of a bad situation like Kathy Clark, seeking help and support like Tekki Lomnicki, or seeking more job training, like Lilly Zook and Alisa Morkides. It means being willing to learn how you can improve your life and then acting on what you learn.

In its Latin roots, courage means *heart*. Having heart pushes you forward to do what's right, even when you know that it might not please—and may even aggravate—those around you. With courage, you can unite heart and mind. The union fosters conscious choice.

Awareness. Courage.

☞ **Conscious choice:**

When life throws you a curve ball, you can refuse to admit defeat. You can choose to find a solution, learn a new way, and opt for a better life. Victory is no accident. It begins with garnering the courage and consciously choosing something better than your current situation.

Unlike wishing for a way out, hoping something good will happen, or praying for divine intervention, conscious choice is deliberate, thoughtful, and purposeful. When you make a conscious choice, you put your mind on alert and can set an intention for a specific outcome or one that encompasses your whole life. You let your whole being—body, mind, and spirit—know that you are taking charge of your fate. As a young woman, Jean Otte felt something deep within her stirring. Intense dissatisfaction and frustration, coupled with the desire for what the good life had to offer, led to the frustration that became life-altering. In an emotional moment, Jean pitted her will against her circumstances. It became *the* moment that changed her youthful existence and put her on a path to victory.

Awareness. Courage. Conscious choice.

☞ **Decision:**

First your heart connects to your mind, and then it *must* attach to your voice. When you know your mind, you must speak it and be heard. You do this by making a decision and verbalizing it to yourself and others.

Making a decision is not always as easy as it may appear. It's not something that another can give you or do for you. Only you can make that all-important choice that whatever isn't good now will improve through your proactive approach. The choice to create a better future admits that you want a better life or pushes you into a decision.

Once you face your challenge squarely, make a decision to overcome it. Alisa's resolve permeated her entire being after she fired her partner. Maureen Ingelsby felt a lightning-like shock. Toni Kershaw's came after a heart-wrenching struggle. Lilly Zook's years of abuse welled up inside of her until she'd had enough.

Each Victorious Woman made a decision when they agreed to tell their story. For some, the decision took more time and thought than for others. In telling her story, the Victorious Woman agreed to open up her life to the world. While some told their story frequently, others seldom told anyone. Still, whether she was accustomed to being in the spotlight or not, the courageous decision to help other women by telling the details of her own story moved each Victorious Woman to a different, more global place in her life.

Awareness. Courage. Conscious choice. Decision.

❧ Goal:

Through decision, direction becomes established. Direction is not outcome. To achieve a successful conclusion, you must set a goal. A decision without a goal to back it up leads to frustration. Lilly Zook wanted to leave her spouse, but it was a nebulous yearning. When she had a concrete goal with a specific time frame, she moved forward. Maureen Ingelsby's goal was to keep her family intact, in spite of the father's desertion. Pattie Painter simply wanted to live...to beat the cancer and to live.

A goal must have five parts: it must be *specific, measurble, attainable, realistic,* and *timed.* In success circles, this is known as the SMART goal. To be more than just a wish, a goal must meet the five criteria.

Awareness. Courage. Conscious choice. Decision. Goal.

❧ Plan:

Positive affirmation and strong emotion can get you through the first four stages. Awareness, anger, and frustration welled up inside of Lilly Zook and she realized she wanted a better life. Purposeful passion filled Maureen Ingelsby after sudden abandonment by her spouse. However, without a plan, neither would have made it too far.

Until you create a plan, a goal is nothing more than a wish with intention. I've spoken to many women who reached the emotional point of making a powerful decision, followed by a goal that went nowhere. What happened? They did not know where to begin, so when they viewed the whole picture, they felt overwhelmed.

Consider the woman who needed to lose fifty pounds. She vowed to get thin, and set her goal. She began a depravation-style diet with a vengeance and had quick success, dropping five or ten pounds in a couple of weeks. However, as her body adjusted, the loss slowed to a normal pound or two per week. Missing instant gratification, she saw only how much, how hard, and how long. Mentally defeated, she quit and gained back more than she lost. Each time she tried, she failed to put a long-term, practical plan into place.

Now consider Nancy Hill and how she planned her move for several years. She found ways to put aside enough money to leave her bad situation, made arrangements to leave, and had a place to go. To effectively go from challenge to victory, each Victorious Woman had a plan to get ahead.

With a clear plan, you know how to get what you want. It is not something you do on a whim. A plan is something you invest some time creating. Rather than counting on emotion to propel you into action, a plan takes you step by step to your goal.

A good plan is one that commits you to doable actions. As you create it, you look at methods, necessary equipment, and expected or potential obstacles.

Without a clear plan, you'll be using the "keep your options open" method. That means you're waiting around to see what comes up before you commit yourself to your goal. You may be waiting to see if the other person will make changes that s/he promised, if the boss keeps his or her word and promotes you, or if you finally win the lottery.

In other words, "options open" means that you are always hoping that there will be some easier way, a way that means you won't have to put yourself out or do something that will make anyone else angry with you or uncomfortable with your change. With your options open, you can keep yourself rolling around a vicious cycle of self-deception for many years.

Conversely, with a well thought-out plan, you allow for new opportunities, but you're not as likely to change course without fully considering the deviation. Maureen Ingelsby's ultimate goal was to keep her family together. She planned to support her children with a full-time teaching career. However, through a part-time job, she found full-time work with more flexible hours and better pay. She altered the short-term plan because it better served her long-term purpose.

There is an old adage that says that if you have no goal, any plan will do. Similarly, if you have no plan, any direction will seem like the right way. When you go any which way, you are more likely to go the wrong way and in a direction that takes you away from your goal instead of closer to it.

With a plan, you have steps to follow. If you get lost for a time or something else comes along and attempts to distract you, a plan helps you determine if it's a worthy change or just a side trip that will deter you from your goal.

Awareness. Courage. Conscious choice. Decision. Goal. Plan.

⚭ Support:

It's important to be clear about the role of support people in creating victory. Each Victorious Woman may have requested and accepted help, but none depended on others to solve her situation. A Victorious Woman uses a proactive approach to her challenge. They did not sit back and wait for a handout, and when an opportunity for help presented itself, they seized the initiative and did their best to make the most of it.

Yet support became a critical component in each woman's victory. Toni Kershaw and Tekki Lomnicki were involved with programs where they met weekly with other people facing the same challenge. Pattie used e-mail to sustain her support network. Lilly Zook relocated to a safe house and then into a government-sponsored self-sufficiency program. Nancy Hill was blessed through her church and Sadie. Kathy Clark had a professional association that helped to shape her success and was there to fall back on when disaster struck. Jean Otte had mentors. Alisa Morkides had vendors. Maureen Ingelsby had a network of older folks.

The truth about us as humans is that while we may not need others in every facet of our lives, some things we just can't weather without someone or some program to back us up. We get tired, worn down, or frustrated. We need others to encourage us, or as Jean Otte puts it, give an "atta girl."

The key to getting good support is making sure it provides positive reinforcement. Whether you choose a group or person(s), consider them part of your team, like your personal board of directors.

As you consider the person or people, take care to choose someone you can comfortably and seriously trust. You must be able to look to the members of your support group not just for pats on the back, but also, and More importantly, for honest and direct feedback. Jean admits that "sometimes it is *very inconvenient* to get to know ourselves better." Yet she asks, "If nobody ever gives you feedback, how do you get better, how do you get promoted?" Jean's mentor did that for her. Tekki Lomnicki had a sponsor in SLAA; a sponsor is a person who guides the new twelve-stepper through the rough spots.

While you may be inclined to choose a girlfriend or sister, sometimes they're too easy on you—and that may not be in your best interest. Instead of being supportively honest, they may want to comfort you when the going gets tough. Rather than see you struggle, they may convince you to let go of your goal or suggest that you aim your dreams at a lesser target.

When you face an obstacle, you need direction, not consolation. You need someone to say that you're off-course and to advise you. Not everyone can do that for you.

During a very difficult period in my own life, close family and friends advised that maybe I was expecting too much from myself and my situation. In contrast, one woman persistently chided me for negating myself. When I spoke with self-defeating words, she stopped me mid-sentence. Though she spoke with kindness, she refused to let me slide into the oblivion of self-pity. Instead she dispensed dogmatic advice, while at the same time professing in her belief in my ability to overcome the obstacles. Though her method sometimes annoyed me, she was the one who helped me push through my challenges. When she praised my efforts, I knew the kudos came from her heart. Throughout that time of my life, I appreciated the comfort of loved ones, but I counted on the strong support of my teacher/advice-giver.

Also, be aware that when you change your course, everyone may not agree with your new direction. Sometimes those who love and care about you the most are the same people who unconsciously sabotage your efforts. Alisa Morkides experienced that when she abandoned her planned career in financial planning to open a coffee shop. Of course, like Alisa, if you change direction regularly, people will be skeptical. Refrain from blame, especially if you've given them reason to doubt you. Instead, prove you are serious and get going. As your victory develops, they most likely will get on board with you, as Alisa's family and friends eventually did.

If you don't have a group, form one. If you don't have a mentor, look for one. If you need a coach, hire one. However, when you choose your support person or group, look for support, not appeasement, and *choose carefully*.

Awareness. Courage. Conscious choice. Decision. Goal. Plan. Support.

☞ **Persistence:**

Whatever victory you are creating, you can expect some obstacles. Each Victorious Woman faced some big ones, but the difference between the Victorious Woman and someone else is that each Victorious Woman stayed the course.

When facing obstacles, you can classify them by severity. Some will only be minor setbacks. For example, you can't get a piece of information you thought easy to find, or you don't get help from an expected source. These kinds of things are likely to happen. As a result, you may face a slight delay in your progress. Usually you can persevere through the frustration with determination.

Sometimes, however, the impediment seems like a brick wall. If that happens, you need more than a commitment to your goal. With dogged determination, you must chip away at the obstacle, often working daily, and sometimes hammering moment by moment, until you clear a space big enough to climb through to victory.

In the year that Jean Otte's spouse and mother died and Jean's sons left home, she felt like giving up. She did not. She went on to become the first woman executive in her company. Lilly Zook knew her children were in danger, but she simply couldn't financially afford a custody battle. She pushed ahead anyway, and though she had to fight in the courts for years, she won. Kathy Clark faced gender bias each day she went to work, but she did not quit. Later on, when left with nothing, she could have crawled into the proverbial hole and mentally died. Instead, she methodically and patiently put the pieces back together. Once again on her feet, her victory rewarded her with a better job, a wonderful spouse, and a beautiful new home.

Toni Kershaw said it best when she advised women, "Stay focused on the things that matter the most, and surround yourself with good people that help you see that most important person...yourself!"

Creating victory is seldom an easy process. If it were, we would all be doing it more often. However, this Victorious Woman Model gives you a track to run on, something to get you started and keep you going:

Awareness
Courage
Conscious Choice
Decision
Goal
Plan
Support
Persistence

There is victory in each of us. Sometimes we don't realize it because the weight of the challenge is at times more than we think we can bear. But remember that pressure creates the diamond: strong, durable, and everlasting.

It's true that not every woman chooses to deal with her challenge victoriously. It's truer that not every Victorious Woman feels she has earned the right to claim her victory.

If you're one to diminish your victories or even if you're one who puffs up your victories from thin air, from this day forward, commit to yourself to change. With new awareness, start demonstrating courage. Make a decision to move forward. Make a plan. Take action. Consistent small steps are better than unconnected great steps. Find your support network. Learn how to be your own champion. Dream big dreams, and bring your dreams into your reality. When challenged, believe in your ability to be victorious.

Each Victorious Woman featured in this book is owed my thanks, and yours. Each woman's story is a gift. Each woman told her story of victory—some with more self-acknowledgment than others, but none with bravado. Each life was simply stated by the one who lived it; the words poured from their hearts. Not one woman told her story for self-aggrandizement. For some, it was easy; for others, it was painful. Yet each woman shared willingly because she knew her victory was hard won and worth telling if it helped someone else through a challenge.

From each Victorious Woman, wherever you are, to each woman thinking about or in the process of creating your victory, I provide you with a final victorious thought:

> *Connect your mind to your heart,*
> *attach it to your voice,*
> *and speak to be heard.*
> *Then*
> *stake your claim,*
> *advance your life,*
> *and*
> *claim your victory!*
> You are *a*
> ### *Victorious Woman!*

SUGGESTED READING

Conklin, Robert. *Be Whole!* Minnesota: Clifftop Publishing, 1997.

Cooper, Robert K. and Sawaf, Ayman. *Executive EQ: Emotional Intelligence in Leadership and Organizations.* New York: The Berkeley Publishing Group, 1997.

de Becker, Gavin. *The Gift of Fear: Survival Signals That Protect Us From Violence.* New York: Little, Brown and Company, 1997.

Jaffe, Azriella. *Create Your Own Luck: 8 Principles of Attracting Good Fortune in Life, Love, and Work.* Massachusetts: Adams Media Corporation, 2000.

Katherine, Anne. *Boundaries: Where You End and I Begin.* New York: MJF Books, 1991.

Klaus, Peggy. *BRAG! The Art of Tooting Your Horn Without Blowing It.* New York: Warner Books, 2003.

Littauer, Florence. *Personality Puzzle.* Michigan: Revell Books, 1998.

Otte, Jean. *Changing the Corporate Landscape: A Woman's Guide to Cultivating Leadership Excellence.* New York: Longstreet Press, 2004.

Sills, Judith. *Excess Baggage: Getting Out of Your Own Way.* New York: Penguin Books, 1993.

Warren, Arnie. *The Great Connection.* Florida: Pallium Books, 1997.

We would love to hear about your victories!

*For details on submitting your stories, or to
subscribe to your free online newsletter, please visit:*

www.victoriouswoman.com

Annmarie Kelly can be contacted directly at:

SkillBuilder Systems
phone: (610) 738-8225
e-mail: annmarie@victoriouswoman.com

ABOUT THE AUTHOR

ANNMARIE KELLY is a speaker, trainer, facilitator, and coach who provides interactive training programs and coaching for personal performance improvement. She is the founder and managing principal of SkillBuilder Systems, a training and development firm specializing in management development, interpersonal communication skills, and goal achievement. As a speaker and facilitator of skill building, she brings the Victorious Woman message to women all over the country.

Annmarie's services include:

- workshops;
- seminars;
- corporate and conference keynotes;
- individual coaching;
- group coaching (Victory Teams);
- retreats.

Annmarie is also a member of the National Speakers Association, Greater Philadelphia chapter of the American Society for Training and Development, Reading Area Trainers Organization, Greater Valley Forge Human Resources Association, Brandywine Valley Alliance of Coaches, and the National Association of Female Executives and its local affiliate, Chester County Women.

She resides in Chester County, Pennsylvania with her spouse, Joseph Eagle.

SHARING VICTORY WITH OTHERS

Three ways to order individual copies of *Victorious Woman!*:

- order online at www.victoriouswoman.com;
- telephone Optimal Living Press direct at (610) 918-0578;
- fax the order form on the next page to (610) 719-0493.

For information about workshops, seminars, corporate and conference keynotes, individual coaching, group coaching (Victory Teams), retreats, the Victory Journal, training materials, or other learning products by Annmarie Kelly and SkillBuilder Systems, call (610) 738-8225.

ORDER FORM

Victorious Woman!   ISBN 0-9746037-0-8
$16.95 ($23.95 CAN)   Optimal Living Press

No. of copies _____   Total price of book(s) $_____.___

Total S/H (see below) $_____.___

Shipping/Handling:

U.S. and Canada: *$3.00 for 1 book, $1.00 each additional (not to exceed $7.00);* **International:** *$5.00 for 1 book, $1.00 each additional.*

Subtotal of above $_____.___

6.00% P.A. sales tax $_____.___

TOTAL ENCLOSED $_____.___

☐ check/money order   ☐ bill my M/C   ☐ bill my VISA

card no._____ expires_____

signature_____

<u>bill to</u>:   name_____

billing address_____

city_____ state_____ zip_____

<u>ship to</u>:   name_____

organization_____

mailing address_____

city_____ state_____ zip_____

e-mail (optional)_____

Make check/money order payable to:

Optimal Living Press
1062 Lancaster Avenue, 15G
Rosemont, PA 19010

Allow 3-4 weeks for U.S. delivery. Allow 4-6 weeks for Canada/Int'l orders.